Confessions
of a
Mullah Warrior

Confessions
of a
Mullah Warrior

Masood Farivar

Atlantic Monthly Press
New York

Published simultaneously in Canada
Printed in the United States of America

FIRST EDITION

ISBN-10: 0-87113-982-0
ISBN-13: 978-0-87113-982-5

Atlantic Monthly Press
an imprint of Grove/Atlantic, Inc.
841 Broadway
New York, NY 10003

Distributed by Publishers Group West

www.groveatlantic.com

09 10 11 12 13   10 9 8 7 6 5 4 3 2 1

In memory of the victims
of Afghanistan's ongoing war

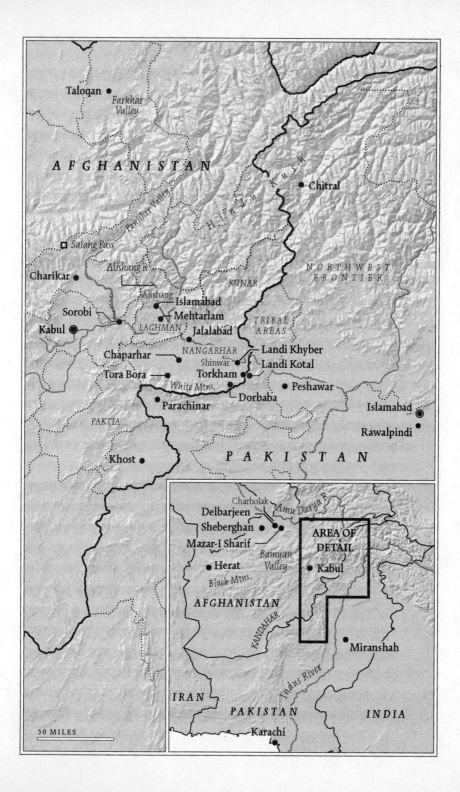

Confessions
of a
Mullah Warrior

Prologue

April 1989—The wind whips across a dry, narrow canal outside Jalalabad, Afghanistan. The afternoon sun warms me through my soiled and sweat-drenched *piran tuban* (tunic and pants) as I stand over a pile of mortar shells, ammunition boxes, rifles, and blankets. To my left, our loader lies in a pool of blood, his right leg blown off above the knee. Doctor Hamid, who is also the mortar gunner, gives him a shot of tranquilizer and radios for help. Now he asks Awalgul to take over.

"Laghmani," Awalgul barks at me, "give me good rounds."

We're taking heavy fire from a hilltop a mile across the plain, and Awalgul wants to respond with "good" mortar rounds, the kind that fly with a beautiful upward trajectory right into the heart of enemy territory. The faulty rounds have bad serial numbers and sometimes explode inside the mortar.

"Laghmani, hurry up," he shouts as he slides another round into the steaming mortar. Putting his fingers into his ears, he cowers as the round shoots out.

This is the third week in the battle of Jalalabad, the mujahideen's final march to liberation. After nine years of occupation, Soviet troops pulled out of Afghanistan in mid-February, leaving behind the embattled regime of Najib. Before their pullout, we were convinced victory would be swift and decisive. Jalalabad would be captured, a temporary government would be established, and Kabul and the other Communist-controlled cities would fall one after the other. But after a few government outposts went down, the battle drew to a stalemate, and the Jozjani militia, which forms the backbone of the enemy defenses and is notorious for its ruthlessness, has received fresh reinforcements. Their guns continue to pound our position for half an hour.

Two pickup trucks suddenly turn up the road. Several armed men sprint across the field toward us, a distance of two hundred yards. As they approach, I spot my twenty-five-year-old cousin Saboor among them. Shy, soft-spoken, and thin as a reed, he's traveled from Peshawar to assist with supplies.

"We need to go to Farm Number Four," he says, referring to a state citrus farm under our control.

Then Saboor turns to Awalgul. Tall and broad-shouldered with boyish good looks, Awalgul is a jokester (he sarcastically nicknamed me Laghmani after the denizens of my ancestral province Laghman, who have a reputation for shrewdness) and tries to keep our spirits up. He decides that I should go to Farm Number Four with Saboor. We load the wounded soldier into the pickup, which then speeds off down the potholed road toward the Pakistan border.

Saboor and I follow in a second truck. I sit in the back with half a dozen other fighters wrapped in woolen *patoo* shawls and carrying rifles. Every couple of hundred yards, we hear the whoosh of an incoming artillery round and the driver slams on the brakes. His timing is good, but when a round lands particularly close to us, I quietly murmur the declaration of faith just in case: *Ashhaduan la illahah, illalahu, wa Ashhaduanna Muhammadan Abduhu wa rasulluhu*—I bear witness that there is no god but God, I bear witness that Muhammad is his Servant and Messenger.

A couple of miles later, we turn onto a narrow dirt road and stop on the edge of the farm. I don't understand why we've stopped in an exposed area until I turn and look over my shoulder. A young man, not much older than I, is chained to the stump of a tall cypress tree, its branches sheared off by shrapnel. Behind the stump is a crater, the work of a SCUD missile. While a plane hums overhead, invisible and out of antiaircraft range, bursts of machine gun fire crackle across the farm. An artillery round explodes in a huge plume of smoke and dust about thirty yards away from the man. He looks anxiously across the open plain and somberly moves his lips.

Standing up in the back of the truck to look closer, we see the man turn his head toward us. His expression reminds me of a virgin groom on his wedding night, his spooky eyes tiny and black, shyly sparkling with anticipation. For a moment I suspect he's an Arab who, as part of a vendetta, must have been tied up by a vengeful Afghan. The driver and Saboor exchange words. Saboor sticks his head out of the window and gestures at the man.

"Do you know who that is?" he asks. "He is an Arab and he wants to become a *shaheed*." A martyr.

As a logistics and liaison officer, Saboor has, over the years, arranged for hundreds of Arab volunteers to fight in Afghanistan.

"Who brought him here?" I ask.

"I don't know, but he's one of the crazy ones. I just wanted to show him to you," he says matter-of-factly.

"Who chained him?" I ask.

"Probably one of his friends. There are a lot of them here, you see. They all want to become *shaheeds*."

Later Saboor tells me that several such men had been spotted around the farm since the start of the battle of Jalalabad. They chained themselves to trees during the day in hopes of achieving martyrdom before the sun went down, and by evening their comrades would come to pick them up, dead or alive.

"He's picked a nice spot," I say, tongue in cheek, because I really don't know what to say at all. "May God grant his wish and make him a *shaheed*."

In the back of my mind, though, this didn't make any sense. Clearly this man wasn't afraid of death. So why did he bind himself? Did he feel his cowardice would get the better of him on the battlefield? Was he fearful of being denied the promise of eternal life in the cool shade of palm and apple trees, and the company of black-eyed damsels? Why did he travel such a great distance to Afghanistan? Not to fight, but to tie himself to a tree?

I hear the unmistakable whistle of an incoming mortar round. The driver hits the gas. Instinctively, everyone in the back of the truck crouches down. As we speed away, the chained man shouts, *"Allahu Akbar!"*—God is great! One of my comrades mouths a prayer for protection against the evil eye.

Since joining the resistance in 1987, and later working as a combat reporter, I'd met dozens of Arab volunteers: young, naive, and fanatically religious men drawn to the battlefields of Afghanistan by the promise of eternal life. When the battle of Jalalabad began in earnest a couple of weeks ago, I met two Arabs near our mortar position. We were taking cover in a trench during a particularly fierce firefight. The Arab men were jittery, and from the way they held their rifles it was clear they had never been in a battle before. Knowing a smattering of Koranic Arabic, I tried to engage them in conversation without sounding like a seventh-century bedouin, but they brushed me off, either unable to understand what I said or uninterested in talking.

They muttered something to each other and leapt out of the ditch, shouting *"Allahu Akbar!"* as they raced across the open plain that separated us from the enemy positions, firing at targets that were far out of range. What were they doing? The enemy encampments were a mile up in the hills. Someone shouted at them in Arabic to come back. But they kept on running. I wondered then if they were acting out fantasies of becoming martyrs like the legendary early Muslim warriors who would fearlessly lunge at the infidels with their drawn swords, leaving their lives in the hands of God. Yet many would-be *shaheeds* failed to realize the Prophet was a shrewd man. He urged his followers "to tie the knee of the camel and then rely on God." What these men were doing was pure folly. As I peered up from the edge of the trench, I heard gunshots and watched both men fall. Drawing heavy fire, we had to abandon our position, and their fallen bodies.

When I look back on the war and how it came to put Afghanistan at the center of Islamic terrorism, I think about that chained man, and thousands of men just like him, who martyred themselves for God. Young and overzealous, these Arabs were war tourists who had bought their way into our country—and most Afghans resented their presence. While we called our struggle a jihad, a holy war, we were fighting first and foremost to liberate our country. The Arabs, who saw us as lesser Muslims, were seeking heavenly rewards. The more politically minded of these fighters declared, with a fierce conviction I could never understand, that "jihad will go on until the green flag of Islam flutters over Moscow and Washington"—an ominous utterance we shrugged off as the rhetorical ejaculation of misguided men.

In a sense, these men symbolized what the war had morphed into by 1989. This was no longer a jihad, a war of liberation against the godless Soviets; it had degenerated into a conflict manipulated by outsiders, each with very different ambitions. The Pakistani military orchestrated the battle of Jalalabad in hopes of bringing friendly Afghan groups to power. The Americans had financed a lengthy jihad and, throughout the war, rallied international support and encouraged volunteers to take part. The toughest fighters received the most American support even if they were in open contempt of America. When the Soviets left, Washington pushed to bring more "moderate" forces to power, but the effort was halfhearted and quickly abandoned. As for the Arabs, they poured into Afghanistan in ever-larger numbers, even after the Soviet withdrawal. Their ambitions wouldn't become fully clear until September 11, 2001.

Many Arabs saw the victory in Afghanistan as the first step in a larger jihad, though Afghans found it hard to call the horrors of the decade-long civil war that followed a victory. I had no idea at the time how long the war would drag on and how many more of my countrymen would lose their lives. No one did. Nor did anyone know that some of these Arab fighters would one day come back to haunt Afghanistan—and America.

Chapter One

Every child who is born is born with a sound nature; it is the parents who make him a Jew or a Christian or a Magian.

—Prophet Muhammad

Summer 1974 or 1975—"Agha, Agha," I said excitedly, "look, there's a fish in the river."

It was a late summer afternoon and I was tugging at Agha's shirttail and tiptoeing over a creaky wooden footbridge, exhilarated and frightened by the rush of the muddy Alishang River twenty feet below. Agha was Sufi Ramazan, my father's father and a beloved, gray-bearded elder of our ancestral village of Islamabad in eastern Afghanistan in the province of Laghman. While my cousins called him by the more formal Baba Jee, I for some reason had adopted the term my father and uncles preferred for him: *Agha,* or Dad. Ever since he'd given me my name and chanted the *azan,* the Islamic call to prayer—*Allahu Akbar, Allahu Akbar,* God is great, God is great—into my ears as an infant, Grandpa Agha had taken a special liking to me, the only son of his oldest son.

I didn't know it at the time, but Agha had decided to introduce me to our ancestral homeland, a world away from my birthplace of Sheberghan in the north. I was happy to get away from Sheberghan for an adventure-filled cross-country trip, but as I clutched Grandpa's shirttail and insisted that I'd spotted a fish in the river, he responded with words that still ring in my ears: "It's a piece of wood, you silly. Now walk carefully or you'll be swimming with the wood."

I was five or six. Agha was pushing seventy and quite fit for his age. He sported a long, neatly trimmed gray beard and a white silk turban. As a district governor in the north of Kabul, he'd earned a reputation for meting out harsh punishments to criminals, but he was kind and gentle with children.

Safely across the river, I let go of Agha and began waltzing through a vast, chest-high field of sugarcane. The village, a cluster of a hundred or so adjoining mud huts and a handful of more sturdily built two-story compounds, lay beyond the field. The sugarcane distracted me. Until Grandpa told me what it was, I thought it was a fatter, thicker variety of *nay,* a species of bamboo used to make calligraphy pens. When I learned what it was, I started pulling at some of the stalks but they were taller than I and much more stubborn and wouldn't succumb to my efforts. Agha, finding me straining and sweating, pulled out his pocket-knife and cut several canes. I remember proudly carrying the canes over my shoulder and following Agha to one of the compounds to spend the night in a cool room.

Only a few other memories from that visit to Islamabad and other villages in our ancestral province of Laghman have stayed with me: meeting old relatives who wore traditional clothes and spoke in a village dialect I could hardly understand; throwing rocks at sheep and cattle; enjoying local delicacies that I associated with the home of my ancestors—corn bread, fried cheese, brown sugar rocks. And one final image: standing next to a cluster of tombs as Agha lifted his wiry hands in prayer. It wasn't the first time he and I had stopped along our journey to pray for the dead, but these little dirt mounds of tombs weren't ordinary—they belonged to ancestors of ours who had brought Islam to eastern Afghanistan, their history closely tied to that of the country.

* * *

I was born and raised in the town of Sheberghan in northern Afghanistan, a very different place from Islamabad. Once a bustling Silk Road trading post, Sheberghan fell on hard times after Genghis Khan's army sacked it in the thirteenth century. While I was growing up in the 1970s, it was something of a backwater town, despite a multiethnic population of some ten thousand. Native Uzbeks predominated, but there were large pockets of Tajiks, Pashtuns, Turkomens, and even nomadic Arabs.

To the other townsfolk, we were Laghmanis—shrewd, industrious, enterprising, and educated. There were so many Laghmanis in Sheberghan that one large neighborhood was informally known as Laghmani Street. Many were close relatives of ours. Grandpa Agha and Grandma Bibi lived there with their three sons, my father, Uncle Khan Agha, and Uncle Agha Shirin. My mother had an older brother and a younger sister as well as two cousins. I knew what to call these close family members, but many others were related to us through blood and family ties so complicated that I sometimes wondered why I called a certain relative a *kaakaa,* a paternal uncle, rather than a *maamaa,* a maternal uncle, or a *khaala,* a maternal aunt, rather than *'ama,* a paternal aunt.

To get answers I'd sometimes turn to Ama Koko, my mother's feisty, slightly hunched maternal aunt. Widowed at a young age and childless, Ama Koko never remarried and instead divided her time between her three brothers and their four dozen children. Whenever she visited us, she'd spend much of her time reading the Koran or the book of Hafez, both of which she'd taught to my mother and her siblings. Like many others in the family, I'd occasionally ask her to consult Hafez to divulge my luck. She would open the book at random and start reading at the first verse her eye fell on. The fourteenth-century Persian verses didn't make much sense to me, but Ama Koko always found a way of putting them in terms a child could understand: "Khwaja Hafez sees fabulous fortune in your future."

When I wasn't asking her to read my luck, I'd pester her with questions about our extended family. A great storyteller, she was open to answering any question except the one that hung over her like a dark cloud: how she'd lost her young husband, the son of a powerful khan near Islamabad, in a tribal feud on the day after their wedding. Everything else was fair game.

"So Ama Koko, where were you born?" I'd start.

"Charikar."

Charikar is a small town north of Kabul.

"Charikar? What were you doing in Charikar?"

"My father was a government officer there."

"What was your father's name?"

"Jalilur Rahman."

"What was your grandfather's name?"

"Jamilur Rahman."

"So how are you related to Father?"

"Don't you know?" she'd say, irritated. "Your father is my niece's husband. Don't you see?"

"No, I mean how else are you related?"

"Well, your father is my mother's stepcousin's son. He is also my sister-in-law's son-in-law . . ."

The interrogation would go on and on, sometimes for an hour or more. By her next visit to our house, I'd forget many of the names and subject her to the same battery of questions. But she could never go back more than three generations in the family genealogy.

Years later I came across an old family manuscript that filled in the holes in Ama Koko's narrative. Titled *Sifat-naamah-I Darwish Khan-I Ghazi,* or *The Hagiography of Darwish Khan Ghazi,* the hundred-page manuscript opens in 1582, the year Darwish Khan, a middle-aged, fanatical general, led an army from central Asia to the regions surrounding Islamabad, the last non-Muslim pocket of Afghanistan. Accompanying Darwish Khan at the head of the army was his octogenarian spiritual advisor and prayer leader, Sultan Quli, my fourteenth forefather. Sultan Quli was no ordinary mullah. He was the grandson of Khwaja Ubaidullah Ahrar, one of the eminent religious figures of his time and the leader of the Sufi brotherhood known as the Naqshbandiyyah.

Sufism was more than an esoteric spiritual pursuit at the time; it was a way of life for millions and a vehicle by which Islam spread through central and south Asia. Among the many mystical brotherhoods, the Naqshbandiyyah boasted by far the largest following, but what set it apart from other Sufi fraternities was not simply the brotherhood's practice of the "silent prayer" but, more importantly, its close ties to the ruling authorities—first the dynasty founded by Timur in the fourteenth century and later Babur's Moghul empire. Ahrar and his descendents served as powerful, behind-the-scenes advisors of both dynasties. As the late German scholar Annemarie Schimmel put it, Ahrar believed that "to serve the world it is necessary to exercise political power" and to bring political rulers under control so that God's law can be carried out in every aspect of life.

The task facing Darwish Khan's army was daunting: conquer and convert some of the Hindu Kush's toughest and most fiercely independent denizens. Darwish Khan did not hesitate to remind his troops what they were fighting for. As he put it, they were part of a battle between God—the One and the Omnipotent—and the gods and idols of the infidels. As the holy warriors took up position on the bank of the Alishang River, native Pashtun tribesmen began to mobilize. While the infidels sacrificed goats to their gods Pandad, Sharwee, and Laamandee, Darwish Khan summoned Allah's help, assuring his troops that "a man needs courage, not a saber by his side." His army likely took his words seriously, as it was believed that Darwish Khan possessed extraordinary powers, an example of which was the ability to gallop headlong into an encroaching army, slicing dozens of infidels in half "like cucumbers."

A total of sixty-six valleys were conquered and converted, but the expedition wasn't a complete success. While the native Pashtuns submitted to the new faith, another, non-Pashtun tribe, living in adjacent valleys, tenaciously resisted conversion. Originally hailing from the Kandahar region, they had fled north to the Hindu Kush some seven hundred years earlier and spoke in strange tongues, worshipped idols, and sang and danced around their dead. Legend had it that they were descendents of Alexander the Great's army, which explained why many of them had blue eyes and blond hair. The Afghans called the region Kufristan or Kafiristan—the "land of unbelief" or the "land of infidels." For the next three centuries, Kafiristan served as a constant reminder that Darwish Khan's mission to bring Islam to the heathens remained unfulfilled.

As for Darwish Khan and Sultan Quli's descendents and the remnants of the army, they settled on the bank of the Alishang and christened the encampment Islamabad, or City of Islam, and built ties with the newly converted Pashtuns. They intermarried with them, acquired land along the Alishang, and built a thriving settlement in the heart of the Pashtun belt. While many lived off the land, the direct descendents of Sultan Quli continued the religious profession of their ancestors, maintaining mosques, running Koran schools, and appointing prayer leaders and preachers across the region. Religion also ensured that every male in the family, and more than a few females, were literate in the midst of an illiterate society. Seeing it as a source of power, they passed it down to their children, generation after generation.

Meanwhile, in matters both important and banal, tribal ways often prevailed despite the injunctions of Islamic law. Murders went largely unpunished. Few, if any, thieves had their hands chopped off. Women only occasionally received the legal right to inherit property promised to them by the new, egalitarian religion. Much to the shock of Islamabad's piety, some desperate tribesmen traded their wives for cattle. People lived their lives according to the guiding principles of *Pashtunwali*—the way of the Pashtun. Its main tenets required showing hospitality to all, providing shelter for those in need, and retaliating against those who have wronged you. *Pashtunwali* made no distinction between rich and poor, landlord and peasant. A khan who looked the wrong way at a peasant's wife could be dragged through the mud, his face blackened, his house burned down, and his family banished. A peasant who stole money could simply pay it back instead of having his hand cut off in accordance with Islam dictates. Everyone, regardless of wealth, was expected to provide lavish hospitality to guests. *Khoday dih ghareeb krhee, chaah dih bih ghayratah krhee* went one proverb: God made you poor, but who took away your honor?

Darwish Khan's wish for Islamic conversion came to pass in the nineteenth century, due to a fortuitous turn of events. In 1893 the British, who had made two futile attempts to conquer Afghanistan, drew a new border between Afghanistan and British India that came to be known as the Durand Line, named after its architect, Sir Mortimer Durand. Their goal: transform the unruly land of the Afghans—Yaghistan, or the "land of insolence"—into a docile buffer state between Czarist Russia and British India.

The Afghan ruler Abdur Rahman Khan, whom the British had christened the "Iron Amir" because of his ruthless and authoritarian rule, saw this as an opportunity to enlarge his domain. While not a religious fanatic, he quashed an uprising by the minority Shiite Hazaras of central Afghanistan in an effort to rally tribesmen to join his motley army in a jihad against the infidels of Kafiristan. Many panicked Kafirs embraced Islam outright, while other tribal leaders offered to pay tribute to the amir to avert war. This was a tactic they had used for centuries to fight off the spread of Islam, but the amir demanded complete and unconditional conversion.

The campaign to pacify Kafiristan was short-lived but violent. Hundreds were killed while thousands more crossed into the neighboring Chitral region of modern Pakistan, where their Kafir offspring live to this day. When the jihad was over, some sixty thousand infidels had embraced Islam and pledged their allegiance to the amir. With the valley subdued, the amir dispatched an army of mullahs to instruct the converts in the ways of Islam. None other than my maternal great-grandfather, Jalilur Rahman Khan, led a troop of mullahs into the valley, with specially trained barbers circumcising men both young and old in accordance with Islamic tradition. My paternal great-grandfather, also involved in the campaign, took into marriage a young girl from the area. She was one of the many women who were taken as spoils of war from the region, which the warriors renamed Nooristan, or the "land of light."

By the time of Nooristan's conquest, little of Islamabad's past power and prestige was left. In fact, the seat of Islam in eastern Afghanistan had declined into a poor hamlet, overshadowed by the fast-growing Moghul-era frontier town of Jalalabad to the southeast. One by one, the men of Islamabad started leaving in search of economic opportunity elsewhere. Many joined the Iron Amir's bureaucracy, some his military. Grandpa Agha started out as a county clerk before moving on to serve as a district chief in several provinces. His older brother became a provincial police chief in northern Afghanistan.

One of the men to strike gold was Grandpa Baba, my maternal grandfather, who was born in 1895. When he was five, he lost his father and was raised along with his two younger brothers and younger sister by his mother and their maternal uncle. He was a mullah who spent most of the first two decades of the last century working as a *mirza* north of Kabul. *Mirza* is an ancient Turkic regal title that had only recently come to designate anyone who was either a scribe or a notary. In an attempt to consolidate his power, the amir went beyond his southern tribal base to build a modern state bureaucracy, commissioning a professional army and centralizing the government. Starting with my great-grandfather Jalilur Rahman, men in my family whose predecessors had for ten generations borne the clerical title *mullah* now were calling themselves *mirzas*. It wasn't that these men were abandoning religion. On the contrary, our family maintained two mosques in Islamabad and pilgrims continued to visit the shrine of Darwish Khan and other pioneers. Yet after three centuries of enjoying the power and prestige that came with their position as men of religion and learning, they realized becoming *mirzas* was a way into the lucrative new world of government service.

As Grandpa Baba mastered the art of official letter writing and penmanship (his apprenticeship required developing a distinct handwriting style—straight *alifs,* curvy *baas,* loopy *seens*—for the entire Arabic alphabet), he seemed destined to follow in his uncle's footsteps. Then, in early 1919, King Habiburrahman Khan was assassinated in his sleep during a hunting expedition near Jalalabad. While the dead monarch's religiously conservative brother and twenty-seven-year-old liberal son jockeyed for possession of the throne, my great-uncle packed up his family and moved back to the secure environs of Islamabad.

Prince Amanullah Khan assumed the throne with the support of the reformist, anticolonialist Young Afghans, who modeled themselves after their Turkish counterparts, and Amanullah soon dispatched a letter to the British viceroy of India declaring Afghanistan's independence. When the British demurred, he did what Afghan rulers had always done when faced with a foreign adversary: he rallied the tribes for a jihad. There followed a series of what Western historians would call "inconclusive skirmishes," fought mostly by southeastern tribesmen, descendents of men converted by Darwish Khan's army. Grandpa Baba spent much of the 1920s as a midlevel district administrator in Laghman. The decade marked one of the most turbulent periods in modern Afghan history, as the young king's effort to transform Afghanistan into a modern secular state, modeled on Mustafa Kemal Atatürk's Turkey, was met with stiff opposition from an alliance of the religious establishment and Pashtun tribes.

By 1929, the liberal regime of King Amanullah was teetering, and Grandpa Baba found himself in the improbable position of defending a monarch who was being accused of heresy. A religiously inspired Tajik movement had overthrown the king, and Grandpa, as a government official and a member of the religious establishment in the Pashtun belt, had sided with a Pashtun general who eventually restored the monarchy. Leaving his post in the Alishang district, Grandpa retired to Islamabad where he reinforced the village's defenses, waiting for months on an enemy force that never materialized. His effort didn't go unrecognized, however. Having struck up a friendship with Mohammad Gul Khan Mohmand, the leader of the Mohmand Pashtuns, one of the tribes fighting the Tajik insurgency, Baba soon found himself in the upper echelons of power as he followed Mohmand to northern Afghanistan.

Running as a surrogate father and son team—Mohmand never sired a son; Grandpa grew up without his father—they governed one of Afghanistan's five administrative regions through much of the 1930s. Mohmand bore the grandiose title of chief executive of the Northern Territories. Grandpa, with his less illustrious title of fourth director, was second in command. Their style of government was ruthless. Justice was swiftly delivered, if only to quash dissent and secure the government's hold on power. To many non-Pashtuns in the north, Mohmand, a self-styled Pashtun nationalist, came to embody the dictatorial rule of the government.

While Mohmand took quarters in the governor's mansion, Grandpa Baba acquired the residence of the former chief executive, an imposing, turn-of-the-century structure of more than two dozen rooms with arched doorways, guesthouses, servants' quarters, stables, and a two-acre pomegranate garden with a large pool surrounded by tall birch trees. Soon Grandpa's clan—his mother, younger sister, two brothers, five wives, and their children—

moved in. My mother and her three dozen siblings and cousins grew up behind the sheltered walls of the compound, where they were attended by a retinue of servants, cooks, and maids. Theirs was the life of the ruling aristocracy.

Adee, Mother's slight, soft-spoken, octogenarian grandmother, was the family's matriarch. With a taste for long black robes and soft linen headdresses, she was a spiritual healer of sorts who attracted a large following from the city. Her son, my grandfather, ran the day-to-day affairs of the household, and while deeply pious, he allowed a liberal atmosphere to flourish within the compound. The adults prayed five times a day, but the children were never forced to join them. Growing up, they developed different degrees of piety. Some, like my mother, were rigidly observant (her own mother came from a clerical background); others, especially the boys, rarely prayed, meekly avoiding Grandpa Baba's stern gaze during the five daily calls to prayer.

For a man of his position and generation, Grandpa was remarkably liberal, which inevitably led to some interesting contradictions. He had a deep sense of justice and fairness and did not play favorites among his five wives. He was pious yet never forced his children to pray. Religion was a matter between them and their God. In social and cultural matters he was open-minded, yet he strictly enforced *pardah,* which assured that nonblood male friends and guests never saw the faces of his womenfolk. He allowed his daughters to attend school, first fully covered and then, when the government made the burka voluntary, with their faces (although not their heads) uncovered. The daughters, out of respect as much as fear, would always hide their short, Western-style skirts and stockings by changing into baggy white cotton pants and linen headdresses before entering Grandpa's room. Once, in Kabul, he was persuaded to venture into the banquet hall where one of his younger daughters was having her wedding reception. Horrified by the sight of so many bare legs, including those of his own daughters, he barged out, cursing them all to hell.

In 1961, when Mother was thirteen, the first girls' school opened in Mazar-I Sharif. This was a bold act, considering that it had been the opening of a girls' school in Kabul during the 1920s that led to King Amanullah's downfall. Rabiah-I Balkhi Lycee for Girls presented a major dilemma to Grandpa, who as a respected member of society had to consider the social implications of exposing his sheltered daughters to the outside world. However, he valued education and, after consulting his two younger brothers, decided that all the girls in the family would go to school. A tutor was hired, and after a year of studying, they took entrance exams and enrolled in different grades. Mother was placed in the fifth grade, but by all accounts she was an unenthusiastic student drawn more to knitting sweaters than solving math problems. So by the time she was in the ninth grade, when Father's family proposed, she was happy to take his hand.

Father was my mother's second cousin, and his journey to northern Afghanistan had charted an improbable course. Unlike Mother, he was born in Islamabad, where his path to become a *qadi*, an Islamic judge, seemed a clear one. His father was a senior government administrator, his mother the daughter of a prominent mullah from the powerful Safi tribe. Although Grandpa Agha himself had chosen public service over a career in religion, he took pride in his clerical pedigree and wanted his three sons to pursue a religious path. While Grandpa served in remote provincial outposts, the family stayed behind in Islamabad, where Father studied first at the family mosque, then later at the local primary school. Along the way he developed a voracious appetite for reading. Years later he recounted how he spent a long winter devouring the bulky *Thousand and One Nights,* and any other classics he could get his hands on, by the glow of a kerosene lamp.

After sixth grade Father was sent to Kabul to attend the Darul Ulum-I Hanafi, Afghanistan's top state-run madrassah, or religious seminary, and a stepping stone to entering the College of Islamic Law at Kabul University. It was distinctly modern in amenities and curriculum, offering classes in both secular and tra-ditional religious subjects.

The madrassah was originally developed during the eleventh century, a full two centuries before its European counterpart, as an institution of religious learning that trained students in Islamic law and jurisprudence. While European colleges would evolve into secular institutions of higher learning, the madrassah re-tained its religious mission. During the late nineteenth and early twentieth centuries, the madrassah's strictly religious curriculum and conservative intellectual outlook were called into question by a growing number of Islamic reformists. Recognizing the central role the scientific revolution and the Enlightenment played in the West's march to progress and prosperity, these modernist think-ers argued that only by embracing European sciences could the Islamic world hope to regain its ancient glory. The ensuing decades-long clash between the conservative religious establish-ment and the reformists produced little change in the madrassah curriculum, but it did lead Westernized governments such as Turkey and Persia to open modern secular schools.

In Afghanistan this clash led to the establishment of the country's first secular public high schools in the first and second decades of the twentieth century. Yet young King Amanullah's radical efforts to reshape Afghanistan in the image of Kemal Atatürk's Turkey backfired. Less than ten years into his reign, an alliance of conservative mullahs and southern tribesmen forced him into exile in 1929. Amanullah's successor, Nadir Khan, a reform-minded, pragmatic prince and former army general, recog-nized the limitations of his conservative society. While reopening the public schools, his government established new madrassahs where modern sciences were taught alongside traditional religious sciences, much like the madrassah my father attended.

Father's education was innovative, especially in its teaching of contemporary spoken Arabic. Young, sophisticated, and friendly Iraqi and Egyptian teachers introduced colloquial Arabic into a curriculum that had emphasized classical Arabic for hundreds of years. Classical Arabic grammar had developed on the basis of the Koran and pre-Islamic bedouin poetry, and its usefulness was limited to unraveling the messages of the Koran and the Hadith, or the sayings of Muhammad. Students learned to say, "Potipher's wife tore Joseph's shirt from behind," but could not share their enthusiasm for their mother's eggplant dish. The Arabic that Father learned in madrassah was, by contrast, a living, spoken language.

As much as Father loved to read, he was drawn even more to the sciences: the thrill generated by solving algebraic problems; the allure of the intricacies of human anatomy; the awe inspired by invisible atoms. This would inevitably lead to complications. While in the ninth grade, Father committed one of the most sacrilegious acts imaginable in a madrassah. Following instructions in his chemistry textbook, he distilled alcohol using simple household pots and pans. The successful experiment, which he secretly shared with more than a few classmates, deepened his passion for science and led him to drift away from the madrassah altogether. Kabul at the time was a charming, well-to-do city with tree-lined boulevards, tranquil neighborhoods, and thriving restaurants and teahouses frequented by the country's growing, largely Western educated, secular elite.

In Kabul, Father spent his weekends and short holiday breaks from school at the home of his uncle, who was the chief justice of the supreme court and a close friend of the madrassah's president. Uncle Insaf exhorted Father to excel in his religious studies, but Father was more interested in tutoring the justice's young, studious son in physics. It was an ideal arrangement, as Father didn't particularly fit in with Kabul's clean-shaven men who wore Western-style clothes and spoke with the refined accent of educated elites. He was torn between a desire to embrace Kabul's liberal culture and an awareness that he was forbidden by his father to do so. Feeling alienated, he would return to his dorm room every night and lie in bed, quietly imitating the Kabul accent he badly wanted to pick up, and painfully conscious he'd have to live with his facial hair for the rest of his life.

Then opportunity knocked: a science school recently founded by the University of Wyoming in Kabul was taking applications. Father took the placement test and scored ninety-nine out of a hundred points. He dropped out of the madrassah, despite his father's refusal to give his blessing, and enrolled at the American Technical School. There he spent the four happiest years of his life. He shaved off his beard, stopped praying, quickly learned English, and immersed himself in mechanical engineering. Although his friends playfully called him *maulana*, which means "supermullah," the title of a distinguished man of religious learning, he socialized at teahouses and befriended worldly university students.

After graduation he took a job as an engineer with the state-run Oil and Gas Exploration Company, spending the next several years working the fields near Sheberghan before winning a scholarship to study petroleum engineering in Soviet Armenia and Azerbaijan.

When Father returned to Afghanistan in 1966, he was thirty-three, well past the marriage age. It was time for him to settle down. At the urging of his parents, he agreed to an arranged marriage to his first cousin's daughter. Theirs was a grand wedding, paid for by Father's family. Payment for the ceremony was the only cost Grandpa Baba exacted. To him the custom of paying a bride price, which was common in northern Afghanistan, was an abomination; it was also un-Islamic. He expected, though, that the would-be groom would honor his family, so instead of pledging a large amount of cash and prime real estate, Father's family threw a weeklong party, complete with separate bands of male and female musicians—for male and female guests—to which hundreds of friends and relatives were invited. Father and Mother then moved to Sheberghan, bringing along several trunks and a young Uzbek servant named Girau.

In Sheberghan, they lived on the oil and gas company's campus, a sprawling development of offices and residential neighborhoods complete with green, manicured lawns, running water, electricity, and central heating—amenities unheard of in most of Afghanistan.

In many respects, however, Sheberghan was like any other small provincial capital: quiet, dusty, low-key, timeless. This was where Afghanistan's national ring road, built by the Americans and the Soviets in the 1950s and 1960s, ended before branching off west and north to the Amu Darya River. The main street was lined by handsome one- and two-story concrete homes, but for the most part Sheberghan consisted of flat-topped and domed mud huts and windy dirt roads that produced dust storms in the summer and turned into mud in the winter.

In the main town square a rusty public address system, hanging from a poplar tree overlooking a posse of parked buggies, alternated between broadcasting scratchy Radio Afghanistan news segments and municipal announcements. For those not lucky enough to catch the broadcast, a *jaarchee*, or professional town crier, went from neighborhood to neighborhood, shouting important and often not very important announcements at the top of his lungs.

While not as big or significant as it had been two thousand years ago, Sheberghan retained something of its Silk Road character as a center of vibrant commerce. A large grain bazaar and a partly roofed produce market carried freshly picked vegetables, apples, pears, apricots, peaches, and mounds of large Uzbek melons; a meat market of about two dozen butcher shops slaughtered animals on the premises; and two sprawling livestock and firewood and fuel markets twice a week, on market days, crawled with peasants from nearby villages, peddling everything from sheep, goats, and camels to cow patties and dried sheep dung.

Like much of northern Afghanistan, Sheberghan had four regular seasons, with brutally cold winters and searing summers and two mild seasons in between. With each season came distinct colors, sounds, and smells. Spring, which classical Persian poets compare to the Day of Resurrection, was the most colorful, complete with black barn swallows and gray sparrows, red tulips and yellow daisies, blossoming Judas trees and pink, red, and white roses—a burst of vitality that followed the gray cold of winter. Walking through town in April or May felt like walking through a medieval Persian perfume market. The scent was more pungent indoors, where most everyone kept rosebushes. Years later it occurred to me that the roses, exquisite as they were, might have served a more practical function besides providing aesthetic pleasure. Strategically planted near outhouses, they were intended to mask the odor of excrement that would become overpowering with the onset of warm weather.

On the modern campus of the oil and gas company, we did not have to worry much about foul odors. Nor did we notice the noise of the bazaar. A *jaarchee* occasionally passed through the neighborhood, and less frequently a peddler of fish or a man on a tricycle bartering trinkets in exchange for recyclable tin and worn-out plastic sandals. "*Koonah bah now. Koonah bah now,*" he would shout. "Used for new. Used for new." By sundown the neighborhood became silent but for the chirping of frogs and the bark of a stray dog or two, until the sun reappeared in tandem with the cock crow and call to prayer. This was a time and place where most people didn't own watches but even a blind person could tell the hour of the day by the sounds alone.

Almost everyone in our neighborhood was an engineer or manager or accountant for the exploration company. Many were products of Kabul University, at the time Afghanistan's only university, children of privilege with professional degrees who ended up working for an oil company with an expanding bureaucracy but little in the way of actual petroleum reserves to justify its continued growth. It was the common fate of most college graduates. In the absence of an established private sector, they became government

bureaucrats, "paper pushers" my father called them, himself included, of course.

The paper pushers who made up Afghanistan's nascent middle
class were a far cry from the men in my family who had spent
most of their lives in the service of God, whether in the mosque
or on the battlefield. "Middle class" was a Western concept used
to refer to the tiny number of high school and university educated
people working for the government. Naturally, wherever they
went, members of this new "class" brought with them the cosmopolitan mores they'd acquired in Kabul and little of their village
ways. The true mark of a middle-class lifestyle was Western-style
clothing, whose purchase the government encouraged by giving
college students an annual "suit" allowance. Not surprisingly,
many felt awkward, even embarrassed, in Western clothes. To
avoid public embarrassment, some would wear traditional baggy
pants and turbans on their way to school and then change into
trousers and don fedoras before entering the grounds. By the
1970s, though, city residents dressed mostly in Western clothes
in public—in schools, government offices, even in courtrooms.

The clash between village and city showed in other ways.
Among my father's relatives and peers, for example, polygamy
was unheard of. In fact, they found it passé, something their fathers did. But while some men had started marrying outside of
the family (one even married a Ukrainian woman at university in
Kiev), most of my relatives, like my father, still preferred first or
second cousins, the way their fathers had done.

Considering its size, Sheberghan offered plenty of diversions.
It had a soccer stadium, a couple of volleyball courts, and a movie
theater that showed Bollywood hits and an occasional Iranian
flick or American western. Whether Bollywood or Western, the
color posters of the mostly black-and-white movies, both current
and upcoming, advertised their *ishq* and *jang* and *khandan*
content—love and war and song—the only things viewers cared

about. What the posters didn't warn viewers, however, was that the films contained plenty of images of Hindu temples and worshippers offering sacrifices to their idols. To register their wounded feelings, the viewers—and they weren't the fanatical, idol-breaking types— would spit between their feet on the floor of the smoke-filled movie theater upon the appearance of the first image of a Hindu god and then curse aloud. Initially I didn't know what it was all about and only later, when I realized something about idols was wrong, did I start joining the adults in spitting bouts during our occasional visits to the movies.

On foot, you could run up and down Sheberghan and visit its every nook and cranny in less than an hour. By car, you could cover the whole ground in less than ten minutes. The movie theater was a ten-minute walk from our house, the soccer sta- dium five minutes farther. But I didn't have to venture even that far in search of entertainment; the boys played plenty of games right outside our house. While my sisters played hopscotch with pieces of gravel, I kept busy shooting marbles, walnuts, and the balls of sheep ankles. We also played a form of baseball called *toop dandah,* and another called *chilik dandah,* with a bat and a six-inch-long stick with sharpened ends. In both games the winner would use his points to make the loser run a certain distance and chant *zoooooooooooooooooo* without catching his breath.

On Fridays, Hasan, our live-in servant, would treat me to a spe- cial adventure for a young boy—a local dogfight. Hasan had a dark face, sun-baked and scarred by smallpox. Kind-hearted and jovial, he'd ended up in our house by accident. The original servant given by Grandpa Baba was Hasan's older cousin, Girau, but he could not bear Mother's harsh treatment and ran away after less than a year, prompting Grandpa Baba to send Hasan as a replacement.

While Hasan endured Mother better than his cousin, a visit from Grandpa Baba was his opportunity to voice complaint.

Hasan knew that Grandpa treated servants fairly. Grandpa summoned Mother.

"Is it true that you curse Hasan all the time?" Grandpa inquired.

Taken aback by her servant's boldness, Mother looked at Hasan and said, "Damn your father, when did I ever curse you?"

The problem didn't go away, and I came to sympathize with Hasan. He lived in the servant's room by the front door. It was a small, spartan room, furnished with a simple rug, a pallet, and a couple of pillows that Hasan would wrap into a bundle and place in the corner of the room after getting up each morning. He also owned an old tambourine that he was trying to teach himself to play.

My ventures to the dogfight with Hasan were the highlight of my week. They were staged on a bare piece of land outside town. A crowd of a hundred or so men—mostly traditionally dressed, illiterate Uzbek peasants from nearby villages and a few boys my age—would gather around a circle. Hasan seemed at home here, greeting strangers and some acquaintances in Uzbek, a language I hadn't yet learned. But with their strong accents, even those who spoke Farsi were hardly comprehensible to me. Profanity flowed from their mouths as readily as drool from the dogs' mouths. This was not the kind of event Father and his friends would attend.

As we waited for the fight to begin, vendors walked around the circle of spectators selling chewing gum, cigarettes, and cookies. Hasan would always buy me a treat. Finally, one by one, the dogs and their owners would walk into the ring. The dogs were large and vicious, not the type that strayed on the streets of Sheberghan, but carefully groomed and specially trained mixed-breed hounds and shepherds. Thrilled and frightened, I'd grab Hasan's arm with both hands, swaying back and forth with the crowd as the dogs moved around. They would go after each other like prizefighters in a ring, trying to pin each other down. Sometimes, but not always, blood would ooze out.

The crowd hooted and jeered when a vanquished dog ran from the circle, the ultimate disgrace. This was a peculiar kind of high-stakes game: little money was wagered, but the personal honor of the owner was on the line. The losing dog would decrease the prestige of its owner, while the winning dog would bring its owner great honor. Fights were declared over as soon as one dog pinned the other down. Their object wasn't to kill or to maim but to defeat.

My dogfight Fridays came to an end when Hasan was drafted into the army the following summer. Having grown close to him in recent months, I was sad to see him go, as though losing an older brother. In his last days with us, Hasan seemed eager to leave, perhaps pleased at the thought of no longer bearing the humiliation of being a house servant. But if he intended never to return to our house, he didn't let on, and Father, handing him a generous sum of pocket money, made it clear that he expected to see him as soon as he was furloughed.

During this time Father was a stern disciplinarian with a penchant for lecturing and prone to tantrums. While I sometimes acted like a spoiled brat with Mother, I always addressed Father using the formal, second person plural form. We had a cold, strictly formal Afghan father-son relationship. He dictated; I obeyed. I had a much closer relationship with Grandpa Agha, father's father, whom I looked forward to seeing on Fridays and holidays. Agha and Grandma, a slight woman with deep blue eyes and soft salt-and-pepper hair that she tied into a ponytail under her white linen headdress, lived with Uncle Khan Agha a mile across town. Without knowing why, I felt I was Grandpa's favorite grandchild. On holidays he'd give more money to me than to my sisters and cousins. At mealtimes he'd ask me to sit next to him and let me feed bread crumbs to his beloved yellow cat. And when Father raised his voice in admonishment, a gesture from Grandpa was enough to quiet him.

Fathers cast large shadows in Afghan society, and no matter what my father had achieved, he realized he'd always live in the shadow of his own father. When Grandpa entered a room, everyone, including Father and his two younger brothers, would rise, bow, kiss his hand, and stand at attention. Out on the streets they trailed behind him like devoted disciples of a Sufi sheikh. Even Father, married with children of his own, stood in awe of him, no doubt aware that, whether he liked it or not, he'd forever be known as the son of Sufi Sahib.

Grandpa Agha was deeply pious, a quality he shared with his beloved (and only) wife. He could have had more than one wife, of course. His religion condoned polygamy, and in fact his social standing called for it. He chose to marry only once, though, much to everyone's bewilderment. Grandpa and Grandma genuinely loved each other, as much as they loved their God. When he wasn't praying, he'd be sitting on his prayer rug, often next to Grandma, fingering his prayer beads or quietly reciting the holy Koran. Religion wasn't simply a hollow expression of piety; it dictated every aspect of his life. In a poor country where appointment to a senior government position was viewed as a road to instant wealth paved with kickbacks and bribes, Grandpa didn't compromise his integrity. He had a clear sense of *halal* and *haram,* the permitted and the forbidden, and he preferred to live a modest lifestyle instead of profiting from the public treasury. Stories attesting to his scrupulous nature abound in our family. Once while serving in a region north of Kabul, one of his closest childhood friends came to visit him expecting a lavish display of hospitality. Day in and day out, Grandpa served him the same simple dish of eggplant stew. Finally the exacerbated friend asked Grandpa why on earth he wouldn't serve him something better—rice and lamb, the staple dish of the well-to-do. Grandpa said he could not afford it because he didn't take bribes. The frustrated friend replied jokingly, "Take that shit and serve me something nice."

Father, on the other hand, had long ago abandoned the turban and the traditional *piran tunban* (baggy pants and tunic). In his enthusiasm for modernity, he encouraged us to don Western garb at all times, not just in school as the other kids did. Although he initially let Mother wear her traditional clothes, she too started wearing bell-bottoms in public. As for my sisters and me, we dressed only in Western clothes, with sometimes graver reactions. Not only did this set us apart from our friends in the neighborhood, members of our own family would voice their disapproval.

One afternoon we went across town to visit Agha in the house of Uncle Khan Agha, Father's younger brother. I was in shorts and a short-sleeved shirt, and my sisters in checkered skirts over low-cut white socks. As we walked in through the unlocked front door, I could see Grandpa's back. He was in the middle of the courtyard, chopping wood, while his turban sat on the edge of the carpeted verandah. Uncle Khan Agha, who was putting away the firewood, warmly gestured toward us. Agha looked over his shoulder. His reddened, veiny forehead glistened with beads of sweat. As we went over to kiss his hand, I waited for a twinkle of recognition in his eyes, but he was fixated on my two sisters.

"Go back to your house and ask your mother to dress you properly," he barked, shooing us away. "Go away and don't ever come here naked."

Terrified and embarrassed, we turned and ran back home, sheepishly reporting to Father what Grandpa Agha had demanded. Father knew that by allowing his children to dress this way he had crossed a line. Yet he had always seen himself as an iconoclast. In his slacks, short-sleeved shirts, and crisp, tailored suits, he felt liberated; he would never ask his children to take chances in confronting relatives with modernity if he wasn't willing to do so himself.

Shortly after marrying my mother, Father took her to see Grandpa Baba at his estate in Delbarjeen, in the Charbolak district. Father wore a suit and tie while Mother was dressed in heels and a skirt that bared her legs, a sight never seen in the village. As they disembarked from the minibus near the village market, villagers converged around them, a commotion my grandfather spotted from the gate of his house up the road. When he realized who they were, Grandpa lost it and quickly dispatched a servant with a pair of horses to retrieve them.

Years later I remember enjoying our once or twice a year visits to Delbarjeen. It was a tiny yet charming village surrounded by large orchards and fields of wheat, much of which Grandpa Baba had accumulated during his tenure as the fourth director. In a country with the most equitable land distribution in Asia, the size of Baba's compound was an anomaly. Standing in the heart of the village, it was an old-fashioned, walled, L-shaped complex of more than a dozen mud-brick rooms overlooking a deep courtyard and a large, murky pool. Grandpa enjoyed long sojourns in the village, usually with one of his three surviving wives and almost always with his only sister, Great-Aunt Koko, who when she wasn't quietly reciting the Koran would practice her favorite hobby of weaving wool robes by their big wood-burning stove.

To Father, however, Delbarjeen recalled Islamabad. These were culturally backward places that represented everything wrong with Afghanistan: abject poverty, rampant and appalling ignorance, deeply entrenched superstitions. A self-styled modern man and an idealist, he preached the benefits of variety in Western cuisine and of using toilet paper over clay to anyone who would listen, demonstrating how to properly fold toilet paper before wiping.

To Father, Grandpa Baba and Grandpa Agha represented an anachronistic world. Like the Enlightenment writers whose work he'd devoured, Father viewed religion as the root of the problem. Growing up, I saw few people say daily prayers and those who did were mainly my grandparents, other older relatives, and occasional visitors from Laghman. At home, Mother fasted and worshipped only on special occasions. Father had long ago stopped praying, unless you counted the occasional wedding ceremonies and funeral services at which he'd join everyone else and mechanically raise his hands in prayer.

It wasn't that my father had lost faith in God. In his most despondent and hopeful moments alike, he'd talk about "the one up there"—an invisible, omnipotent, supernatural force that "always looks after me, and I don't know why." What he could not stand were the demands and trappings of the folk religion practiced in places like Islamabad. That form of religion was for illiterate peasants who had to be taught like children. Father would try to explain away much of the Koran as allegory. The "rivers of wine and honey" were meant to appease the ever-thirsty, water-deprived bedouin Arabs. The "fair-skinned, black-eyed *houris*" of paradise were for lechers who wanted multiple wives but couldn't afford them. The promised handsome young boys known as *ghilman* were clearly meant for pederasts. Father found the power these stories held over ordinary believers ironic, given that the Koran says its stories are meant for "those who think" and "those who ask questions."

What Father didn't find ironic were his only son's telltale signs of genius shown from an early age (how many fathers *don't* think that of their only sons?). Talent was a big part of genius, but nurturing it played an even larger role. To Father, building a genius was like building a piece of machinery. It was simply a matter of putting the parts together. He liked to say that there were "Einsteins and Newtons and Galileos" all over Afghanistan—even in Qizilayaq and Khojadokoh, small, impoverished hamlets on the edge of Sheberghan. The reason we didn't know of them was that no one had given them the opportunity to reach their potential. He wanted to give me, the genius in progress, that opportunity.

We got off to a rocky start. Before I entered first grade, Father decided that I ought to learn the alphabet a year ahead of schedule. Much to his chagrin, I proved thoroughly incompetent. The first letter in the Arabic alphabet, *alif,* a straight vertical line, proved the most daunting. For whatever reason, I'd draw a curved line, or a line extending from the upper right-hand corner of the notebook to the lower left-hand corner. The more I tried, the curvier my *alifs* got. Forget about the rest of the alphabet. I never got to the second character.

Father was clearly frustrated. He thought my inability to draw a simple straight line resulted from a learning impairment. He took me to a counselor employed at the school for the children of Soviet contractors working for the oil company. I spent half an hour sitting next to the plump, middle-aged counselor in her cluttered, brightly decorated office as Father and she spoke in Russian. At the end of their conversation, the woman handed me a pile of coloring books and a box of crayons. I didn't have a steady hand, she explained to my father, meaning I'd have to practice drawing to steady my hand.

After a week or two of drawing, the problem vanished and the genius project was back on track. I remember the look of triumph on Father's face when I wrote the entire alphabet without a mistake. By the time I began reading and writing simple sentences in the first grade with the competence of a second-grader, he was as proud of me as he was of himself for diagnosing my problem and finding a solution. Perhaps because of his pride, I started school a half year before the minimum age of seven. Starting first grade six months early was supposed to work to my advantage, a fact frequently remarked upon by relatives. Had Father gotten his way, I'd have entered right into the second grade, but after a half hour of proselytizing on my behalf, he couldn't convince the admissions officer to promote me on my first day.

Ibn-Yamin Lycee was Sheberghan's only first- through twelfth-grade public school for boys (its girls' counterpart was called Khadijah-I Jozjani Lycee). With its three large one- and two-story classroom buildings, a small soccer field, and two volleyball courts, the school was one of only a handful of modern structures in town. Looking on one side of the building, where the main paved street ran past the soccer stadium, you could forget how antiquated the rest of the town was. Yet looking on the other side, you would see a much more familiar scene: a dirt road lined with old shops that sold trinkets, spices, and groceries. This was the site of one of Sheberghan's two livestock and fuel markets.

Our classroom was on the second floor overlooking the market. Most of the students at Ibn-Yamin were the sons of oil company managers or government bureaucrats and lived within easy distance of the school. A smaller number of students walked much farther from villages outside Sheberghan. Mostly ethnic Uzbek, these students dressed traditionally but outside the gate of the school slipped Western pants on over their ethnic garb.

Inside the classroom education was a mix of old madrassah methods (learning by rote) and modern accessories (sitting on benches instead of the floor and learning the alphabet from textbooks). Yet mechanical learning by repeating and committing to memory every letter, word, and sentence would start in the first grade and last through most of my school experience.

Having learned the alphabet prior to the first grade, I was named "captain" of the class. Among other tasks, the captain brought the class to attention with a loud "All rise!" when the teacher entered. Thanks largely to my academic aptitude, I went through the first grade without receiving a single beating. In those days beatings were expected, even encouraged. As the poet Sa'di said, *Jawri-I ustad bih zi mehr-e padar*—The teacher's cruelty is better than the father's love. The school was governed by strict rules, and violations could get you a beat-ing, especially troubling when the severity of the punishment outweighed the gravity of the offense. Failing to turn in your homework might get you only ten raps on the hand, while repeated tardiness might result in the ultimate punishment, a beating on the soles of your feet.

Having finished the first grade at the top of my class, I did then skip a grade. That summer I spent long hours studying with my older sister, who herself was preparing to skip the third grade. In the evenings Father, who was delighted at our progress, would test us. Whenever I floundered in a subject about which he was unable to motivate me, he'd send me for three days to his brother's house to learn my assignment. Uncle Khan Agha lived at the other end of town. He was smaller than Father, quieter too, and wore sunglasses to mask a defective eye that had been replaced by a plastic one. Uncle Khan Agha was supposed to have become a *qari,* a professional reciter of the Koran, but instead earned a degree in agricultural engineering in Kabul and went to work as a bureaucrat at the local office of the Department of Agriculture in Sheberghan. Clean-shaven and wearing Western clothes and sunglasses, it was hard to imagine him doing a sonorous rendition of Koran verses, though some relatives still called him *qari*. He was a kindly man who let me relax, even laze about. I could spend my three days however I chose as long as I mastered my lesson by the time I returned home. Knowing how my father would react if I hadn't learned the assignment, I always did.

I hated that summer. I wanted to be outside, shooting marbles or walnuts, engaging in theatrical, profanity-laced shouting matches with neighborhood boys. We belonged to various ethnic groups but all spoke Farsi. This was important because we could exchange insults and know we were understood. Each of us had learned cruel epithets about our ethnic rivals. A Tajik, for example, would refer to the bulkiness of the Pashtun's behind, while a Pashtun would comment on the smooth privates of a Hazara's mother. Dirty words were taboo in our home, but during the scant moments Father let me go outside, I unleashed a torrent of profanity that would last until the other kids' offended parents appeared on their doorsteps and shooed me away.

In any case, Father's hard work paid off. I passed the second grade exam and was admitted into third grade. My new teacher was named Ghaffar Khan, a large man who coached the school's new boxing team. Now I found myself surrounded by kids two and three years older than I was. They brazenly discussed subjects like sex that were baffling to an eight-year-old. Less baffling was the experience of being punished in class, which I finally got a taste of. Ghaffar Khan's favorite method of discipline was to put three ballpoint pens between the four fingers of the hand and to squeeze tightly. It was the most painful thing I had ever experienced—but it wouldn't be for long.

On my way to school, I'd run into Salih and Atta, distant relatives who were in eighth or ninth grade. One of them had green eyes. The taller one had dark, narrow eyes. I had dirty blond hair at the time, and on seeing me, one or the other would taunt me, "Hey German, how are you? Hey German, where are you going?"

I don't know why they called me German rather than Russian or American, but the epithet hurt, made me feel self-conscious and estranged. If I couldn't avoid them, I'd just smile shyly and mumble something as I ran away.

While I never shared the insult with my parents, I couldn't keep it from the neighborhood boys. One day a schoolmate named Nazeer, who lived near us, heard Atta and Salih call me German. The next day at school, Nazeer started calling me German too. I told him to cut it out, but he wouldn't listen. After school let out, we squared off for a fight. He was older, at least nine or ten, and bigger. I thought the fight was a bluff until he hit me. The punch landed on my right cheek. I stumbled back, my head buzzing. I looked around to take a swing, but Nazeer was nowhere to be found. Holding my cheek with my hand, I went to my cousin Rooin. He was furious and went straight back to the schoolyard, which by this time had emptied out. He said he would deal with it the next day.

Rooin had taken Ghaffar Khan's class and was still close to him. The next day Rooin told Ghaffar Khan what had happened. Ghaffar Khan said I was to identify Nazeer. I pointed him out, but

Nazeer said he had done nothing wrong. Ghaffar Khan asked
Nazeer to come to the front of the room and told him to lie face-
down on the desk next to the blackboard. Nazeer wouldn't com-
ply, so Khan asked one of the janitors to put him on the desk.
Ghaffar Khan got a bunch of tree branches and, with the janitor
holding the kid down, started flogging him on his buttocks.
Nazeer yelled and screamed, but Ghaffar Khan would not let up.
After fifty lashes he stopped and asked Nazeer to go home. The
next day after class, I was walking home near the crowded bus
station when I heard someone running behind me. It was Nazeer.

"Hey German," he said.

"Fuck your mother," I said, and lunged at him.

We started pushing and shoving. I held Nazeer by the shoulder
with my left hand and threw a punch. It was perfect. I could see
it before it hit his face, could feel the bone and then the softness
of his eye. He fell back. The late afternoon crowd paid little heed
to our fight. As he tried to get up, I took off, running as hard as
I could, looking back to make sure he wasn't following me.

I felt good about knocking Nazeer down but was nervous
about going back to school the next day, fearing the consequences
of my action. Within minutes of my arrival in class, Nazeer appeared with his teacher. The teacher talked to Ghaffar Khan and
told him I'd hit the kid. Ghaffar Khan was furious and asked the
janitor to get branches.

I started shaking. "I didn't do anything," I blubbered, sounding like Nazeer the day before. "He started it," I said. "He hit me
first. It wasn't my fault." The janitor reappeared with freshly cut
branches. I was forced to lie faceup on the concrete floor while
Ghaffar Khan bound my feet with his turban. With the janitor
holding my feet above the floor, the teacher started the flogging.
The pain was sharp, like bee stings, then the soles of my feet got
numb and I couldn't feel anything. Ghaffar Khan hit me twenty
times, after which I put on my shoes and limped to the back of
the classroom.

My feet were swollen. They felt as if I had received shots of Novocain. I was in pain, but I hadn't learned any lesson: I still felt good about knocking that bastard down. Nazeer never called me German again, and fortunately my parents never found out about the incident. I made sure of that as I clumsily stood upright on my blistered feet when I entered the house walking straight to my room. I knew by this point in my life that I was supposed to be a good kid. If any of my father's friends discovered I had been beaten at school, it would have disgraced Father and would probably have earned me a beating from him too.

On the contrary, Father remained thrilled with my progress at school. One afternoon Annan Khan, an engineer and neighbor who played card games with my parents on Friday nights, stopped me on the street near my house. He was holding a folded copy of the local paper *Deewah* in his hand.

"Your father says you can read newspapers," he said. "Is it true?"

I blushed. "*Balay*," I said meekly.

"Here," he said and opened the paper. "Read this. You're a very intelligent boy."

I hated being put on the spot. I hesitated, afraid that I'd be stumped. What if Father found out I failed a simple reading test? To my relief, I breezed through the article, a short piece with big words that I could pronounce without understanding their meaning.

"*Aafareen, Aafareen!*" Annan Khan exclaimed, patting me on the shoulder—Bravo! Well done.

Here was an eight-year-old third-grader reading a newspaper in a country where 95 percent of the population could not read or write. This, Annan Khan felt, was surely an achievement worthy of *Aafareen!*

When he asked me what I wanted to become when I grew up, I regurgitated something I'd picked up at school: "I want to serve my country."

Aafareen. Aafareen.

While I enjoyed accolade for my intelligence from Father, Grandpa Agha was a tougher sell until I learned my daily ritual prayers. It happened one day when Bibi Shirin, Uncle Agha Shirin's plump and kindly wife, was visiting us. She called me inside our house, where she and Mother were sitting around a large cloth spread on the floor, rolling dough to make scallion pancakes.

"Do you know how to say your *namaaz*?" she asked. *Namaaz* are the ritual prayers performed in the direction of Mecca five times a day. I said I didn't, and I was about to run back outside again when she asked, "Do you know your *kalimah*?"

Kalimah is the Islamic declaration of faith: I bear witness that there is no god but God, and Muhammad is his Messenger. Grandpa Agha had chanted the words into my ear when I was a baby.

"Of course I know my *kalimah*," I said, standing in the doorway. This was not unusual, as Muslims of all ages know the words of the declaration of faith.

"If you know your *kalimah*," she said kindly, "then you should learn your *namaaz*. Come here, my dear son. Let me teach you the prayers."

I wanted to go back outside and play, but Mother and Bibi Shirin insisted I sit down and learn my prayers. I didn't understand why they were making me do this. No one my age prayed. I was still too young. I suspected this was my mother's idea, and even though I was irritated, I sat down and waited.

Bibi Shirin said that I first had to learn how to perform the ablution. "To start," she said, "go to the bathroom and wash your private parts." I told her I was already clean.

"That's how it's done," she insisted. The *istinjaa*, the washing of the private parts, comes first.

When I emerged from the bathroom and proclaimed myself clean, she commended me.

"Now, let's go outside and I'll show you how to do the ablution," she said.

In the courtyard I sat on my haunches while Bibi Shirin held an ewer filled with water. She gave me directions about the order in which to wash and how many times to do it. First I washed my hands and arms, then rinsed my mouth, nose, and feet, making sure I washed each part three times. Then she taught me a few simple verses from the Koran. I disliked the sound of the words. They were strange and hard to pronounce. I was getting impatient. After a couple of hours of practice, though, I mastered the rhythm and began to enjoy how sonorous the words really were. In particular I liked how they sounded almost like poetry, which Father had started teaching my sisters and me.

When Bibi Shirin felt I had memorized the verses, Mother got a prayer mat and spread it on the floor. Facing Mecca, I stood on the mat. Bibi Shirin taught me how to stand upright and express a verbal intention to pray, how to bring my hands up to my ears and touch them with my thumbs and then lower my hands and put the right over the left and place them both over my navel. Of course we didn't have a prayer book, not that it would have helped, as Bibi Shirin was illiterate. I began to like the rising and bowing, prostrating and kneeling, turning left and right. It was like learning a new game.

When Father came home later that day, Mother told him that Bibi Shirin had taught me my prayers. He looked tired. "Well done," he smirked, and went to the bathroom.

In 1977, when I was eight, Father asked for and received a transfer to western Afghanistan near the border with Iran. A gas field had been discovered nearby, and seismic studies suggested the presence of oil. Father would be running a much smaller office in Herat, but he saw it as an opportunity to live in a "historic" city and to introduce us to our country's culture and history.

A month or so before our departure, Father took the bus to
Herat to get the lay of the land. He returned with enchanting pictures and postcards of the city, even more enthusiastic about the
move. One depicted the famed Masjid-I Jami, a congregational
mosque built in the fifteenth century, Afghanistan's finest house
of worship. Another showed the Seven Minarets. There was also
a beautiful hilltop public park known as Takht-I Safar. It was like
looking at holiday snapshots, which was essentially what our entire year in Herat was like once we moved there. While Father's
office occupied two floors at the Mo'afaq Hotel downtown, we
lived in the guest quarters of a large house rented by the company
until a permanent residence was found for us.

Located on a quiet, tree-lined street off the main boulevard
that ran from downtown to Takht-I Safar, our temporary house
had a unique ventilation niche built across the top of a sidewall in
each room. A common architectural feature in the city, it served
as natural air-conditioning, letting cool air in during Herat's famous four-month-long windy summer season. In addition, it had
a large garden and playground where my sisters and I played with
the little blonde-haired daughter of a Soviet engineer, one of hundreds of contractors who worked for the company. The company's
local director, a potbellied, vodka-swilling man Father had befriended, lived across the street.

Herat was unique among Afghan cities in that much of its heri-
tage had survived over the centuries. The city's history dates as far
back as Sheberghan's, to the time of the Persian king Darius the
Great and Alexander the Great, but Herat is most famous for the
hundred or so years of enlightened rule by the Timurids, the dynasty founded by the Turko-Mongolian world conqueror Timur,
also known as Tamerlane, in the fourteenth century.

Timur took Herat in 1382, but it wasn't until his death, in
1405, when his son Shah Rukh succeeded him, that the city entered a golden age. Shah Rukh moved his capital there from
Samarqand, and under the rule of him and his wife Gowharshad

Begim, Herat flourished as a center of learning and culture, attracting poets, writers, painters, calligraphers, and architects from around the Islamic world. Art in painted books flourished, some of the finest Islamic architecture was built, and several great Sufi poets became beneficiaries of the enlightened court.

Herat's golden age ended abruptly with the rise of the Moghul empire founded by Babur. After Babur turned west to India, Shiite Safavids of Iran controlled the city for the next two centuries. Then, in the 1800s, Herat became a proxy battleground in the "Great Game" between the British and Russian empires. The Russians backed Persian claims to Herat, while Great Britain, wary of Russian intentions in India, supported the Afghans. The Iron Amir finally incorporated Herat into the Afghan nation-state in the late nineteenth century.

By the 1970s, Herat had become a gateway for hundreds of thousands of Afghan laborers trying to cross into Iran in search of lucrative employment. Lured by the prospects of riches in Iran's booming oil economy, many paid human smugglers to sneak them across the border. There they toiled as construction workers for a year before returning to their homes with a few hundred dollars in savings, along with Seiko watches, Sony boom boxes, and foam mattresses. Some unscrupulous smugglers reportedly would pick up the unsuspecting villagers at night, drive them around Herat, and drop them off outside the grand mosque, telling them they were outside a famous mosque in Iran.

By the time we arrived there, Herat had become a tourist trap, popular with Western backpackers on the "hippie trail." They would pass through Afghanistan on their way to India. Father nicknamed Herat's main drag Tourist Street because it was lined with antique stores, restaurants, teahouses, and pastry shops. One afternoon, while we were window-shopping, Father asked me to talk to a tourist, a stocky man with a thick blond beard over a reddish face. He was standing on the sidewalk outside a pastry shop. He looked as if he had carried his worn backpack all day.

"What should I tell him?" I asked.

"Ask him what his name is," my father replied.

"What should I say?"

"Say, 'What is your name, please?'"

It was the first English sentence Father taught me. I was not familiar with the English alphabet, so I simply learned the entire sentence as opposed to the individual words.

Shyly, I went up to the man and uttered my best "What is your name?"

Taken aback, the man looked at me and said, "John." I didn't know what else to say. I ran back and told Father his name was Jaan. Wherever the tourists went, it seemed, we went too—the grand mosque, the minarets, the citadel. Then there were Herat's many shrines, mausoleums, and monuments to saints—friends of God—that attracted a handful of foreign tourists but flocks of pious Afghan pilgrims. The biggest was Gazargah, a hilltop shrine complex built during the Timurids around the tomb of Khaja Abdullah Ansari, a famous eleventh-century mystic poet. The shrine also houses the tomb of Dost Muhammad Khan, the Afghan king whom the British unsuccessfully tried to replace. We visited Gazargah several times. What I remember most vividly is an ancient tree, just outside the tomb, with hundreds of pieces of cloth nailed to it. Men, women, and children stood before the tree, prayed, and entered the tomb, awestruck and supplicant. Cloth was tied to the tree as a supplication, my father explained. Upon entering the tomb, men whispered prayers and women wept softly with their children following.

Watching them from the shade of the tree, I wondered what we were doing there. Supplication was not on Father's mind, but Gazargah was a great historic site, and Father took pains to explain its history, "Khaja Abdullah Ansari was a prominent poet and . . . Dost Muhammad Khan was king and fought against the English."

As far as Father was concerned, Heratis were the most sophisticated, progressive, knowledgeable, and cultured people of Afghanistan. They were models for the rest of the country. Men were educated, and women didn't wear the full body covering called a *chaadaree*. It had a thriving artist community of not only Afghans but Iranians as well. Theaters staged productions involving both male and female actors. As the year wore on, we started taking road trips to more remote monuments and resorts outside Herat. Proud to show off his new city, Father announced to relatives that they had a standing invitation to visit us. Having a close friend in Herat, Uncle Izmaray, Mother's younger brother, accepted the invitation the following spring with his blonde Ukrainian wife and two much less blond sons.

With the long Afghan New Year celebrations under way, the week our visitors stayed with us was hardly enough to visit even the most prominent sites. Nevertheless, I insisted that we go to one of my favorite shrines, the Khwaja Ghaltan, or "Rolling Khwaja."

The tomb of the Sufi saint was located outside the tiny compound, guarded by an old, shaggy midget who held out her dark, sun-baked hand for money. The caretaker, apparently her husband, a bearded man younger than she, wore a tightly folded old turban. The sand-covered, slightly sloping courtyard inside was about ten meters by ten meters. At the end of the courtyard sat a marble brick. To receive the saint's blessings, the visitor was to lie on the sand and put his or her head on the stone, making a wish.

"What should I wish?" I asked Mother the first time we visited the shrine.

"Wish that you will pass your exams," Mother said.

As I lay down with my eyes closed, the caretaker spun me around. I began rolling all the way to the end of the courtyard until I came to a stop.

"*Alhamdulillah*," the old man said, his eyes brightening— Praise be to God.

I got up, almost convinced that I'd pass my exams with flying colors. My sisters and parents followed me before Father slipped a bill into the old man's hand.

On the surface, this was a time of peace and prosperity. The king had been overthrown in a bloodless coup in 1973. The new ruler, his cousin, Prince Muhammad Daud, who had declared himself the president of the new Republic of Afghanistan, largely continued the king's reforms. This was still a time of law and order when you could travel freely around the country. Murder was unheard of. I was stunned to hear about a notorious bandit who had robbed and killed several members of a family. Yet unbeknownst to most Afghans, the Daud years were the beginning of the end of peace and prosperity in Afghanistan. Daud had come to power with the help of Soviet-trained military officers. Prodded by his communist supporters, he began locking up Islamic activists (their main rivals) and in some cases executed them. A fierce nationalist, Daud later expelled communists from his government on suspicion of pro-Soviet sympathy. By then the seeds of his demise had taken root.

Of course none of us knew this on that fine spring day in 1978. Walking into the compound, Uncle Izmaray lay on the ground and did what he was told by the caretaker. But when the old man tried to pull him, Uncle Izmaray moved to one side and stopped. He lay still on his stomach. I giggled as I watched him. Legend had it that your wish would come true only if you rolled all the way to the end of the yard. The caretaker flushed as Uncle Izmaray got up, rubbed the sand off his hands. "This doesn't work for me," he said. Years later it would prove to have been an ominous sign for my uncle.

Chapter Two

April 1978—It was a balmy Friday in late April, the kind of day we'd normally spend at Takht-I Safar. Instead we were at home, where Father had gathered his coworkers on the shady lawn of our courtyard. The unexpected guests had dropped in just as we were leaving the house and ruined the day for me. Mother was miffed but did her best to seem hospitable.

Bringing out cushions and pillows and spreading them on the lawn, she asked everyone to make himself at home as she dashed into the kitchen to prepare tea. Father and his friends sat in the shade of the apple and apricot trees lining the wall of our court-yard, listening to the news on the radio.

I helped Mother carry trays of tea and sweets but was disap-pointed our Friday plans had unraveled. I filled everyone's cup and decided to join them on one of the cushions. Father was holding his shortwave radio, flipping through stations in search of a clear news broadcast. His friends sat cross-legged in a circle, their ears perking up at each scratchy sound bite that came over the radio.

"There it is," one of them said nervously, pointing at the radio as though the broadcaster sat inside it. "It's Radio Tehran, Maulana Sahib. Let's listen."

They listened. Someone named Mir Akbar Khyber had been murdered in Kabul, the second political assassination in four months. Thousands of demonstrators had taken to the streets condemning Daud, demanding justice, and calling for democracy. Father and his friends listened to the news and talked for hours, trying to make sense of what was happening. Who was Khyber, this obscure figure who had thousands of followers? Who wanted him dead? And who were these protestors who had thrown Kabul into turmoil? I don't remember if they got far in their search for answers, but when Father's guests anxiously departed late that afternoon they left every impression that something big was happening in Kabul.

From that day on, Father obsessively followed the news. Little else seemed to interest him, which was fine with me because he'd stopped bothering me about my schoolwork. Often I'd join him, listening for hours at a time to Radio Kabul, Radio Tehran, the Voice of America, and finally the BBC. I didn't exactly understand what was said, and I'm not sure Father did either.

A week later we both understood things more clearly. On April 28, 1978, Radio Kabul heralded the "Democratic Revolution of Afghanistan" and the end of President Daud's regime. I remember hearing the phrase "People's Democratic Party of Afghanistan," and that a certain "Comrade" Noor Muhammad Taraki headed the new "Revolutionary Council." It was the first time I'd heard the word *inqilab,* Arabic for *overthrow* or *coup d'etat,* but in Persian a word for *revolution.*

Soviet-trained military officers sympathetic to Afghanistan's underground Marxist Party, the PDPA, had overthrown Daud and killed dozens of his family members. The coup wasn't supposed to take place that spring, but when the assassination of Khyber, a royal police officer and liaison between the Communist Party and Communist sympathizers within the military, led to widespread protests, Daud jailed the senior leadership of the party and threatened to execute them. The jailed leaders decided to act, ordering infiltrators to take over Kabul's radio and television stations, to bomb key ministries and the presidential palace, and finally to kill Daud and his entire family.

On the surface the coup was far from remarkable in Afghan history. Since the death of the Iron Amir at the end of the nineteenth century, no Afghan leader had come to power peacefully. Daud himself had seized power through a coup with the help of the same men who eventually engineered his demise. Ordinarily, who ruled in Kabul mattered little to the average Afghan, but this time was different. The Communists had launched a "revolution" and were intent on transforming Afghanistan. They called it *Inqilab-I haft-I Saur,* the Saur 7th Revolution (Saur is the second month in the Afghan calendar), a "people's revolution" modeled on the Bolshevik Revolution.

Within days the government-run newspapers splashed their front pages with grainy photos and official bios of the new revolutionaries. There were new ministers and deputy ministers, new members of the party's Central Committee, new regular and auxiliary members of the Politburo, and a new Revolutionary Council. Some had several titles, and most had adopted noms de guerre. These were our new "comrades," our new *rafeeq,* the Farsi word for *friend,* and *malgary,* its Pashto equivalent, both of which made the new government sound foreign and strange.

Father was acquainted with a couple of *rafeeq,* including Sulayman Layiq, a former classmate at his old *madrassah.* The son of a revered Sufi master, Layiq was expelled after leading his fellow students in a protest march to Kabul before becoming a die-hard Marxist. Father and Layiq had long ago lost touch, but Father remembered smuggling a Persian translation of Karl Marx's *Das Capital* inside a radio from Azerbaijan to Layiq. Now, in a nod to his old friend, one of his first orders of business was to make me memorize one of Layiq's poems about the corruption and profligacy of the old regime—

Last night, from a towering, glorious palace
Rang the laughter of wine-worshipping girls.

Layiq and his comrades condemned Daud's despotic rule and his father's reactionary regime, and they promised democracy, social justice, and human rights. This was music to my father's ears. But Father was too sober-minded and rational to embrace any ideology. He was definitely not a "sympathizer" like Kharkash the Thorn Gatherer, his overweight friend in Sheberghan. Yet in the days and weeks that followed the coup, Father, like many educated Afghans, also welcomed Daud's ouster and believed the new regime's vow to end corruption and "to establish democracy, equality, and social justice." He now openly supported slogans against the "feudal" and "oppressive" government of Daud, and cheered as they chanted the likes of "Death to Daud" and "Long live the People's Democratic Party of Afghanistan!"

In hindsight, Father's enthusiasm doesn't surprise me. In those early days no one knew that the new rulers were communist. The Communists themselves never used the term. They were simply members of the People's Democratic Party of Afghanistan, and their promises had popular appeal.

All across Herat, in schools and offices and public squares, Communist firebrands led boisterous rallies complete with red revolutionary flags and banners that blared *istibdad, hizb, istismar* —despotism, party, exploitation. At one school rally I recited Layiq's poem and later, having been introduced as the top student in my class, got to sit in the front row next to the gruff, hulking new governor of Herat.

In those early days, the Communists had not yet begun to implement their Marxist view of religion as the opiate of the masses, and in keeping with Islamic tradition, they began all official events with a Koranic recitation. On one such occasion, Father's new Communist boss had learned that he was a *maulana* and listed his name on the official program to deliver the Koranic recitation. Father learned about this only an hour before the start of the ceremony and had to break the news that not only was he no *maulana*, but he'd long since lost his recitation skills. The Communist operative then went around frenetically looking for an authentic substitute.

In schools, improv plays were performed depicting the corrupt world of the ancient regime where a bloodthirsty, fat, tyrannical landlord, through his cunning overseer, exploited the peasants. *Exploited* and *peasants*—two more new and unfamiliar words in a country where the average farmer tilled his own plot and distribution was among that part of the world's most equitable. If these "exploited masses" had not risen up against those who possessed the means of production, disillusioned members of the urban elite would have done it for them. Afghanistan was now a long way from the time of King Amanullah, who in the 1920s introduced a series of such radical and disastrously received social reforms as creating the first schools for girls, allowing women members of parliament, and encouraging modern education in the madrassahs' curriculums. Among the city-dwelling middle class was a growing acceptance of modernity, but the larger Afghan society remained conservative. Instead of drawing lessons from this failed experiment, the Communists extolled Amanullah, who had pro-Soviet sympathies, as an anti-imperialist and progressive leader.

Within a few months, Father was transferred to company headquarters in Mazar-I Sharif. His boss had been fired, so Father was asked to assume a more senior position. It wasn't clear this was a promotion, but it also was not a political appointment, as those were reserved for party members. Father arranged for our belongings to be transported to Mazar, while we took a company bus for the journey. To entertain the few passengers on the bus, Father asked me to get up and recite a poem. Blushing, I stood up and recited Layiq's poem. The passengers looked stupefied, as if to say, "What strange language was that?"

In Grandpa Baba's house in Kabul, the revolution had become the butt of everyone's joke. My aunts sarcastically referred to the new Communist leader Taraki as "the Great Teacher" and Hafizullah Amin as his "Loyal Disciple." Uncle Kamkay, my mother's twenty-two-year-old brother, joked how he could now get married for three hundred Afghanis (the equivalent of six dollars at the time) because the government had declared the traditional bride price illegal. He teased me mercilessly until I read him my now ubiquitous poem: *"Last night, from a towering, glorious palace . . ."*

"Well done, revolutionary boy," he said as he picked me up and threw me in the air.

By then the Communists had grown in their zeal. The more radical faction of the party, known as Khalq, or Masses, had taken over and exiled members of the rival Parcham, or Banner, faction. Under Khalq, the government began implementing a series of revolutionary measures starting with land redistribution. This meant land was confiscated from large property holders and often given to the landless peasants who worked it—an illegal landgrab, as Baba saw it. To ensure he wasn't completely deprived of his property, Baba dispatched Uncle Kamkay to the village with orders to knock down every fruit tree in every house and orchard, lest it fall into Communist hands.

Early the following spring, after six months in Mazar-I Sharif, we moved back to Sheberghan. It was quite different from the place we'd left two years earlier. The town had more enthusiastically embraced the revolution than the rest of the country had. Shop shutters, gates to government offices, facades of practically every building—hardly any surface had not been painted revolutionary red. Red banners emblazoned with words of wisdom from the Great Teacher and his Loyal Disciple hung from every available pole lining the main street, at entrances to schools and government offices. Even Sheberghan's grand mosque was not spared.

For those who could not read the banners—not that the literate could make any better sense of them—public-address systems had been helpfully set up around town blaring radio broadcasts of the Great Teacher's speeches. The local Communists running Sheberghan were unmistakable in their appearance. Hailing primarily from the southern Gilazay Pashtun tribe, they wore thick, flamboyant, handlebar mustaches and swaggered around town in military uniforms. Even their civilian operatives carried automatic rifles, as the AK-47 became the symbol of the revolution.

It had been a year since the coup, and my father had now started speaking openly against the revolutionaries and saying Afghanistan was headed for trouble. This would have been unusual for anyone other than my father, but quiet notes of dissent could also be heard elsewhere if you listened close enough. April 27th had replaced July 6th, the date of Daud's coup in 1973, as a national holiday. The date was celebrated with pomp and circumstance, including military parades and marches by schoolchildren, office workers, peasants, and nomads shipped in for the occasion. Marching to the stadium grounds in the middle of town, the parade leaders would shout revolutionary slogans we were supposed to repeat: "*Long live the Great Teacher, Noor Muhammad Taraki!*" This was followed by a strange new word: "Hurrah!" In Persian, *hurrah* sounds the same as the phrase "that way." As our march leader shouted "hurrah," some of us in the back of our procession would devilishly mutter *eeraah,* Persian for "this way."

Shortly after the first anniversary celebrations, Ahmad Zahir, Afghanistan's king of pop music, was killed, purportedly in a car accident. I loved Ahmad Zahir's music and had gone to one of his concerts. In Kabul tens of thousands attended his funeral, turning it into a rambunctious display of mass mourning and protest. Within days rumors swirled that Ahmad Zahir had been murdered. Had he made a crude joke about Taraki at a concert that Taraki then found out about? Had he been having an affair with the wife of Taraki's bodyguard who therefore ordered his assassination? Whatever the reason, few doubted that he had fallen victim to communist atrocities.

While Afghanistan was devastated by the loss of its beloved entertainer, in my grandfather's house in Kabul, our sorrow was equal for Uncle Kamkay. On the day Ahmad Zahir was killed, unaware of the death, Kamkay left the house for work. As my aunts recalled later, he left that morning with his usual bright smile, wearing his favorite pink shirt. It was the last time they saw him. He had joined the thousands who simply vanished. Word of his disappearance reached us weeks later. Mother was devastated and hurried with Father to Kabul to find out if they could do anything to locate him. They returned broken and bereaved, reporting the disappearance of half a dozen other close relatives and with no clues on Uncle Kamkay's whereabouts.

In the summer of 1979, Amin, the Loyal Disciple, seized power by having his Great Teacher strangled during a palace coup. During his six months in power, Amin unleashed a reign of terror, the magnitude of which Afghanistan had not seen since the time of the Iron Amir. Thousands of intellectuals, clergymen, and other suspected dissidents were jailed, tortured, and executed. "Counterrevolutionaries" were everywhere and the government was paranoid; many activities were criminalized, including listening to foreign news broadcasts. On summer nights when we ate on the verandah, Father turned down the volume of his radio, afraid that passersby might hear it over the walls of our house and report us to the government.

Later that summer Uncle Khan Lala, Mother's oldest cousin and a close friend of Father's, and Uncle Ghulam came to visit us to celebrate their release from prison. They had both been picked up by the secret police on the same day the previous month and kept at a detention center. After being forced to profess that they were not counterrevolutionaries, they were released and each given a hundred Afghanis, the equivalent of two dollars.

Uncle Ghulam had been tied to a chair, wires attached to his hands and feet, and the interrogation, which occurred every day for a week, began. He had never been tortured before, but he had heard from several friends who had been incarcerated that the machine made you "jump like a rooster." One day, sitting in the interrogation room, he recognized the man operating the machine.

"He looked at me and winked, and I winked back at him," Uncle Ghulam said. "Then I remembered we both had once worked at the office of the campaign against malaria in Mazar-I Sharif. I know after that he lowered the voltage. God bless him." The electrical discharge was indeed mild—"like touching a car battery," he said, not jolts that made you "jump up and down like a rooster being slaughtered." Uncle Ghulam, though, moaned and shrieked and kicked his legs, giving the impression he was in excruciating pain and hiding nothing.

"I'm glad he didn't attach the wires to my tools!" he said, laughing. "Still, it made me jump like a cock."

We laughed at Uncle Ghulam's ability and good fortune in maneuvering out of harm's way. Uncle Khan Lala, on the other hand, was anything but lighthearted. He had not been tortured, but he was extremely paranoid. He spoke in hushed tones, afraid he would be taken away again. What he wanted to know, he said to Father, was who had informed on him.

"There are spies everywhere," he said, taking a deep drag on his cigarette. "You can't trust anyone anymore."

"Like the Soviet Union," Father said, "the husband spies on the wife, the wife spies on the son, and the son spies on the sister."

Uncle Khan Lala was about to say something, then stopped. He looked at me and then at Father as if to ask if it was okay for his son to be around. I took the hint and headed for the door to avoid the embarrassment of my presence being questioned, but Father said, "You can stay."

This was an important moment for me. I felt like a part of Father's inner circle. Uncle Lala went on with his story: One evening two police officers were driving down a road outside Mazar-I Sharif when they saw a hitchhiker. They pulled over. The hitchhiker told him his wife, who was standing nearby shrouded in a burka, was sick and needed a ride to the hospital. When the policemen walked up to her, the supposed "woman" under the burka, a man with a gun, shot both officers. The assailants grabbed the policemen's weapons, tossed the bodies off the road, and drove away in the officers' Jeep.

When he was finished, Uncle Khan Lala turned to me and said, "Don't you ever tell anyone what you just heard—understand?"

I nodded and left the room feeling exhilarated. It was the first I'd heard about a growing popular resistance among people whom the Communists called "bandits," "rebels," and "counter-revolutionaries."

The night the Soviets invaded had been a Thursday, a night for visiting friends and family. We had Uncle Shah Lala's large family over for dinner. Mother had prepared her specialty, *turdi palow,* Uzbek-style veal and rice cooked in sesame oil with carrots and raisins. As she hustled between the living room and kitchen to make sure everyone had enough to eat, she received compliments from the guests. After dinner she brought out dessert—dried mulberries, raisins, walnuts, and a surprise: a large watermelon that we'd kept for the longest night of winter.

Outside was a dark, moonless night. Snow covered the ground. Father and Uncle Shah Lala, sitting at the far end of the room away from the woodstove by the door, were huddled over a portable shortwave radio. Father started flipping through the channels looking for the BBC Pashto Service. It was a nightly ritual. Father had become an expert at finding the frequency. On this night, though, every station he tried was jammed. Then a booming, clear voice came on.

It was Babrak Karmal, the head of the Parcham faction of the Afghan Communist Party, who, along with his comrades, had been exiled by the rural Khalq faction a few months after the 1978 coup.

"I, Babrak Karmal, Secretary General of the People's Democratic Party of Afghanistan, declare . . . limited contingent of our friendly Soviet forces . . ."

"Incredible news," my uncle said.

"Indeed," Father said. "Very incredible."

As they talked animatedly, we found it irresistible to run outside. We wanted to deliver the news to our friends.

My elder sister, Par, and I dashed out of the room and climbed the ladder leaning against the wall that separated our house from our neighbor's. We shouted for Ghani and Ghotay, the son and daughter of an old artillery officer who had lost his hearing during a military training exercise.

Par said in Pashto, "I have news for you," to which Ghotay, plump and pretty, replied, "I have news for you." That was how we greeted one another, a way to try to outwit the other. We knew all of us had been listening to the radio, but Par went ahead and asked, "Did you listen to the news?"

Ghotay said, "Did you listen to the news? The Russians have come."

We sprinted back into the house. In the living room, Karmal's speech was booming over Radio Tajikistan. Father was frenetically hunting the BBC, but it was nowhere to be found. It didn't really matter. The Russians had indeed come.

"The war," Father later said, "will not end for twenty or thirty years." The war? Did he mean the popular uprising that was spreading around the country? Or a new war the Soviets were about to launch against our people? A student of history, Father recalled the decades of bloodshed it took the Russians to pacify Central Asia.

As one of his first acts in office, Karmal announced general amnesty for political prisoners. A nervous cheer buoyed the room.

"God willing, Kamkay will be released," said Aunt Samargul, Uncle Shah Lala's wife.

"*Inshallah*," Mother said with a mixture of hope and sadness—God willing.

The Soviet invasion was well executed. Before they flew Karmal in from exile, they dispatched Soviet commandoes to seize the presidential palace and assassinate Hafizullah Amin, the Loyal Disciple. In the days that followed, columns of Soviet military transport trucks and tanks rumbled through Sheberghan. Russian soldiers—young, pink-faced, blue-eyed—peered out from tank turrets or sat tightly next to each other in the backs of military trucks, holding rifles between their knees, the bayoneted barrels pointing up. The convoy moved down the main street and around the town square. Traffic stopped for hours as townsfolk watched in awe and fear until the dust kicked up by the last truck settled.

I was on winter break when the invasion happened, so by the time I returned to school several days later, the immediate shock of the attack had worn off. A few changes had been made at school, however. The old red banners with revolutionary slogans painted on them had been replaced with ones praising the "new phase" of the revolution. Gold-framed portraits of President Babrak Karmal now hung where those of the Loyal Disciple had been before. In class we were afraid to talk about what had happened, especially the teachers, who were waiting to learn the new party line before they could teach it to us.

Several weeks later my paternal grandmother came to visit us from Kabul. She had aged considerably in the year and a half since I had seen her. She always carried herself with quiet grace, but newly gray hair and bloodshot eyes made her look confused and disoriented. When she saw Mother, she hugged her and the two broke down into sobs.

Grandma told us that a week after the invasion Aunt Nasreen and Aunt Najia, encouraged by Karmal's amnesty, had gone to the gates of the notorious Pul-I Charki prison outside Kabul to look for Uncle Kamkay. Karmal's amnesty had opened Pul-I Charki's gates, and more than ten thousand haggard prisoners streamed forth. "Ghulam Ali, Ghulam Ali," Aunt Nasreen and Aunt Najia shouted, using Uncle Kamkay's given name, alongside throngs of other anxious family members. The prisoners released that day, far from being hardcore counterrevolutionaries, were mostly ordinary people who had been picked up by the previous regime's secret police for small offenses against the state. They were Kabul University students, junior army officers, village mullahs, government employees—those who needed to be purged if the revolution was to succeed.

Having reunited with their relatives, the pardoned prisoners boarded buses provided by the government to take them to the city. With the crowd thinning, Aunt Nasreen and Aunt Najia pressed their way forward, Aunt Nasreen slowing their progress with her cleft feet. There were still thousands of people waiting, shouting names as lone prisoners wrapped in dirty *patoo* shawls walked outside.

Finally the guards announced that all prisoners had been released and began dispersing the crowd. Convinced their loved ones were still inside, the crowd refused to move. Some pointed at figures peering out the windows of prison cells. The soldiers and guards insisted that no prisoners remained and forcibly pushed the crowd onto the buses. As the prison gates closed, Aunt Nasreen and Aunt Najia walked up to some of the last prisoners to walk out, tearfully asking them if they'd seen or heard about their brother. "A tall fellow," they said, "with thick black eyebrows and a black beard, always smiling, always joking." They got hurried and confused answers. "No, sister, by God, I don't remember seeing him," said one man. "Oh, yes, I remember seeing someone with that description being taken out of prison, but I don't know where," said another.

Deep in their hearts Mother and Grandma knew Uncle Kamkay was dead. Yet between crying fits Grandma told Mother of how she had met former prisoners who had seen Uncle Kamkay alive. Rumors were rife saying some prisoners had been taken to the Soviet gulags from where notes from them had been smuggled in matchboxes back to Afghanistan. There were plenty of tales in Afghanistan to give those without hope reasons to believe.

It was 1982, the third year of the occupation. Travel by road had grown increasingly dangerous, as spontaneous acts of revolt against Communist rule ballooned in response to the occupation. Around this time I first became aware that the resistance fighters the Soviets called *dokhi*—meaning *ghosts*—preferred a different name: mujahideen. Better armed and better organized, the mujahideen brazenly stopped cars and buses in broad daylight looking for suspected Communists. The road between Sheberghan and Mazar-I Sharif became so dangerous that the government started providing military escort to civilian vehicles. Ironically this only made them more obvious targets for mujahideen attacks. The convoys were inevitably ambushed, with several neighbors and distant relatives of ours among the victims.

Up to that point, you could live in Sheberghan and not know a war was raging around the country. The Soviets had encircled the city with several security rings. Sheberghan wasn't the most strategically important town in the country, but the Soviets valued the oil company and wanted to protect the hundreds of Soviet engineers who worked for it.

The security ensured the fighting happened far from Sheberghan, but it didn't always succeed in hiding it. Gas pipes outside the city started blowing up late at night, around eleven or midnight. Without so much as a sound, the sky would suddenly light up in orange and crimson and burn for hours like a fiery desert sunset. To catch a glimpse, neighbors would get on their rooftops, while I'd join Father and an occasional guest in the courtyard as they tried to figure out what section of the pipeline had been blasted. The pipelines carried all of Afghanistan's limited gas output to the Soviet Union. Though relatively insignificant in value, it was meant to defray the cost of the occupation.

One night while drinking tea after dinner, we heard the sound of gunfire. Walking out onto the verandah, I heard barrages of automatic rifles in the distance. Then came single shots, followed by loud machine guns. Tracers ripped the dark sky. A heavy firefight broke out. Some of the gunfire was so loud it seemed to come from across the street. The fight lasted an hour or two before dying down to sporadic outbursts for the rest of the night.

The next day as I walked to school I saw that the building housing the Department of Agriculture had been incinerated, its windows gutted and facade blackened. The movie theater across the street had absorbed rocket propelled grenades but stood intact. Other buildings on my way to school bore bullet holes.

The damage was minimal, but the mujahideen had sent a message: the security rings were not impenetrable. A week or so later I caught a glimpse of the supposed faces behind the attack. It was late in the morning, and we were asked to assemble in the schoolyard for a "meeting." Another new entry in the national lexicon, a meeting was a government-organized standing rally. A marching rally, also organized by the government, was called a *marsh*. Essentially they were powwows meant to inspire the masses. Supposedly voluntary, they were in fact mandatory, but in the years since the Communist coup, I had managed to skip some without being punished. On this sunny day, however, I found myself standing in the middle of the crowd, about fifty yards from the huge makeshift stage erected for the occasion. Large posters of Karmal and revolutionary banners decorated the stand.

One after another, a parade of student leaders, teachers, and administrators walked up to the podium and rambled about the revolution. Then a party official, a slight man in a crumpled suit and tie, came up. Addressing us as "dear students," "champion youths," and "future leaders of the revolution," he recalled the recent incident precipitated by the enemies of the state.

As he spoke, two bearded men in dark traditional pants and tunics emerged from the back of the stage and limped forward. As the men stood a few feet to the left of the podium, the party official, punching the air with his right fist, let loose a barrage of stock epithets: "These traitors, these enemies of the state, these counterrevolutionaries, these agents of Pakistan and America . . ."

"Death to America! Death to Pakistan!" came the cry of a twelfth-grade student leader standing a few rows in front of me. To which the rest of the assembly responded in unison: "Death to America! Death to Pakistan!" Amid the uproar, I tried to look closer at the two men. One was in his thirties and wore a hat, the other was closer to middle age with a shaved head. In their blank expressions and soiled clothes, they could easily have passed for common criminals pulled out of prison for the occasion.

Then the party official turned to the middle-aged man and spat on him. As the man jerked away, one of the guards kicked him in the back of the thigh, sending him stumbling forward. Before falling, the man regained his balance and was pulled back to his spot. I decided he must be a mujahid holy fighter, and I felt excited and sad that he was probably going to meet the fate of tens of thousands of others who had taken up arms against the Soviets.

In the weeks that followed, the government began to organize neighborhood militias. Ours took up a position in an abandoned government building across the street from our home. They erected a watchtower and protected their position with sandbags, watching over us with rifles and heavy machine guns.

Father decided it was time to leave Sheberghan. He felt the militia outpost would mean trouble, plus he didn't want "protection" from a puppet regime. Leasing our house to the company, we moved into one of Uncle Khan Agha's two houses, a modest place with three domes and a bare little yard, but we were closer to our relatives and felt more secure.

There Father started acting strangely. He'd get into loud arguments with anyone who had sympathy for the government. He would say to anyone who would listen how much he hated the *watanfrooshan*—the "nation sellers," the Communists who had handed the country over to the Soviets, just as Shah Shujah, the notorious Afghan king, had handed it to the British in the 1830s.

As the year went on, Father's public behavior turned from bizarre to reckless. One summer night I heard the sound of a motorcycle stopping outside our house, then a commotion. Going out I saw neighbors gathered on the street. Father was standing next to a young man on a motorcycle who was dressed in plain clothes but with a gun strapped on his side, a sign he was either a Communist Party member or a Khad secret police agent.

Father was shouting at him, telling him how ignorant he and all the Communists were. The conversation had apparently started at a party and grew heated when the man dropped Father off. The neighbors were trying to get Father to go home, but he was undeterred. In the faint light of the doorway, I could see the bulging veins on Father's neck. He was swaying his arms in the air, ready to strike. Never before had I seen him so belligerent.

The young man just sat on his motorcycle, his hands shaking on the handlebars. His gun was clearly visible. Once or twice he tried to dismount but then changed his mind. I was terrified. I could smell alcohol in the air, though I couldn't tell which man was drunk. Finally the man rode off, and Father stormed into the house and went to bed.

I was thirteen, going on fourteen. In an attempt to beef up its demoralized army, the Communist regime began aggressively enforcing the draft, lowering the mandatory age to sixteen, and rumors circulated that it would be lowered even further, putting me only a year or so from joining the army. While much of the country was beyond the government's reach, press-gangs started scouring city and town neighborhoods for recruits. High school students were drafted upon graduation unless they arranged for an exemption or obtained a scholarship in a Soviet-bloc country —benefits that were offered to people with connections. Father had plenty of connections, but the last thing he wanted was to send his son to one of those other countries while Afghanistan remained under Soviet occupation. On more than one occasion I heard him say to relatives, "I have two choices. I can send my son to Babrak's army, or I can send him to Masood's army. Why would I want my son to fight in a country-seller's army and not alongside a great hero?" At the time, Ahmad Shah Masood was the toughest mujahideen commander, fighting the Soviets from his base in the Panjsher Valley north of Kabul. His Afghan admirers, and later his Western fans, dubbed him the "Lion of Panjsher."

It was a provocative comment, Father's way of telling people where his allegiance lay. He hated the Soviets and was willing to put his son's life where his mouth was. And he urged others— especially Uncle Agha Shirin and Uncle Khan Agha, who had sons of their own—to do the same. I pictured myself in the mountains, carrying a gun, running alongside the Lion of Panjsher, killing Russian soldiers, and bringing honor to my family. For days I thought about nothing else. Was I, at the age of thirteen, old enough to fight? I heard from relatives visiting from Islamabad that boys as young as eight had taken up arms in Laghman. My fantasy, though, quickly became a way to joke about what my father was saying. Everyone in my extended family caught wind of it.

A few days later, when I visited an aunt's house, her servant, a friendly young Uzbek, greeted me with a sheepish grin. "So when's your father going to send you to Masood?" he said.

"It doesn't concern you," I said, taken aback by his question.

"So you're going to become a mujahid?" he said.

"Yes, and it's none of your business," I said and ran inside the house.

When I went to Uncle Daud's house the next day, I knew he wasn't happy with Father. Uncle Daud was a pious and conservative man who had nonetheless arranged for his oldest son to study in the Soviet Union on a scholarship so as to avoid military service.

"Tell your father that he can send you wherever he wishes but to leave my sons alone," he said.

Father had more things to tell me. He said state education, the same system he'd once wanted me to star in, was a farce and, to the horror of Mother and my uncles, briefly pulled me out of school. He quickly realized, though, that I had to stay in school if I was to avoid conscription.

"In our country," he said one day, "there are two roads to success. You either take bribes or you run your own business. There is nothing in between."

What about being a doctor? I wanted to ask. Many of our relatives were successful doctors, and I'd long wanted to follow in their footsteps. Doctors and engineers were the most respected professionals. But it no longer mattered to Father. Where once he cheered my desire to become a heart surgeon, he now denounced the Communist-influenced education I was receiving. He didn't even care when I dropped to third place in class. Not that much learning occurred in our classrooms of late. Teachers stopped showing up. Some joined the resistance. Others were drafted into the army. Still others had taken up positions in the Communist Party. By winter, my classmates and I had transformed the classroom into a playground, breaking up chairs and desks and throwing them into the woodstove to keep warm. During the warmer months, I started skipping school altogether, playing cards in Uncle Agha Shirin's house or joining in volleyball games.

Father realized I was headed for trouble, so he started a study group to teach the works of Sa'di, the thirteenth-century Persian poet whom he described as "the greatest teacher of life." Sa'di's *Gulistan,* or the *Rose Garden,* had been a classic of Persian education, one which generations of students, including Father and Mother, had studied. All across Afghanistan and Iran, it was the second text that boys delved into after the Koran. Long a believer in modern education, Father had told us little about the classical training he'd received as a boy. To him, that education—starting with the *Baghdad Foundation* and moving on to the Koran, the Hadith, and the *Rose Garden*—was part of a world he had turned his back on. Now that I was practically a delinquent, he changed his mind.

We didn't have a copy of the *Rose Garden,* unusual for an Afghan household, so Father and I went looking for one in the alleys of Sheberghan until we spotted an old Pakistani edition with yellowing pages at an herb store run by an elderly man. Then three or four evenings a week for the next several months, we got together after dinner—my sisters, three of my cousins who were headed for college, and I—and listened to Father expound on the wisdom of Sa'di. We read stories about just and righteous kings, naive princes, capricious and civil dervishes, youthful in-transigence, Sa'di's youthful homoerotic inclinations, and his forty-year adventures around the world.

While this gave me something to occupy my time, nothing could stop Father's increasing vocal denunciations of "treacher-ous Communists." It was only a matter of time before he had run-ins with the authorities. On the way back from Mazar-I Sharif he was detained and questioned several times, and warned each time to keep his mouth shut. Most people did exactly that. As I'd learned by now, Father wasn't like most people. It was then that he started laying out plans for something no one else in our ex-tended family in Sheberghan had contemplated: escaping from the Soviet occupation.

It started with an elusive character we came to know as Hajji Sahib—the Pilgrim—*hajji* being an honorific for someone who had gone on the pilgrimage to Mecca. Father first met the Pilgrim's son, a local engineer named Khan Mohammad, at the oil company. Recently married, Mohammad was thinking about moving to Pakistan, where his parents and siblings lived. Father confided to him how much he wanted to get his own family out of Sheberghan.

"I feel as if I have been strangled, the oxygen has been sucked out of me," Father told him one night. "I look forward to the day when I can cross the border, look at the sky, and breathe freedom." Mother, who was sitting on a pallet in the corner of the room beside Khan Mohammad's young wife, rolled her eyes. *Crossing the border to breathe freedom,* I could see her thinking. Yet Father said those words with such earnestness that I began to imagine the air across the border would smell sweeter, could actually feel better in the lungs. I imagined Father stepping across an invisible line in the desert, looking up at the sky, and taking a prolonged deep breath.

The Pilgrim visited Sheberghan from Pakistan the following spring. Like his son, he was tall and sturdily built with a clipped salt-and-pepper beard and a shaved head covered with a silk turban. A man of few words, he had the affected courteousness of a country man. He put his arm over his chest in deference to Father, got up every time Father would leave the room to go to the bathroom, and answered obsequiously with many *yes sirs*, *no sirs*, and *I'm your humble servant, sirs*. This was the kind of sycophant Father normally had no patience for but now, out of desperation to leave his country, pretended to politely acknowledge.

As Hajji Sahib put it, leaving the country would be a piece of cake, the obvious danger notwithstanding. He'd take care of everything. When we got to Pakistan, he said, we wouldn't have to worry about a thing. He had a big house where we could all live together. "Then we can try to get you to Saudi Arabia," he said. "We have a lot of relatives there. You speak Arabic, Maulana Sahib, don't you?"

"Yes, a little," Father said. "It's been thirty years since I last used it, but I know the language. It's one of five languages I speak."

"Then you should have no problem getting to Saudi Arabia," the Pilgrim said. "A lot of Saudi sheiks come to Karachi, but we can't communicate with them, because we don't speak the language."

But nothing comes free. We'd have to pay the smuggler ten thousand Afghanis, or the equivalent of two hundred dollars. Each of us. In total, roughly the cost of an average house. The Pilgrim warned Father that the journey would not be easy. Father said he was aware of the perils, but went on to say that to stay in Afghanistan was not an option. The country was in the throes of war, and our family was suffering as a result. Not a month went by that we didn't learn someone we knew had been jailed, executed, or killed in combat. The year before, Uncle Izmaray, Mother's younger brother who'd visited us in Herat with his Ukrainian wife, had been executed. He'd joined a Maoist splinter group, and as the leader of an urban cell, he'd participated in assassinating Soviet and Afghan Communist officers and blowing up government installations—acts of terror that I found thrilling and heroic despite his misguided politics. With Uncle Izmaray's execution, following the disappearance of Uncle Kamkay, Mother had been robbed of her two full brothers, and she became increasingly protective of me.

Meanwhile, fighting raged everywhere, even in villages and towns near Sheberghan. Rumors of military operations were followed by columns of tanks and armored personnel carriers roaring out of town, and later with war casualties streaming in. Many of the dead brought into Sheberghan were young Afghan conscripts killed by the mujahideen fighting the Soviets. Although most of these Afghans had been conscripted against their will, I saw them as traitors. Why didn't they simply desert and join the mujahideen? As the war dragged on, tens of thousands asked themselves that same question, making the government even more dependent on Soviet troops for protection.

One day while I was visiting an ill uncle in the hospital with my cousin, I stumbled over a dead body in a dim corridor. I had often wondered about violent death but had never seen a corpse up close. My heart was pounding. I wanted to leave but grabbed my cousin by the shoulder for support so I could look closer. Draped in a white, bloodstained sheet, it was the body of a big, fat man, his face swollen and blue. There were no visible wounds on his face, and we learned shortly after that he had been shot in his stomach.

"When that happens," my cousin explained, "the bullet makes a much bigger hole in the back."

I did not understand how a man could die by being shot in the stomach. Weren't the head and the heart the only fatal spots? I was terrified and started imagining myself as that man, struck dead by a bullet, with people stumbling over my lifeless body. I left the hospital shuddering.

Father's preparations were soon under way, and we left Sheberghan for Mazar-I Sharif and ultimately Kabul early in the summer of 1983. It was still dark that morning when our carriage pulled up outside the small ticket office on the main square in Bandar-I Akhchah. Taghayee, Uncle Khan Agha's skinny, jovial Hazara servant, helped carry the trunks while Father ran into the ticket office. Mother, her eyes red from sleeplessness, stood next to Uncle Khan Agha and my sister Fay, who was quietly crying.

When Father emerged with tickets in hand, he looked around warily, as though we were being watched. We knew most everyone in this neighborhood. Many of Father's colleagues and my classmates were on the street each day. He wanted to get out of Sheberghan before word of our flight got around.

"Finish your good-byes," he demanded as mother held Farkhundah in her arms.

Fay, my father had decided, was going to stay behind with my uncles, a necessary prop of deception, a ruse to make the government believe we were only going to Kabul for vacation, not fleeing to Pakistan, an offense against the state.

As Mother let go of Fay, tears streamed down their faces. With Fay pulling away, Mother wiped her tears with her white scarf and climbed onto the bus.

We pulled out of the station, passing familiar sites—Bandar-I Akhchah's shops and bakeries, my school, Father's office, the Soviet engineers' housing complex. On the edge of town, we passed through the arched gateway, a relic from Sheberghan's days as a heavily fortified walled city. Yet the gate was well defended that day, with a checkpoint manned by armed policemen, army soldiers, and secret police stopping traffic. It was a marked departure from the days before the war.

As the driver pulled over, armed police officers climbed in, looked around, talked to the driver, and asked a few men sitting in the front rows for their documents. Although I had a letter from my school stating that I was a student in good standing and not of draft age, I was relieved that I wasn't asked to produce documents.

I hadn't taken the road to Mazar-I Sharif in several years. It had become too dangerous, controlled in turn by mujahideen, renegade government militia, and highway robbers. Shortly after the Soviet invasion, an old Uzbek neighbor of ours had taken the bus to Mazar-I Sharif. About halfway through his journey, the bus was stopped by particularly vicious mujahideen who targeted Communists and Communist sympathizers. It was Ramadan, the fasting month, and he was discovered to be chewing tobacco in violation of religious rules. As the rest of the passengers watched in horror, one of the mujahideen shoved his bayonet into the old man's mouth, leaving him dead on the side of the road. Father had chosen for us not to travel as part of a military convoy, though I don't know if it was out of precaution or principle. He certainly didn't want a Communist escort while escaping from Communist rule.

About an hour into our trip, the driver suddenly hit the brakes. The desert lay barren on either side of the road. A cluster of washed-out old mud huts were barely visible in the distance. Looking out the window, I could see men on the roadside. Two who were carrying rifles under their shawls, with their pant legs rolled up, got inside the bus. I'd been looking forward to meeting mujahideen, but I couldn't immediately be sure if these were fighters or bandits. One of them stayed on and asked the driver to move, while the other ran alongside the bus, directing us down a side road to a village a couple of miles away.

We pulled up outside a large compound of mud huts. The driver said, "Brothers, please get out of the bus and wait outside. Everyone out except women and children."

Armed men were waiting outside, some of them hiding their faces with turbans. One of them asked the passengers to empty their pockets and hand over their watches and jewelry into a big sack he was carrying. Father tossed a few small bills into the robber's sack with an angry look. The smart travelers had handed over their valuables to the women on the bus, knowing that if the robbers were gentlemen, they wouldn't press the women. Although the thieves looked disappointed with their meager catch, they didn't enter the bus.

"This is what the country has come to," the driver said, hitting the gas and speeding past every car in sight, all the way to Mazar.

After two days in Mazar-I Sharif, we set out for Kabul. This was a road I had taken many times as a child. Now it was ravaged. A new pipeline ran alongside the road, supplying fuel to the Soviet military. In Tangi Tachqurghan, a narrow gorge an hour north, carcasses of destroyed Soviet tanks lay by the roadside. When we neared the Soviet-built Salang Tunnel, I saw deeply tanned, shirtless Soviet soldiers sunbathing on their tanks. I was afraid they would stop us. I'd heard how a Russian soldier a couple of years earlier had dragged an Afghan woman from a bus. That prompted an enraged passenger to grab the soldier's rifle and shoot every Russian in sight. The Russians retaliated with a killing rampage of their own. I was thankful that we passed the sunbathers unscathed.

The night before we left for Jalalabad, my cousin Rooin stopped by. Having said good-bye to him in Sheberghan, I didn't expect to see him again, but I was glad he showed up. Two years my senior, Rooin often deferred to me intellectually, but on this evening he questioned Father's decision to flee Afghanistan. "You have a great future ahead of you," he said, "why risk it? You'll be languishing in a camp, recruited by fundamentalists to go out and kill. You know, so many people who left the country have come back," he said wistfully, "kissing the soil with tears in their eyes."

While I was well aware that Afghanistan was our sacred land, I also knew Rooin had grown up accepting the Soviet occupation as a fact of life, much like every boy growing up in Sheberghan. As long as the war didn't affect them personally, it didn't bother them. Few if any questioned the morality of living under occupation. While I felt sorry for what Rooin would face after I left, I also felt lucky that Father had chosen this path for me, and I was certain it was right.

The next morning we took a taxi to the Jalalabad station, a walled area the size of a football stadium teeming with people, battered cars, and minibuses. The Pilgrim was waiting for us. He introduced Father to our smuggler, a short middle-aged man who looked suspiciously at Father as if taken aback by the sight of a beardless supermullah. Dressed in traditional clothes and sporting a woolen hat and an unshaved face, Father looked awkward, like a new prisoner in a jumpsuit.

Father had already paid the smuggler fourteen thousand Afghanis each for him and Mother and ten thousand each for me and my two sisters, more than the Pilgrim had told us the trip would cost. It was a huge sum of money, equivalent to the annual salary of a civil servant, and was clearly a no refunds kind of deal. Human smuggling had grown into a lucrative business. While many refugees living in the border areas knew their way out of the country, well-off city dwellers often relied on smugglers to guide them through the mountains and deserts into Pakistan or Iran. Our smuggler, an Uzbek from the north, specialized in northern refugees.

On the edge of town, we stopped behind a line of vehicles at a checkpoint called Pul-I Charkhi, named after the nearby notorious Communist prison where tens of thousands of dissidents had been tortured and killed and where Aunt Nasreen and Aunt Najia had stood at the gates looking in vain for Uncle Kamkay. Stories were already circulating about what kind of place Pul-I Charkhi was, but it wasn't until much later that I would learn how prisoners had their fingernails plucked, their genitals tied to electric prods, how they were blindfolded and machine-gunned in the dead of night, and how Uncle Kamkay spent the last months of his life there before being shot by a firing squad.

The Kabul-Jalalabad road was the last leg of our journey through Communist-controlled territory. It had been built in the 1950s to replace an ancient, parallel road that ran a mile or two through the mountains. The Soviets knew that a British army sixteen thousand strong had been slaughtered on that ancient road following England's first attempt to install a puppet ruler in Kabul in 1838, and this new paved road ran through the same mountains, still offering no immunity from periodic mujahideen attacks. To protect it, the Soviets and the Communist government posted thousands of soldiers along the road.

Driving through the mountains, Mother asked in a whisper through her burka if I had my document with me. "Yes," I said curtly, afraid others on the bus might find out we were fleeing, but it turned out everyone on the bus, some thirty people in all, were being handled by the same smuggler. Along with women and children, there were several men in their sixties and seventies. Father, at fifty, was the youngest. This made him the hardiest man, but it also meant he'd stand out if we were caught.

In Jalalabad the bus dropped us off around noon by the side of the road near a small market. Father bought a bag of lemons before we set out. The temperature had risen noticeably, and being out of the overheated bus brought no relief. We started walking up a dirt road leading to a hilltop fort that belonged to a landlord who was on the smuggler's payroll. The women went inside while I joined the men in the one-room mosque. I was promptly stung by a bee. Having no medicine to treat me, Father asked the mullah to say a prayer. I was astounded. Standing beside him, I saw his outward posture of rising, bending, and prostrating to be as good as any proper madrassah student, but I didn't know what was going through his mind. Clearly he felt that he had to pray in present company, but was he sincere or was he putting on a show? Father wasn't a hypocrite. Perhaps today he believed in God.

We took a nap after evening prayers and were awakened around eleven p.m. The donkeys had arrived. Men started loading them as a full moon brightened a cloudless sky. Mother and my sisters Par and Lachi came out of the house, followed by the other women. They said the womenfolk inside the compound had treated them well, businesslike but hospitable. After several unsuccessful attempts Mother climbed on her donkey. I chose to walk. We set out into the desert.

Some hours into our journey spotlights began to illuminate the sky. You could see the origin of the light four or five miles from the horizon. I asked one of the donkey riders where it came from, and he said it was the Soviet base protecting Jalalabad, headquarters of an army division responsible for counterinsurgency operations in eastern Afghanistan.

A couple of hours later we reached a paved road. In the dark it was hard to tell whether it was the Kabul-Jalalabad road or the Jalalabad-Torkham road. An airplane hummed overhead. Concerned we would be spotted, the smuggler and donkey drivers admonished us to conceal anything white. "Make no sound," they insisted. All you could hear was donkey hoofs. We crossed the road, straggled up another hill, and disappeared further into the desert.

Walking in the dark, I recalled a Communist propaganda cartoon that showed poor villagers crossing the border into Pakistan, where "rebel" leaders robbed and enslaved them in their mansions. What the cartoon left out was the fact that the Soviet military targeted refugees on the Afghan side of the border. This was because refugees took the same goat trails through the mountains that the mujahideen used to ferry supplies across the border. Mujahideen or refugees, whoever was crossing the border was going over to the enemy. Better to eliminate them now rather than have to do it later. Thousands of civilians lost their lives in these attacks. Judging from his expensive clothes and glittering gold watch and silk turban, though, I could tell our guide had, so far, been very successful.

Early the next morning, we arrived on the bank of the Kunar River, a tributary that flows into the Indus River in Pakistan. Little Lachi was dehydrated, so Father gave her some lemons. Passing out the remaining lemons, he warned us not to touch the muddy river water, saying this as others in our caravan eagerly helped themselves to the water. I put a lemon in my mouth. It tasted awful. I didn't understand how it would quench my thirst and, feeling even thirstier, went down to the river and took in several gulps.

We rested until the sun came up and the dinghy boys pulled the boats across the river. Clumsily boarding one, we sailed across the fast current. Back and forth the boats went until everyone in our party had been taken over. It was now noon, and we spent the day and the evening in a nearby village, the smuggler determining that it was not safe for us to leave until the next afternoon. We'd been on the road for nearly seven hours and had several more to go. I could see the long shadows of our exhausted party in front of us, and the rising dust that trailed our lumbering donkeys.

Entering a valley, we heard a single shot. Then several more. Everyone started panicking. The donkey riders and the smuggler shouted at everyone to get down. Out of nowhere, there appeared parapets. Did this mean mujahideen were nearby? We scrambled off our donkeys and took cover in the parapets. Our smuggler deduced the fire was coming from mujahideen who'd mistaken us for a rival group. As I lay behind the parapet, I could see the donkeys grazing on the barren valley floor, oblivious to the shooting. Lying not far from Father, one of the donkey riders asked if anyone knew how to write. I said I did. Handing me a piece of paper, the smuggler dictated a message: "We are refugees. Please do not fire at us." As the shooting continued, I scribbled down his words and handed the note to him. He asked one of the donkey riders to make his way down the parapet and somehow try to reach the gunmen. But as quickly as it had started, the firing stopped.

Relieved, we left the valley at once and got to a caravanserai late that evening. The next day we switched to a tractor-trailer and arrived at the border crossing, which was not exactly what I had imagined it would be. There were no signs, ropes, barbed wire, or fences. Just gray barren mountains as far as the eye could see.

"Over there is Pakistan," the smuggler announced as we disembarked. The moment of truth had arrived, the moment we'd been awaiting for more than a year. I was expecting Father to stop here, look up, and inhale that symbolic breath of freedom I'd longed to see. He was too much of a romantic to have forgotten what he said, but he was also too busy unloading our bags to actually do it.

The smuggler smiled with satisfaction as he did a head count. This was the first time, he said, that he had not lost a single member of his party. On previous trips, one, two, even ten people had died under different circumstances. Still, despite the miracle of our safe arrival, no one asked, or was asked, to bow down before God to offer thanks.

The money we had paid the smuggler covered the journey up to the mountain pass. From there we were on our own. Scaling the mountain, I looked down below and saw for the first time in a week signs of civilization: cars, paved roads, power lines.

Down by a busy taxi and bus station, freedom greeted us in the form of cheap Pakistani colas. I'd drunk Coca-Cola and Fanta before but what was Pepsi? To quench the day's thirst, we gulped down a few bottles and after a short rest hired a pickup truck to head to Peshawar. As we drove through rustic countryside, even the signage looked exotic. In Sheberghan, billboards were nowhere to be found; in Pakistan they were everywhere, enticing you to indulge. Crammed in the back of the pickup, I looked forward to my new life in Pakistan.

Chapter Three

Summer 1983—"*Maajirah,* get up. *Maajirah.*"

It was the morning after we crossed the border when I first heard my new name—refugee. A skinny cop with a baton towered over me on the concrete platform of the Peshawar raiload station, where I was lying next to my parents and sisters. *Muhajir* is a Koranic term given to one who flees from infidels to a new land, but in Pashto the word had been butchered into *maajir,* the slang word used by Pakistani cops harassing Afghan refugees crowding the streets of Peshawar. The cop was Pashtun, one of several scouring the filthy, overcrowded station, ostensibly clearing out refugees but more interested in cleaning out their pockets.

Hearing the commotion, Father got up and faced off with the cop. "*Moonj Afghanan yu*"—We're Afghans, he barked in Pashto. "We arrived from Afghanistan last night. We escaped from the Russians and the Communists, and it is our right to stay here. We're not going anywhere."

Taken aback, the cop muttered something unintelligible and moved on to harass the next poor devil.

It was our second day in Pakistan. All along, the Pilgrim had intended for us to head straight to Karachi, Pakistan's commercial capital on the Arabian Sea. But Peshawar had advantages over Karachi. It had been the winter capital of Afghanistan during the nineteenth century, and its residents were predominantly Pashtuns who had ended up on the wrong side of the border when Sir Mortimer Durand, humble servant of the crown, put pen to paper and drew up the artificial boundary to keep out the unruly Afghans. In the 1980s, as one of two major Pakistani cities near the Afghan border, Peshawar was home not just to a large number of Afghan refugees but also to the headquarters of mujahideen groups fighting the Soviets.

Several relatives of ours worked for these groups. Our closest relative in Peshawar was Mother's uncle, a former judge known in our family by his nickname, the Evangelist. Never enthusiastic about relocating to Karachi, Mother suggested we settle in Peshawar, where the Evangelist could get us lodging.

"We should look up Uncle the Evangelist," she pleaded. "Perhaps he could help Father find a job and get us a place to live."

After tea, Father left with Par to track down the Evangelist, leaving me behind to keep an eye on Mother and Lachi. When I wasn't guarding them, I walked around the busy station. Red-jacketed teenage porters hauled luggage onto trains. Old men carried dirty trays of tea on their heads. Haggard refugees clumsily boarded the Khyber Express as its aging steam engines lumbered out of the station. At the end of the platform an old man was folding his prayer mat. It was too late to pray. In the week we trekked across the mountains, I had missed only one of my five daily prayers, and that was when we'd been caught in the crossfire.

As the hours went by, Mother and I grew worried. "What happened to your father?" she asked, her dress soaked in sweat. I kept reassuring her that he'd return, but I also knew Peshawar was a sprawling, boisterous city with a population of millions. Despite the large number of Afghans and many mujahideen offices, it would be easy to get lost.

It was almost noon when Father and Par returned, accompanied by one of the Evangelist's sons. Handsome, with a clipped beard, and wearing the traditional *shalwar kameez* that was popular locally, he looked at home in Peshawar and not like a refugee living in a strange city. Dodging the pestering throng of porters, he helped us carry our belongings to two big rickshaws.

The brightly painted scooter-driven cabs zigzagged through traffic, leaning on their sides, their engines choking out thick black smoke. Soon we arrived at the end of a winding alleyway. The Evangelist greeted my parents warmly. When his surprised wife and his daughters emerged from their house, Mother embraced them and broke into a sob. She hadn't seen the Evangelist's wife since Uncle Izmaray's execution and had to engage in the mourning ritual.

The Evangelist was a fabulously wealthy former provincial chief justice who had left his big house in Kabul for this modest brick one. He carried himself with pomp and circumstance: crisp, freshly ironed clothes that he changed twice a day, and generous amounts of musky perfumes applied all over his body. Thick, black eyeliner—kohl, worn by men in some parts of Afghanistan in keeping with the Prophet Muhammad's practice—outlined his shining, dark eyes.

He was a born mullah, and when it was finally time to sit down for a late, hastily prepared lunch, he ate like one. His hands, strengthened by a lifetime of prostrating, voraciously shoveled large handfuls of rice and juicy chunks of lamb into his mouth. As I watched him, I wondered how many hungry refugees could be fed with what he ate, even as chunks of the tender lamb melted in my own mouth. After wiping his plate clean, the Evangelist expressed surprise at our arrival.

"Why did you leave Afghanistan?" he asked Father.

The Evangelist was making a point. From his perspective, he was a man of God, a *muhajir,* who had fled his country in the name of God. He wondered what could possibly bring a man of no faith like my father here.

"I felt suffocated," Father said, pointing to his thick, veiny neck in explanation. "I couldn't breathe any more. I wanted to breathe freedom."

The Evangelist raised his eyebrows. "You would have been better off in Sheberghan," he said. "Your life was not in danger. Peshawar is not the right place for you. It is too conservative."

"Mister Evangelist," Father replied, "we've come to you only to seek your advice."

Mother giggled nervously as Father mentioned the Pir, the Sufi sheikh then leading one of the Peshawar-based resistance groups. "I remember the Pir very well," Father said. "We were classmates at the madrassah, if you remember, Mister Evangelist. Perhaps I can pay him a visit. Surely he'll remember me."

"No one can see the Pir," the Evangelist snapped. "He's a very important person, too busy keeping up with his followers to see you."

The Pir's followers came from all over Afghanistan. Poor illiterate farmers and powerful tribal chiefs alike came to him with goblets of offerings in exchange for the opportunity to prostrate at his feet. The water Pir used for ablution was the most sought after item; followers believed it possessed healing powers. In the pantheon of Afghan resistance leaders, though, the Pir was relatively minor, his power overshadowed by Abdul Rab Rasul Sayyaf and Gulbuddin Hekmatyar, two ideologically extremist mujahideen leaders. These two men virtually ran Peshawar and protected only proper refugees, men with long beards and limitless religious zeal, not clean-shaven supermullahs with dubious religious credentials like my father.

"That's the reality, Mister Supermullah," the Evangelist told my father.

"If these are the leaders of our fight against the Russians," my father said, "then I have no use for them. Thank you, Mister Evangelist. You're absolutely right. I surely don't belong in this city."

"Karachi is a great city," the Evangelist said. He did not come out and urge my father to leave, but this was his way of telling him to keep moving. Like a travel agent he rattled off a list of the city's fantastic attributes: millions of people; big, tall buildings; a fantastic metropolis by the sea.

"You'll love it, Mister Supermullah," he summed up. Father nodded with no interest. The floor was cleared and tea was served. Satisfied, the Evangelist was now looking forward to watching his favorite TV show: professional American wrestling.

If my father was disappointed, he didn't let us see it. He treated the rest of our week in Peshawar like a holiday, taking me to the Old City district to visit other relatives, and fattening up on the hearty meals prepared by the Evangelist's wife and daughters. At the end of the week, we took rickshaws to the railway station where we boarded the Khyber Express for a grueling thirty-hour journey to Karachi.

The rickety ceiling fan with a missing blade hissed and clattered to a stop. A thin man standing next to me in a loincloth looked up and muttered something. He was as dark as an African and spoke Punjabi, Pakistan's most popular language. Next to him was Ayoob, the Pilgrim's burly son who, like his father, was uneducated but had a pleasant, courteous manner. Inside this vast, stiflingly hot factory, men stood at rows of tables wrapping matchbooks into bundles. Ayoob moved his hands like an expert juggler, shoving the wrapped bundles into trays. I tried and failed to imitate him, realizing for the first time the futility of my schooling. Father had been right all along. I might as well throw my degree in the outhouse; it wasn't worth *gooh*—crap.

I was a long way from Sheberghan.

It was the second or third week after we'd arrived in Karachi on the ironically named Khyber Express. We'd been living in Sohrab Goth, a sprawling Afghan refugee camp a half-hour walk down a dirt road from the match factory. The camp was a hodgepodge of houses built with different materials depending on the owners' financial means—concrete walls for those who could afford them, baked bricks for the less affluent, and so on down to bricks and simple clay for those one step away from homelessness. Below the haze-blanketed tips of the high-rise apartment buildings in the distance, noisy cars, buses, vendors hawking their wares, and donkey-drawn carriages all contributed to the clamor of what was Paki-stan's largest city. You'd also see hulking SUVs and sedans with tinted windows driving toward the walled compounds. These traffickers were usually Pathans, Pashtuns from Pakistan's tribal areas near the Afghan border (Pakistan's main source of opium and heroin), and were a common sight in this drug-infested environment.

The Pilgrim graciously welcomed us into his house, but it was far from the palace I'd imagined. Made of brick, it showed him solidly in Sohrab Goth's middle class, but it bore no resemblance to middle-class houses anywhere else. There was a squalid court-yard and the front door of the house was missing, the entryway covered instead with a rough tapestry of cloth, stitched together, the way many villagers back in Afghanistan had done. The house itself had only two rooms, one for the Pilgrim, his wife, and their children and another for guests. We stayed not in the guest room but in a cramped pantry made from timber and thatch next to the outhouse.

For many refugees Sohrab Goth was an improvement over the life they'd left behind. Tents popped up every day. New houses were under construction, and the mosque was being expanded. Several shops opened for business along the dirt road, including a minimarket and a kebab stand. Many a camp resident, it seemed, had relatives around the Persian Gulf, mostly in Saudi Arabia, and nearly everyone in Sohrab Goth dreamed of making it there.

During our first few days in Karachi we explored the camp and the city, visiting its great green spaces, beaches, and amusement parks. With a population of more than ten million at that time,

Karachi attracted only a small number of Afghans, and the few who did go there went primarily as a stepping stone to the Persian Gulf. For identification purposes, we got membership cards in an Afghan resistance party, the same party the Evangelist worked for in Peshawar. Father also served as something of a translator, using an antiquated English he hadn't spoken in close to thirty years to communicate with Pakistanis schooled in a pedantic South Asian version of Victorian English in which, for instance, a pharmacist was called a "dispenser" and an overpriced item was always "costly."

To leave Sohrab Goth's laborers, peasant boys, carpet weavers, and drug smugglers, Father started looking for a job in the city. Within a few days, he stumbled upon the Iranian Cultural Center where he not only became a member, but on the spot had himself hired as an assistant librarian. Those first few months in Karachi were filled with promise and were the happiest I saw my father.

Within a couple of months, we left Sohrab Goth for a small apartment in a quiet, middle-class neighborhood. I quit my factory job and started working at a printing shop, but the job lasted only a couple of months. Without a job I became a loner and spent long hours at home reading books Father brought in from the Iranian Cultural Center. Par was less generous than Father in sharing her books with me. One day I found her immersed in a book. I picked one up from her stack.

"Why do you sit around the house all day instead of going out and looking for a job?" she yelled. She stood up and took the book away from me.

I was furious. Mother tried to stop her.

"Why don't you give him the book?" she asked.

"If you can't find a job, why don't you join the jihad like everyone else?" Par said.

Mother rolled her eyes. "Stop talking about jihad and just give him the book."

Stop talking about jihad? I was confused. Wasn't our flight from Afghanistan in support of the jihad? Didn't Father tell everyone back in Sheberghan that he wanted me to fight under my great namesake, Commander Ahmad Shah Masood of the Panjsher Valley? Jihad was being waged first and foremost in defense of our *namoos*—our women, our honor. *Namoos* is what defines every male Afghan. The worst insult he can suffer is *bee-namoos*—a man whose womenfolk have been violated. Back in Sheberghan, shortly after the Soviet invasion, I'd overheard my father recite to a relative the famous Afghan motto about the three most important things to every Afghan man's honor: women, land, and gold (in Farsi, they all start with the letter *z*— *zan, zameen,* and *zar*). The easiest way to provoke an Afghan is to violate one of the *z*'s, he said, and the Russians had violated all three.

Yet jihad seemed so distant from Karachi. Except for the nightly BBC and VOA news broadcasts, we had lost contact with our home. We had no telephone (not that there were direct phone lines to Afghanistan), so my Father wrote a short letter on a piece of white cloth and gave it to an old man from Sohrab Goth who was traveling to northern Afghanistan; he promised to deliver it to our uncles in Sheberghan. We never learned if it reached them. Most information came from recently arrived refugees who told us where the fighting was when they left. Boys my age and older had fled with their families to avoid conscription into the Communist army and were working hard to survive or save enough money to travel to Saudi Arabia.

In 1984, about a year after our arrival, I found a job through a friendly Pakistani neighbor and started working as a *kampooder*— a compounder of medicine—for the neighbor's friend. He was a doctor and, like the man who had arranged the job, a *muhajir,* a refugee from the India-Pakistan Partition in 1948. I liked my job title. In Persian, the butchered version of the word sounded like "little powder," and since I spent part of my time mixing and grinding tablets in a mortar, I thought I'd cleverly figured out where the word had come from.

"Daaktar Sahib" or "Mr. Doctor" drove me five miles each way on the back of his motorcycle through the chaotic streets of Karachi to a slum where I spent seven hours a day in a cubicle grinding tablets in a mortar, filling prescriptions, and giving people shots. Yet I didn't lose contact with the boys from Sohrab Goth. One day, Hajji Sahib's son Ayoob stopped by the apartment with a young man I didn't know. Declining my invitation for tea, they suggested to taking a walk and having a chat. Ayoob said a sheikh was visiting town to interview prospective workers. Ayoob's friend, Abdullah, knew the sheikh, which is what both boys called him.

An aspiring mullah from northern Afghanistan. Abdullah had dropped out of a madrassah, fled to Pakistan, and then somehow made his way to Saudi Arabia, to which he was now trying to return. Apart from his white flannel prayer cap and thin longish beard, little of the madrassah education had rubbed off on him. Affable and gregarious, he laughed and joked and wore a large gold ring inset with a shining red stone. He didn't exactly look like someone who'd taken the Prophet Muhammad's credo "Poverty is my pride" to heart.

The best jobs, Abdullah said, were either working in a bakery or running a store or shop. Ayoob agreed. "With your education," he said to me, sounding a lot like his father, "you should be able to get the best job. Running a store. You know how to use an abacus, don't you?"

I'd played with an abacus as a kid but never learned how to use it.

"Oh, no, no, you don't need to know how to use the abacus," Abdullah interjected, "just the calculator. Do you know how to use a calculator?"

That I did know. So the following day, we dressed our best and took a rickshaw to meet the sheikh at the Sheraton, the only five-star hotel in Pakistan. According to a family friend who worked as a concierge, a room cost two thousand rupees a night—more than I got paid in a month. My imagination was fired up. Perhaps with the sheikh's help one day I'd be sitting at the front of an expensive store next to a big bronze scale flanked by shelves of merchandise and serving long lines of white-robed customers.

The lobby was quiet and cool. It gave me the false sense of being in a foreign country. The sheikh opened his hotel room door and invited us in. He was in his late forties and had a wisp of a goatee. He offered us Pepsi from the minibar and took a seat across from us.

Abdullah started mumbling in Arabic but it was clear that he couldn't communicate with the sheikh. He was not reciting the Koran—but I wondered how much of his conversation was peppered with the Arabic he'd learned at the madrassah and not with the Arabic that he obviously had failed to learn in Mecca.

Frustrated, Abdullah turned to me. "Say something in English, please. The sheikh," he said, "speaks English."

"I . . . work . . . calculator," I said.

The sheikh, smiling in approval, said something in English I didn't understand. I'd barely touched my can of Pepsi, but the meeting was over. He handed each of us five hundred rupees and said something in Arabic I likewise didn't understand. When we were down in the lobby, Abdullah told me it was a deposit for our future services. We were going to work for him and no one else.

Weeks passed. When I next saw Ayoob, he said the sheikh had never showed up again. I was disappointed but realized this was not uncommon. The sheiks picked a handful out of dozens they interviewed. But Ayoob was still determined to get to Saudi Arabia. With him was a friend, a refugee who had already been to Saudi Arabia and returned. It's very simple, the friend said with a smile. Hundreds of Afghan refugees, even Pakistanis, had already done it. We would get fake Pakistani passports and travel across the border into Iran, then move through Turkey and Syria, until we finally reached Saudi Arabia. The whole journey would take four or five weeks, a month or two at most. We didn't need a lot of money. "We just work our way along," Ayoob's friend said.

Once in Saudi Arabia, he would take care of everything. He knew people who would give us jobs. This was the second time I heard the best job was working at a bakery. The pay was great—about fifty Saudi rials a day. That's how much the doctor paid me in a month. Fifty rials a day!

"How much money do I need for the trip?" I asked.

"Not much. Probably five thousand rupees," he said.

"Is that going to last two weeks?"

"We'll have no expenses," he said. "We'll sleep outside apartment buildings. We don't need to stay at a hotel."

What about the passport? The going rate for a Pakistani passport was about ten thousand rupees, not the kind of money I could easily come up with.

"The great thing about you is that you don't have to spend too much money," he said. "You speak Urdu fluently, so you should be able to get a genuine passport for a lot less."

I went home, as excited as when I was eleven years old and my Mother told me she was going to buy me my favorite Chinese bicycle with a nickel-back seat and a carpeted saddle. Flipping through the pages of the Iranian calendar hanging on our wall, I pictured myself walking the streets of Tehran, Shiraz, and Isfahan en route to Saudi Arabia.

Our landlord downstairs told me he could get me a Pakistani passport for a thousand rupees. "I'll give you the money anytime you want," I said. "I need a passport as soon as possible. How long will it take you to get it?"

"Two weeks," he said in thickly accented English. Although not highly educated, he'd picked up the middle-class habit of dropping English words and phrases into conversation.

The landlord said it was "no problem," so I decided to tell my parents that I'd bought my ticket to freedom and riches out of Pakistan. That night we got a telegram from Peshawar. My sister Fay had arrived from Afghanistan. This was welcome news as we had not had contact with her since we left Sheberghan the year before. Mother said she and I should leave for Peshawar at once. So I told Father that he should give seven hundred rupees to the landlord for a passport.

"What do you need a passport for?" Mother asked.

"I need it."

"What do you need it for?" she insisted.

"I need it to travel to Saudi with Nemat and Nabi and the son of Hajji Sahib," I said.

"Get lost, my crazy son. Stop thinking crazy thoughts," my mother said.

Ignoring her, I asked Father to deliver the money to the landlord. Father said he would, although I was sure he didn't mean it.

The day after we got to Peshawar and saw my sister at the Evangelist's house, Mother and I went to visit Uncle Jaan Agha, her second cousin. I liked Uncle Jaan Agha, whom I remembered hunting with in the woods near the Kabul zoo. Witty, erudite, and disarmingly charismatic, he could hypnotize anyone. And he loved throwing people off their guard.

"How are you doing, young man?" he asked me in English. I blushed. I had no idea what he said, only that he asked a question in English that I needed to answer. Switching to Farsi, he said how glad he was to see me and then led us onto their verandah. Relieved to be let go so quickly, I greeted his two sons and tried to avoid him.

A couple hours later he said he wanted to "have a word" with me. Sitting on an overstuffed cushion next to a giant fan at the end of the verandah, he was drinking tea and taking long drags on his Marlboros. I shyly sat down next to him. He placed his arm over my shoulder.

"So what do you do in Karachi, my boy?" he asked. I told him about my job working for the doctor.

"You don't go to school?"

"No, I don't."

"Why not?"

"There are no schools for Afghans in Karachi."

He moved his arm off my shoulder to take another drag on his Marlboro, letting out a cloud of smoke that floated over his piercing green eyes. I knew he was trying to charm me because he wanted me to do something. I just didn't know what that was or why. His intentions quickly became clear.

"Your mother tells me you want to go to Saudi Arabia," he said quietly. "Is that true?"

I was furious. How dare Mother discuss with others what I was planning to do!

"Yes, I suppose," I said, trying to hide my anger.

"What are you going to do in Saudi?"

"I'll take whatever job I can get."

He chortled and put his arm back around me. "Listen, my boy, you haven't finished school. Finish your studies. You can come stay here with us, and I'll help you get into a school." There were several refugee schools in Peshawar, he said. His son Muhammad was attending one of them.

"When you finish school, you can do whatever you want. I don't care. But going to school will be an asset you will always have."

Education would turn thorns into roses. It didn't sound like a bad idea. I liked Uncle Jaan Agha, I could get out of Karachi, and I could finish my education. Of course, Uncle Jaan Agha didn't really offer me a choice. He and mother had already decided this was the right thing. They had simply made it seem like I made up my own mind about what to do.

Returning to Karachi with Mother and Fay, I learned Father never gave the money to the landlord to get the passport. He thought it was a bad idea from the beginning. It was only a few days before I was on a bus back to Peshawar.

Chapter Four

Autumn 1984—"Ah, son of the supermullah," the Evangelist said.

It was a muggy July afternoon in Peshawar, and the Evangelist was weeding the small garden of his house. I was fifteen years old and had never been insulted by anyone who wasn't my own age. Was this how true believers saw my father? How they saw me?

"Where have you been?" he asked. "How is your father? How's your mother?"

"They're good," I said. "They send their greetings."

I shut the gate behind me and kissed the back of his hairy hand narrowly missing a pinch of snuff between his thumb and forefinger. I straightened up without receiving the customary kiss on my head.

"What brings you back so soon?" he asked, picking up a spade.

"I've come here to study, Uncle," I said. "I'll be living with Uncle Jaan Agha. I got here two days ago."

After my visit with the Evangelist, I was reeling from my moment of humiliation. Perhaps that's one of the reasons I was so strongly influenced by Uncle Jaan Agha. Unlike my father, he was a pious man living in a household with other devout men. He had not always been so religious, though. At University in Kabul during the 1960s, he and several classmates had turned to leftist politics. A gifted writer and poet, Uncle Jaan Agha published fiery polemics in the group's newspaper. His sociology professor once told his class, "In this environment you turn to either radical politics or masturbation."

This period was a fortunate one in Afghanistan's tortured history. My uncle witnessed the so-called "decade of democracy" from 1963 to 1973, during which the increasingly assertive King Zahir Shah promulgated a liberal constitution, allowed more freedom to the press, and took steps toward legalizing political parties. It wasn't long before clashes broke out among various political groups, student groups, and the police. The government, deciding the students had overstepped their bounds, moved to disband them and jail their leaders.

At the age of twenty-five Uncle Jaan Agha found himself imprisoned in Pul-I Charkhi. Convicted of sedition, he spent five years in jail, where he renounced politics, taught himself English, read Shakespeare, and imbibed heavily from the Koran. Shortly before his release in 1973, he dreamed that a blind man took him around a foreign city, stopping in front of statues of Marx, Engels, and Lenin and asking, "What are these idols that you worship?"

He went home to his wife and two sons. The next day, he picked up the Koran from his bookshelf, the copy Great-Aunt Koko would read during her visits, and started reading where a green, silk-string bookmark had been left: "And what are these idols that you worship?" It was a verse he'd never read before in the Koran but was attributed to a young Abraham addressing his idol-making father.

"That's when I accepted the truth of the Koran," he said with the conviction of a born-again believer. "The Koran is the only miracle in Islam. Other supposed miracles are all superstitions. We don't need other miracles. We have the Koran."

Uncle Jaan Agha added other books to the old bound copy of the Koran in his house. Now, sitting next to books on literature were an extensive collection of religious texts, several handsome copies of the Koran and commentaries on it, and biographies of the Prophet.

Yusuf, Uncle Jaan Agha's oldest son, was also living in the house along with his younger brother Muhammad. Yusuf was reading *Muhammad: A Reappraisal of the Prophet,* a Persian translation of a biography by a Hungarian scholar. Yusuf had been a medical student in Kabul and was now taking English language classes as well as working at an aid agency. Muhammad, who was a year older than I, kept several books on his bedroom bookshelf. A recent top graduate of a refugee school run by a radical mujahideen group, he was impressive not only in his knowledge of Islam but in how seriously he took his prayers.

Bismullah, a quiet relative, lived in the guest room. He was extremely religious and had piercing black eyes and a foot-long beard that he stroked as if it was a cat. His reticent yet firm handshake, furrowed forehead, and long string of olive green prayer beads added to his serious demeanor. Everyone called him *Maulana.* He was not a learned scholar, but people weren't shocked when they heard his title, as they were with Father.

In the mornings everyone woke up at the sound of the *azan,* the call to prayer that rang out from a cacophony of loudspeakers perched atop mosques across the city. The first call came from the neighborhood mosque, chanted by a one-eyed dour muezzin and prayer leader. Clearing his throat, he would deliver an unpleasant rendition of the *azan* that made even the most pious cringe. Uncle Jaan Agha would quote from the Koran to skewer the muezzin's vocal performance, "Verily, the worst voice is that of the donkey."

The Supermullah worked as a low-ranking official at the Ittihad-I Islami Afghanistan (Islamic Unity of Afghanistan), one of the seven mujahideen groups based in Peshawar. Like most Afghans in the resistance bureaucracy, he'd gotten his job through a connection, in his case through the second in command. I never learned what his official position was, but he had good handwriting and could add and subtract, which may have been enough.

Bismullah offered to help me get into his party's recently established high school.

"All you need is a picture," he said.

I went out and had my picture taken. When I returned with the photo, he looked me over and said, "You're not going to let me down, are you?"

I didn't know what he was talking about. Before I could respond, he said, "No movies. And never miss your prayers."

"That shouldn't be a problem," I assured him.

And as simply as that, I was a member of the Islamic Unity. It was run by Sayyaf, one of the two most powerful mujahideen leaders and the man whose name the Evangelist had tried to scare Father with.

With a couple hundred students, the Islamic Unity of Afghanistan school was one of three high schools for three million Afghan refugees living in Pakistan. The two other fundamentalist parties had been running their own schools for a few years, and Sayyaf had decided to start his own.

The school was a pell-mell operation, still getting off the ground. It was a shoddy knock-off high school with an inordinate emphasis on religious subjects. In Afghanistan students take one religion class, beginning in middle school. Here, in addition to the regular high school academic fare, the curriculum included several religious subjects no longer taught in Afghanistan, including Arabic grammar, the Koran, Koranic exegesis, the Hadith, and the laws of inheritance. There were no chairs or desks so, like village students, we sat cross-legged on tarp-covered concrete floors facing a large blackboard and, during winter, we wrapped ourselves in woolen blankets. No attendance was taken. The instructors were mostly former teachers from Afghanistan, but they didn't seem to care if you showed up late or didn't show up at all. There was no bastinado for tardiness here. Our books were either reprints of

Afghan textbooks or hastily written "improved" copies. In some subjects, there were no books, so the teacher would simply read from his own notes. All of this suited me perfectly, and while I never missed a day, I also assumed I could quit whenever I wanted to.

It didn't take me long to get bored. While the combination of contemporary subjects and religious studies offered a curriculum that resembled my father's education, I felt the pace was too slow. I also didn't feel any closer to my goal, which was to go to Saudi Arabia. I'd heard rumors that Pakistani authorities were shutting down refugee schools because they either didn't approve of the curriculum or because of disputes between party officials and the landlords. I wondered whether ours was next.

The Supermullah always smirked when he had something on his mind. It was a twisted, almost devious grin that lasted a full minute or longer before he finally said whatever he had to say, good or bad. This time the news was very good indeed. The Saudis, the great patrons of the jihad, had opened a religious school for Afghan refugees. It was just up the road and it came with all sorts of perks—daily meals, a generous weekly stipend of 250 rupees, and a future opportunity to study religion in Saudi Arabia.

"It's just the right place for you," the Supermullah said. "I can help you get in."

Out of work, out of money, and now out of school, I liked the suggestion, especially the hope to study in Saudi Arabia. Uncle Jaan Agha wholeheartedly agreed.

"It's a good way for you to study Arabic," he said philosophically, "which is key not only to understanding the Koran but also to understanding Persian literature." He even encouraged Muhammad to join.

Armed with letters of reference from Bismullah, Muhammad and I eagerly boarded a minibus to Upper Tahkal, a dilapidated neighborhood of mud huts a couple of stops up the road. We wore our best attire: white linen tunics and freshly ironed pants, checkered summer scarves thrown over our shoulders, plastic sandals, and white flannel prayer caps. From the bus stop, it took us a while to find the whitewashed building amid the squalid alleyways lined by ramshackle storefronts. Teenage boys with books under their arms streamed out of its large metal gate. A bored old man with a rifle stood guard. When we held up our letters of reference, he waved us in without bothering to look at them. At least he was honest, unlike many guards, who were illiterate but would grab your documents anyway and stare coldly at them.

Inside the large courtyard, chants of students echoed out of the classrooms and filled the heavy summer air. I saw what looked like a prayer ground, covered by a large tarp and shaded by tall evergreen trees. The main building housed classrooms and offices, its hallways smelling of dust and fresh paint. At the end of one corridor, a noisy group of boys had crowded around a desk. They were pushing and shoving, like a throng of refugees around an aid truck. A fat man in a turban sitting behind the desk was trying to shout them down.

"We're full," the man barked at one sad-looking fourteen-year-old. "Do you not understand? No letter, no admission. A camp card is not good enough. Go back and get a letter from your commander." I can't say if he relied on these letters to sort out the religious from the desperate, but rules were rules, even in one of Peshawar's most decrepit neighborhoods.

The fat man grabbed my letter from my hand. It was written by a legitimate mullah I didn't know, vouching for my high moral character and religious credentials. He gave it a quick glance and put it down, looking satisfied. I was fortunate to have people pulling strings for me. He took our names and basic information. When he was done filling out forms, he told us to come the next day.

"Early," he said. "Eight o'clock sharp."

The next day Muhammad and I arrived almost a half hour early only to find other kids already waiting to be assigned to classrooms. The fat administrator, acting friendlier than during our first meeting, showed us to a room at the end of the hall. It was small and bright, illuminated by generous amounts of sunlight streaming through two big windows. The walls were a freshly painted white and decorated with two simple posters, saying ALLAH and MUHAMMAD, in gold letters against a black background. A teaching desk with a chair stood in the corner beside the window, faced by crude and unpainted benches and desks for students. I was disappointed; I had grown to enjoy sitting on the hard, barren floor of my classroom at the Islamic Unity school. Muhammad and I took seats in the front row next to several uncomfortable-looking twelve- and thirteen-year-old students. The room filled up until the desks were gone and students had to lean against the wall.

A middle-aged, heavyset teacher with a tightly wrapped white turban lumbered in. From his bushy salt-and-pepper mustache, his appearance was that of a traditionally schooled mullah, but with so many bearded men in Peshawar, it was hard to tell which were mullahs and which weren't. Placing the oversized book he was carrying in his hand on the desk, he turned to us with a serious expression on his face.

"*Assalamu alaikum wa Rahmatullahi wa Barakatuhu*"—May peace and God's mercy and blessings be upon you. He intoned this greeting slowly, as if reciting a favorite verse from the Koran.

We responded in unison, "*Wa alaikumu assalam wa Rahmatullahi wa Barakatuhu*"—And may peace and God's mercy and blessings be upon you. This was the longer and more elaborate version of the simple Islamic greeting of *Assalamu alaikum,* often shortened to *Salam,* or peace. I'd heard this longer version at war rallies in Peshawar, and I'd taken to mouthing it in jest when greeting friends. I found this exchange funny, and almost snickered, wondering whether I was back in Sheberghan in my noisy first-grade classroom, where we used to greet each other the same way. Our teacher surveyed the class, walked over to his desk, cleared his throat, and intoned, this time more loudly, *"Awuzu billahi mina shaytaan I rajeem, bismillah I rahman I raheem"*—I seek shelter in God from the damned Satan, in the name of God, the merciful, the magnificent.

This was a familiar incantation, usually said before reciting verses from the Koran. I thought he was going to say a verse or two before launching into his lecture. Instead, he said in Pashto, "Does anyone know what the word *Qur'an* means in Arabic?"

I was confused. What kind of question was this? The class fell silent as the teacher looked around for someone clever enough to reply. I'd considered myself smart before this, but now I felt embarrassed; it had never occurred to me to ask what the word *Qur'an* actually means. Much to my relief, Muhammad was equally stumped, staring at the teacher with his chin buried in his palms.

When no one answered, the teacher explained that *Qur'an* means "recitation" in Arabic and has the same linguistic root as the words *qiraa'at,* or recitation, and *qaaree,* a professional reciter of the Koran, both common words in Farsi and Pashto.

"In fact, the first word revealed by God Almighty to the Messenger of God, may peace be upon him, was *iqrah,* recite," he said. "Surely, you all must know that."

Anyone familiar with the briefest outline of the Prophet's life, of course, did. According to Islamic belief, the archangel Gabriel appeared before Muhammad in a dark cave outside Mecca and beseeched him three times to "recite." Illiterate, Muhammad pleaded each time: "I cannot read." Gabriel finally replied, "Recite in the name of your Lord." These divinely revealed words marked the beginning of Muhammad's twenty-three-year mission as a prophet. But who would have guessed that the word *Koran* itself had a meaning? I'd always thought it was simply a proper name, like God and Muhammad. Sitting on the rough chair that day, I felt more than a little stupid not to have made the connection myself, especially in the company of my intellectual inferiors.

"By the grace of God, you're all pious, learned young men," the teacher continued. "You recite the holy Koran, but here we teach you its meaning."

He sat down in his chair, opened the immense volume of Koranic exegesis, and started reciting the first *surah*, or chapter, of the Koran, *al-Fatihah*. Every Muslim child knows the Fatihah, the Opening of the Koran, by heart. I knew the Opening's meaning well enough, but that was the extent of my scriptural knowledge. Even so, I felt encouraged when the teacher said that the Koran was the easiest book in the world and then translated the Opening word by word and delivered a brief lecture on the traditional interpretation of the chapter.

This kind of education couldn't be that difficult. If I had already learned the Opening, surely I could master the entire Koran too. I was ready to match wits with the Evangelist any time, even though he was not only a *qadi* and a *qari,* a judge and a professional reader of the Koran, but a *hafiz,* one who has committed the entire Koran to memory. I looked forward to my next day at the madrassah.

I had not so fully embraced the Prophet's call to education, "Seek knowledge even unto China," which rang out from the cover of every refugee school textbook, nor had I imagined myself as one of the learned men of legend who traveled to far-flung corners of the world, wandering from master to master, madrassah to madrassah, "journeymen in the cause of God until they return," as the Prophet called them. That phase would come later. During these first few weeks, I thought learning Arabic and studying the Koran and contemplating the sayings of the Prophet would help me become a better Muslim. It would not only put me in proper company but would win the approval of men I now considered learned.

The madrassah I attended was a far cry from the Abu Hanifah where Father and the Evangelist had gone in the 1940s and even more removed from the original institutions which sprang up in the eleventh century with the express purpose of training jurists. Back then young pupils were expected to know basic Arabic and Islamic theology before they even enrolled. The madrassah was a place of rigorous legal training, much like the medieval precursors of modern western universities, with students poring over dense texts and engaging in heated classroom debates in preparation for the legal profession. By contrast, the hundreds of madrassahs that sprang up in Pakistan in the 1980s and 1990s were more like village Koran schools than colleges of law. They were built by Islamic missionary groups and Arab charities nourishing the Afghan jihad. Arabs built other facilities, such as hospitals, orphanages, and aid distribution centers, but Arab-funded madrassahs numbered in the hundreds, many of them placed near refugee camps along the Pakistan-Afghanistan border with the explicit intent of countering the influence of more secular schools set up by Western aid organizations.

Most Afghans appreciated the efforts but realized the Arabs had ulterior motives. Accepting Arab-funded madrassahs also meant accepting a severe form of Islam known as Salafism and Wahhabism. Many Afghans found this offensive, being adherents of the Hanafite rite, one of the four main Sunni schools of jurisprudence. Hanafism is an orthodox school but also relaxed in ways, allowing room, for example, to continue local customs of visiting shrines. Strictly monotheistic and vigorously literal in their interpretation of scripture, the Wahhabis frowned upon such practices, equating them with idolatry and labeling their adherents infidels. Along with their madrassahs, Arabs had started to marry Afghan women. According to Afghan custom, a man may marry a foreign woman, either Muslim or non-Muslim, but an Afghan woman is forbibben to marry a foreign man. It was believed that many Arab men had married for pleasure, abandoning their wives as soon as they completed their brief stints in Peshawar. Rumor also had it that some Arabs were running a syndicate in Afghan slave girls. "Son of a Wahhabi" quickly became an Afghan insult, the equivalent of calling someone a "son of a bitch."

I kept my mind on my studies. The teacher I grew most fond of was our Arabic grammar instructor Ustad Fazil, or Master Fazil. A tall, lanky fellow with a small beard that could barely pass for a mullah's, he was, in fact, not a mullah but was from a clerical family in northern Afghanistan where he attended a state high school. Had the war not broken out, he probably would have become a high school teacher. Instead he fled to Peshawar after the invasion, where he found work with a mujahideen group. Ustad Fazil then got a scholarship to study the Shariah, or Islamic law, in Saudi Arabia, where grammar became his passion. Grammar study is at the heart of the madrassah curriculum, as it is the key to unraveling the language of the Koran and understanding its unusual turns of phrase, word orders, and verbal patterns.

Fazil started us off with the basics of Arabic grammar. *Sarf* is a branch of grammar that explains how a change in a single verb ending can alter the meaning of an entire sentence. Such changes can have profound legal and theological implications. Pronouncing a verb one way instead of another can mean the difference between a Sunni and a Shiite, or a believer and an infidel. For an hour each day, in keeping with centuries-old pedagogical tradition, we'd conjugate verbs, using *zarb* ("to hit") as a model. *Zarabah, zarabaa, zaraboo*—he hit, two men hit, they hit. *Zarabat, zarabataa, zarabatoo*—she hit, two women hit, they hit. I loved the guttural sound of Arabic and paused frequently while I dipped into each syllable. Occasionally Ustad Fazil would break from tradition and have us conjugate different verbs. *Qatl* (to kill) became a hit in class, not because of any homicidal fantasies we shared but simply because it had a nice sound to it. As for me, *zarb* remained my favorite.

The idea behind this repetition was to learn how to properly explicate the words of the Koran. One of Ustad Fazil's examples was to look at the verb *tukazibban* in the well-known verse "O which one of your Lord's bounties will you and you deny?" Being in the second person dual form, the verse is addressed not just to men but also to jinn (ghostly creatures made of smokeless fire), which was a lively way to illustrate some meaning behind our rote memorization. Ustad Fazil also had an uncanny ability to explain the logic behind the inconsistencies and irregularities of Arabic grammar.

"What if two people is comprised of a man and a woman?" I asked Ustad Fazil one day.

"In that case, you say 'two men hit,'" he said. "In the Arabic language, men always take precedence over women."

I picked up new things every day, nuggets of wisdom I was using to make myself a better Muslim. One such piece involved the answer to an old theological question: Is the Koran "created" or "uncreated"?

Maulawi Sahib, my Koran teacher, started this debate in our class. Now I knew the words *khaliq,* creator, and *makhlooq,* creation. *Khaliq* is the subject form of the verb *khalq* and *makhlooq* is the object. God is *khaliq* and everything else in the universe is his *makhlooq.* There was a clear-cut distinction between the two. I found the question absurd because I thought everything apart from God the creator is part of his creation. This sounded suspiciously like a trick question, similar to "Are you an Afghan or a Muslim?" In Peshawar, the correct answer was, "Of course I am Muslim," but this was a far more serious question, and no one had dared answer it.

"The Glorious Koran is the speech of God, and speech is one of the attributes of God," Maulawi Sahib said finally. "The letters and words printed in ink in the Glorious Koran you are holding in front of you, and the sounds that form the words, are created. But the words themselves are the speech of God. Therefore, the Glorious Koran is uncreated."

The question, intensely debated by serious theologians in the early days of Islam, had been put to rest long ago, he said. A

Muslim sect known as the Mu'tazilah believed the Noble Koran was created, but they were heretics. "The Noble Koran is eternal and uncreated," he insisted. "It is the eternal and uncreated speech of God Almighty. This means that there was no time at which the Noble Koran did not exist. It has always existed—it's been on the Preserved Tablet—and it will always exist.

"They lived in the time of the Caliph Amin, the son of Harun al-Rashid," he said, referring to the eighth-century Abbasid caliph. He paused then added, "I beg your forgiveness. They lived in the time of the Caliph al-Ma'mun. He was the other son of Harun al-Rashid. The wicked al-Ma'mun threw the great Imam Ahmad ibn Hanbal, may God be pleased with him, in jail and tortured him and had him executed because Imam Ahmad did not accept the Mu'tazilah doctrine."

We sat in silence. This was a lot to absorb in one sitting. The Noble Koran is uncreated. The Mu'tazilah believed it was created, but we believe it is uncreated, so to believe it was created is a form of unbelief. The point of the lesson was to teach us correct belief. The main text we used was *Fiqh-I Akbar* (*The Great Theology*), a standard introductory text written by Abu Hanifa, the great eighth-century theologian and imam of the brand of Sunnism practiced in Afghanistan. I found the fact that we were being taught orthodox Sunni Islam, not Wahhabism, reassuring, but I sometimes wondered what position the other three Sunni religious rites took on various questions. That knowledge was not to be gained here. There was no room for debate. In fact, we never learned what the theological implications of the debate were. Perhaps the teacher himself didn't know. Or perhaps he thought we were not intellectually advanced enough to be exposed to the dangerous beliefs, ironic given that the Mu'tazilah, as I later learned, were strict monotheists who believed that associating God with attributes such as speech was actually a form of polytheism.

The more time I spent at the madrassah, the more entrenched my beliefs became. I began reading religious books and started memorizing long passages of the Koran. I committed to memory a lengthy list of prayers for every occasion—before and after eating, drinking, sleeping, looking at women, even having wet dreams or "Satan's deceptions" as they were known among young men. Before going to bed, I prayed, "O God, keep us away from Satan, and keep Satan away from what you've granted us." As I woke up, I'd praise God who "gave us life after we were dead and guides us his way." Upon entering the bathroom, I begged the "scent of heaven" to mask the odors of the toilet. After finishing up, I'd thank God for the relief. Some of the prayers I had plenty of opportunities to say. "O God, I beg your mercy and seek refuge in you from Satan," was to be uttered every time I heard a cock crow or a donkey bray, both common sounds in Peshawar.

In the mornings I no longer had to be awakened by the Supermullah. I would be washing up in the bathroom before everyone else. Instead of taking a nap after saying my prayers, I'd recite the Koran for an hour. The English translation of the Koran may sound a bit dull and even boring, but I found the "clear Arabic" Koran beautiful and soothing. Unlike readers of other holy scripture, I did not recite for inspiration—I still did not understand much of it anyway—but as part of an act of worship that every Muslim was obligated to perform. Reciting the Koran, the Prophet once said, cleanses the heart, and I felt my heart could use some cleansing. Most Muslims know by rote a few short chapters of the Koran but I started memorizing some of the longer chapters. Muhammad also started memorizing some of these passages, but I wanted to outdo him. He and I often tested each other. Sometimes he would beat me, but I was proud the day I completely memorized the Ya-Sin, the thirty-sixth chapter of the Koran, called by the Prophet "the heart of the Koran."

All this was a little amusing to Uncle Jaan Agha, and to register his amusement, indeed his irritation, at my new extremist views, he started calling me Mullah Masood. He knew too many mullahs already who grew long beards, prayed five times a day, recited the Koran every morning at sunrise, yet were every bit as sinful and certainly more hypocritical than those who didn't pretend to be pious. Whenever we walked past a pair of stern, bearded men with big turbans, he'd versify, "Ouch! These herds of mullahs are all beard and wool like mountain goats." I brushed off his sarcasm and focused my energies on rigidly following everything I was learning.

Aware that the Prophet was the perfect man, a model for emulation by all Muslims, I tried to practice every piece of wisdom he'd uttered. Small things now mattered a great deal to me: how to bow and prostrate in accordance with the Prophet's preferred style; how to train my eyes on the mat while praying; how far to lift my forefinger while uttering the declaration of faith: *I bear witness that there is no god but God and Muhammad is his Messenger.* Only one thing seemed impossible to change through piousness: my almost utter lack of facial hair. In Western cultures this may seem a petty concern, but in Peshawar your beard was a measure of your piety. The longer, fuller, and bushier the beard, the more pious its wearer. I remember a mullah at a refugee camp one day sermonizing to a handful of congregants with short, clipped beards. "Your beards serve no good," he said. "It pleases neither God nor your wives, because God wants a long beard and your wives want no beard." The Evangelist had been right. Father didn't belong in Peshawar.

I was almost seventeen and embarrassed by my baby face. I wanted a beard as thick as the Supermullah's and as long as Sayyaf's. So I began to shave the peach fuzz on my face as often as three times a day, eagerly awaiting facial hair that was sure to come any time now. While I was waiting, my increased religiosity imbued me with a hefty degree of moral superiority. I frowned on the mechanical prostrations of those who constantly fingered their prayer beads and prayed five times a day without knowing the meaning of their prayers. Hadn't God said in the Koran that hypocrisy was worse than adultery, and adultery was punishable by death? I'd learned only a tiny sliver of the vast body of Islamic teachings, yet I figured my teachers had furnished me with solid religious arguments. For instance, I believed looking at women was un-Islamic because one of my teachers had quoted the Prophet as saying it was sinful. "The right course of action," he said, "when you see a woman, is to cast your eyes down or try to look at a green pasture." Peshawar was not the most verdant place in Pakistan, so on the rare occasion a pair of beautiful female eyes peered at me from behind a white scarf, I'd curse Satan, ask God for forgiveness, then look up at the trees.

One day, a classmate lent me a slim, dog-eared copy of *A Picture of Life after Death*. This was a welcome gesture as I had little interaction with my classmates outside the madrassah. Living mostly in refugee camps on the outskirts of the city, they had little time to spare when classes ended for the day. Poor, bedraggled, and mostly uneducated, they weren't boys I wanted to associate with anyway. The few students who did linger after school lived in town and had already received some schooling, though they didn't share my religious zeal.

I eagerly read the book, wanting to enhance my vision of life after death, which admittedly hadn't evolved much from what I learned when I was a boy back in Sheberghan. An older neighborhood friend named Ahmad Shah had once described the Day of Resurrection to me with the earnestness and ardor of a fiery preacher.

"All you've done in this world will be weighed against what God has given you," he said, standing outside his house, holding a large aluminum hoop boys used to roll down sidewalks. I listened carefully, gripped by the subject. "A single eye," Ahmad Shah said solemnly, pointing to his own eye, "will weigh more than all the good things we've done in this world. Not your whole body, but a single eye." I imagined a giant set of scales suspended in midair. One scale was weighed down by an eyeball, but, as I was unable to imagine the forces of good with a concrete image, the other side of the scale was empty.

This simplistic picture was a far cry from the scenes of absolute depravity in *A Picture of Life after Death*. Although the Koran devotes equal space to descriptions of hell and heaven, this book dispenses entirely with the delights awaiting the virtuous and instead focuses exclusively on hell. It starts off with "life of the grave," the period between death and resurrection on the Day of Judgment. While in the grave, the body decomposes but the soul remains alive, receiving a taste of what awaits it in the afterlife. Drawing on the Koran, the sayings of the Prophet, and the author's imagination, the book describes how infidels will learn their fate on the Day of Resurrection, biting and gnawing their hands in fear. Manacled and chained like prisoners they will be dragged by their hair and feet through boiling water "that will blister their innards and melt their skins; for them there await hooked iron rods." They will try to escape, but guards will drive them back into the fire and say to them, "Taste the chastisement of the burning." It detailed with frightening authority various punishments that awaited different types of sinners—liars, adulterers, masturbators, those who skipped fasting and prayers.

When I finished, I shuddered with fear that I might end up in hell for even such a minor infraction as forgetting to say a prayer before going to the bathroom. Rereading the book, I realized I was in deep trouble. There was no way I could escape punishment. I was devout, perhaps more so than most people, but what about my sinful past? Later, when I felt weak or feared I had sinned, I'd fall into severe depression, sometimes waking up in the middle of the night sobbing. I nonetheless redoubled my efforts to atone, but I felt trapped in an endless cycle. For instance, deliberately skipping a single daily prayer requires one week of compensatory prayers. Once I started counting how long it would take me to make up for the missed prayers, I gave up, dumbfounded by the math and daunted by the impossible task of being pious.

Back at the madrassah, whether we were deciphering passages of the Koran or obscure sayings of the Prophet, classroom discussions often veered to the topic of jihad. Jihad was the consummate religious act, we were taught, the surest way to martyrdom and the ultimate glory to which a Muslim should aspire. Our jurisprudence teacher said the Prophet's words were unequivocal: "Nobody who dies and finds good from God would wish to come back to this world even if he were given the whole world and all that is in it, except the martyr who, upon seeing the superiority of martyrdom, would like to return to the world and die again." Martyrdom was a religious end in itself.

One day several new students joined our class, young soldiers who had returned from the front and with the help of their commander had gotten into the school. The presence of young mujahideen in our midst was not unusual—several of my classmates had already participated in the jihad—but these fighters had recently come from the front and, sitting in the back of the room, they were more than willing to talk about the fighting in Nangarhar province. I looked over my shoulder and listened as they talked about how they had endured bombing "day after day, night after night" without sleeping, as well as how they had suffered "several martyrs." I'd heard stories like this many times, but knowing that these mujahideen were only two or three years older than I made it hard not to feel jealous.

We rose when our Hadith teacher walked in. Someone told him these students had just returned from the front. "May God accept your jihad," he said, making small talk before proceeding with the lesson of the day. As usual, he'd chosen several hadiths, recorded sayings of the Prophet, about the merits of jihad. While he listed the long chain of transmitters of the Hadith, one of the new students in the back raised his hand.

"Is jihad," he asked "a *fard al-ayn* or a *fard al-kifayah*?" That is, is jihad a personal religious obligation or a communal religious obligation? This was a question I'd heard adults animatedly discuss, but I had not understood what the debate was about or what the right answer was. I was eager to hear the teacher's answer.

"Jihad," the teacher replied, is a "*fard al-ayn.*" A personal obligation. He was anxious to resume the lesson, but he'd obviously misread his new student.

"I heard it is a *fard al-kifayah,*" the student said, wrapping his shawl around him, looking keen to spark a debate. The teacher agreed that jihad was in fact a communal as well as a personal obligation. He then explained the difference. A *fard al-ayn* (personal obligation) is incumbent upon every individual—praying five times a day is an example—and neglecting such obligations constitutes a great sin. A *fard al-kifayah* (communal obligation) is not obligatory to everyone. If enough members of the community perform the obligation, the rest of the community is absolved of the duty. Jihad and the funeral prayer are examples.

"But jihad becomes a personal obligation for every Muslim when infidels attack a Muslim country," the teacher said.

The student in the back wasn't buying it. Why had he asked this question in the first place? He and his friends did not need to hear that it was their obligation—religious or otherwise—to take part in jihad. Perhaps they were looking for converts in our classroom? I was grateful our teacher had explained the legal difference between a communal and personal obligation and became more convinced that jihad was something each Muslim had to decide for himself whether to participate in. Yet at the madrassah, as well as in the mujahideen publications I regularly read, the jihad our compatriots were fighting in Afghanistan was presented in the context of the seventh- and eighth-century Islamic military expeditions. This made it seem more like a communal obligation. We were winning not because of some innate strength that any of us as individuals possessed but rather because God was on our collective side. If this weren't the case, how could a small, poor nation repulse the mighty Red Army with its tanks, fighter jets, and helicopter gunships? Wasn't it often said that our jihad was like the battle of Badr, the legendary first skirmish between the Prophet's nascent Muslim army and the pagans of Mecca? Even though they were outnumbered three to one, the Muslims vanquished the infidels. Surely our odds against the Russians were no better.

It was soon time for exams. We had both Koranic recitation and an Arabic grammar and vocabulary test. I had spent the previous evening studying my *surahs,* trying to recite them again and again out of fear of making a disastrous mistake. After we had taken the grammar and vocabulary test, Ustad Fazil informed the class that he himself would be administering our recitation test since our Koran teacher had not shown up. Now I was even more nervous. Ustad Fazil had faith in me, however. I knew I had done well on the Arabic test, but what if I made a mistake here? What if he discovered I was not as smart as he thought I was? We waited in the back of the classroom as he called each one of us to come to the front and recite a chapter. Some breezed through the exam, others stumbled while Fazil corrected them. Finally it was my turn. Muhammad trailed right behind me as I prepared myself for the recitation. Fazil looked at us and smiled. "I trust you both," he said. "You know your Koran. You can go home."

Not long after exams, we were told a sheikh from Saudi Arabia, a representative of the organization that provided funding for our school, would pay us a visit. Money was going to be handed out we were told. Lots of money. This was exciting. Some of my classmates imagined how they would spend it. One even boasted he would buy us all Fanta sodas if he received more than a thousand rupees.

As it turned out, the sheikh wasn't an elder but a young man not much older than twenty-five, dressed in the traditional Arab robe and red-and-white-checkered head scarf. An even younger-looking man accompanied him. They walked into our class accompanied by the head of the madrassah. We stood up in respect and were told to sit down. Then Ustad Fazil began teaching, and the two sheikhs and the head teacher watched with interest.

After lunch, we gathered on the prayer grounds. The tarps had been swept clean. The entire class, about a hundred of us, sat cross-legged as we were ordered to form a neat row and sit properly. When we were all at attention, the sheikh delivered a brief statement, which was translated by Ustad Fazil. Like most everyone, I could make out only a word or two of what the sheikh said, especially when he recited the Koran or quoted the Prophet, and without Ustad Fazil's translation, we'd have been completely lost.

"He says you are the children of jihad," Ustad Fazil said in Farsi after the sheikh had finished speaking. "One day you'll be participating in the jihad, but knowledge is also a form of jihad. You can help the jihad in many different ways."

I wondered how faithful his translation was and how much of it was his own embellishment. It didn't matter much, since most of the Pashto-speaking students also didn't know Farsi.

Handing a stack of magazines to the teacher, the sheikh continued speaking. "One of the ways we can support the jihad," Fazil translated, "is to donate blood. Tomorrow cars will be here taking you to an Arab-funded hospital to donate blood."

When the sheikh finished, the class was quiet. I thought someone would lead us into a boisterous *Allahu Akbar!,* as was the custom on such occasions in Peshawar, but no one said a word. The sheikh turned to the young man accompanying him, who pulled out several large wads of money and handed it to him. I couldn't wait to see how much they would give us. Five hundred? A thousand? Five thousand rupees? I couldn't see how much the sheikh was handing out because I was standing at the back of the line being pushed and shoved by kids trying to get in front of me. When I finally reached the head of the line, I was handed two five-hundred-rupee bills, the equivalent of four weeks of my stipend. I said in Arabic, *"Shukran jazeelaa"*—Thank you very much—and shyly walked away. The boy who had promised to treat us all to Fanta was nowhere to be seen. As Muhammad and I walked out into the afternoon heat, he said, "What a generous man."

"Yes, what a generous man," I repeated. "May God bless him."

* * *

In my year and a half in Peshawar, I had little contact with my parents. I visited them once, but only for a few days. Besides that our contact was limited to an occasional phone call or exchange of letters. Father liked what I was studying, and in his short, formal, handsomely written letters, he would urge me to pay attention to my studies. Mother's letters were different. Long, clumsily written, and formulaic, they were a diary of gripes about Karachi's blistering heat, nocturnal mosquitoes, and the violent race riots that had spread to their neighborhood. "Uncle Jaan Agha is like your father," she'd conclude before signing her letters and imploring me to treat him and his wife as my own parents.

Such a reminder was hardly necessary. Uncle Jaan Agha and I had hit it off, and as the year wore on, I came to look up to him as a father figure. I was envious of the relationship he had with his own sons, however. Unlike the cold relationship my father had with me, Jaan Agha's relationship with Muhammad and Yusuf was a genuinely warm friendship. Throughout my days in Peshawar, Uncle Jaan Agha—part professor, part philosopher, and part poet—was a constant and positive influence in my life. He was an assortment of contradictions: devout in his religious practice but a hopeless romantic, a dispenser of irreverent humor yet fiercely rigid in his political and social views.

Both inside and outside the house, Uncle Jaan Agha entertained a coterie of faithful disciples who called him "Professor" and relished every word of wisdom he uttered. Whether the subject was politics, literature, or philosophy, he spoke with the authority of a Renaissance man. My favorite evenings were the informal poetry gatherings he held in the guest room or on the verandah for select friends. I'd serve them tea as they discussed obscure and complex poems of Rumi or Baydel, serious intellectual discussions that went far beyond the nightly sessions on Sa'di that Father used to organize for us in Sheberghan. When the guests left, I'd occasionally pluck up the courage to ask Uncle Jaan Agha about a certain line of a poem they'd discussed. Always generous with his literary knowledge (perhaps a little too generous) he'd patiently deconstruct a verse down to its literary and linguistic parts. Despite his somewhat pedantic approach to literature, he was a mystic at heart, his worldview shaped by a lifetime of reading the poems of Baydel, Mawlana, Sa'di, and Hafez, the bright stars in the firmament of classical Persian literature. A leading authority on Baydel, a free-spirited seventeenth-century Sufi poet with a cult following in Afghanistan, Uncle Jaan Agha liked to cite one of his most accessible works:

What does all this beard mean?
What does it mean other than worrying?

But more often he quoted Hafez, that irreverent and biting critic of the religiously extremist rulers of his time:

Oh Hafez, drink wine and be profligate and merry.
Do not turn the Qur'an into a snare of hypocrisy.

"Be merry," I could understand, but drink wine and be profligate? "*Toobah na'oozu billah,*" I said. God forbid.

"No God forbid," Uncle Jaan Agha chuckled. "Listen, my boy, Hafez is not urging you to drink wine, not that you can't easily find it in Kaar-Khanoo." *Kaar-Khanoo* was the smugglers' market right outside Peshawar's gates, rife not only with alcohol but contraband of every conceivable stripe: electronic equipment, heroin, even pornography. Hafez, however, was not talking about the booze sold in *Kaar-Khanoo*, Uncle Jaan Agha explained.

"Wine," he continued, "is a metaphor for love of God, the spiritual drink that intoxicates the Sufi. In this verse, Hafez is saying that pure-hearted profligates are superior in the eye of God to mullahs who use the Koran to deceive people. Do you understand, Mullah Masood?" he asked, making sure I wasn't taking the conversation too seriously.

I appreciated his levity, but as the year wore on I grew increasingly religious and outspoken in my views, not just at home but also outside with strangers, encouraged no doubt by Uncle Jaan Agha's open and accessible style of conversation. I'd get up in the middle of the night and pray for an hour or two on the verandah. In the mornings I'd remain immersed in the Koran, sometimes ignoring repeated calls to breakfast. And on Fridays I'd follow the Prophet's practice of drawing a bath, putting on clean clothes, and wearing perfume and kohl before heading to the congregational mosque half an hour early so I could claim a spot in the front row and absorb every word of the preacher. When I proudly announced to everyone one morning that the Prophet had commanded that we all should wash the inside of our nostrils three times in the morning because Satan had spent the night inside our noses, Uncle Jaan Agha wryly observed, "Make sure you don't mix up your *istinshaaq* and *istinjaa* prayers." This was a reference to a well-known Rumi story in which a pious simpleton says the prayer for washing your privates while he is actually cleaning his nostrils. Of my perfume, Jaan Agha again cited Rumi, as translated by Coleman Barks. "If you want your wretchedness to vanish," he said, "try to make your 'wisdom' leave you. You are musk scented but not musk. You smell like musk but you are only dung."

Uncle Jaan Agha was patient with me, but even his patience had limits. One night in his presence, I argued that women were inherently inferior to men in every respect, intellectually, physically, and temperamentally. "History is full of great men," I said, intent on provoking a debate. Muhammad nodded in agreement, while Yusuf wasn't so sure. "Give me a single example of a woman achieving greatness," I demanded.

Uncle Jaan Agha, who was sitting next to his wife, was quiet while he looked at Yusuf, clearly stumped. Usually he jumped to Yusuf's rescue. Finally Yusuf said, "All right, Indira Gandhi?"

"No good. She was Hindu," I countered, "and clearly deficient in her judgment of her bodyguards who assassinated her."

"What about Rabiyah al-Adawiyyah?" Yusuf asked.

I'd heard of Rabiyah al-Adawiyyah, an important female Sufi figure born in the eighth century, but I wasn't about to concede defeat.

"What great act is she famous for?" I demanded.

I'd crossed a line and Uncle Jaan Agha had heard enough. "Listen, my boy," he said. "Do you see this woman?" he asked me, putting an arm around his wife. She tried to push him away, but Jaan Agha's heavy arm stayed on her shoulder. "This is your aunt," he said, raising his voice. "But she is also half my heart." He put his right hand on his heart. "She's behind every poem I write, every essay I write. She's been my partner since the day I fell in love with her and when she leaves me, half my heart will be gone. I will be no more." Uncle Jaan Agha and his wife were a rare couple in Afghanistan, a husband and wife in love with each other.

"Don't look down on women," he said finally. "I don't care where you get your ideas. Remember, they're all your sisters, your mother."

I said nothing, staring at the carpet, but I'd gotten the message. Apparently, though, that was only the beginning of his attempts to reeducate me. A few days later he summoned me and told me an anecdote about the Prophet. On the day of a festival, the Prophet had allowed his favorite wife, Ayeshah, to rest her head on his shoulder and watch a concussion band and a camel race.

"That," Uncle Jaan Agha said, "shows the Prophet had nothing against music."

Was this so? While I occasionally listened to music at home and even enjoyed it, I'd feel guilty about it, as I believed it was forbidden in Islam. Uncle Jaan Agha, however, was citing none other than Ghazali, the eleventh-century theologian and philosopher and the author of the celebrated *Kimmiya-I Sa'adat*, the *Alchemy of Happiness* and the monumental *Ihyaay-I Ulum al-Din*, the *Revival of Religious Sciences*.

Regarded by many as the greatest Muslim after the Prophet Muhammad, Ghazali became a celebrated professor at Baghdad's prestigious Nizamiyah madrassah in his twenties, only to leave a few years later when he had a spiritual crisis. He felt that his theological knowledge, as vast as it was, was not leading him to the truth, or to happiness either for that matter. Much to the shock of his colleagues and students, he quit his teaching job in search of spiritual fulfillment, spending several years in meditation and in the company of Sufis in Damascus and Jerusalem. The fruit of his spiritual wandering was the Arabic *Revival of Religious Sciences*, of which the *Alchemy of Happiness* was an abbreviated, popular version written in Ghazali's native Persian.

Uncle Jaan Agha owned a two-volume edition and encouraged me to read it. No other book I'd read was like this one. The *Alchemy* offered an education far beyond learning the correct mechanics of prostration. For example, I learned the meaning of the introductory Arabic phrase *Awuzu billah-I minah shaytan al-rajeem*—I seek refuge in God from Satan the accursed. I had no idea that my madrassah knowledge was as much drilled-in, mechanical, rote memorization as the education I received when I was a young schoolboy. Ghazali wrote, "Satan laughs at such pious ejaculations," and compares the man who utters this phrase to a man who meets a lion in the desert and says, "I seek shelter in that fortress," without taking a step toward the fortress. "What will such an utterance profit him?" Ghazali asks. "In the same way, simply saying, 'I seek refuge in God from Satan the accursed' will not save you from the terrors of God's judgment unless you really seek refuge in him."

Ghazali was a revelation and a breath of fresh air, laying bare my superficial piety and exposing how petty and small-minded I'd been all along. As I absorbed his wisdom, I began to realize my devotion, while sincere, lacked the depth Ghazali and other Sufis demanded. The more I read his works and the works of other Sufis, the more the madrassah's version of Islam struck me as blinkered, provincial, and shallow. If I ever considered pursuing a career as an *alim,* or religious scholar, I realized the knowledge I'd gained thus far wasn't going to be of much help.

If the madrassah's version of Islam was about form, Sufism was about substance. Uncle Jaan Agha liked to quote a Sufi poet who said, "One intoxicated prostration before God [equals] a hundred years of ritual prayer." What mattered was quality and sincerity, not quantity. When Uncle Jaan Agha stood on his prayer mat late at night, he closed his eyes and recited his prayers loudly, both of which I knew were against orthodox practice. I realized, though, he had abandoned formalism in favor of spiritual sincerity.

Uncle Jaan Agha's education continued one late afternoon when he called for "Mullah Masood" and invited me to sit down next to him on the verandah. The big swamp cooler sat idly in the corner. Across the street the trees had started shedding their leaves.

"If everyone became a mullah, who would treat the sick, build the roads, and educate the children?"

"God Almighty," I said provocatively.

Uncle Jaan Agha chuckled. It was a familiar laugh, one he'd use just before he debunked one of my more extreme comments. "Listen, my boy," he said. "Every society needs doctors, engineers, and teachers. Besides, if everyone became a mullah, what would all the mullahs be doing?"

Uncle Jaan Agha was saying the world doesn't need one more mullah, in the same way an American parent might say to his child, "The world doesn't need one more lawyer." I still didn't know what I wanted in life—I was only seventeen years old—but I was ready to move on. Muhammad had already dropped out and was working as a translator at an aid agency while taking English language classes.

Uncle Jaan Agha had been thinking about what I should be doing next too. Recently he'd taken a job as head of a United Nations–funded employment agency for Afghan refugees, a link between Afghan refugees and dozens of Western relief agencies operating in Pakistan. When his secretary quit to move to America, he offered me the job; I took it without hesitation.

I began working and taking English classes at a language school run by the International Rescue Committee, an American charity, though I still clung to my daily religious routine and rituals. Quitting the madrassah did not mean I should be any less firm in my commitment to God. On the contrary, I viewed my madrassah education as an asset, a foundation for my spiritual development. So while I no longer believed that people who were less religious than I were going to hell, or that women were inferior to men, I said my daily prayers, fasted during Ramadan, and remained close to God.

Chapter Five

1986–1987—Not long afterwards, my parents and sisters moved to Peshawar. Mother liked to joke they'd become refugees all over again, this time victims of Karachi's spiraling race riots. The deadly violence pitted native Sindhi nationalists of Karachi against the *muhajirs,* Indian Muslims who'd fled to Pakistan when British India split into a predominantly Muslim Pakistan and Hindu India in 1947. Caught in the middle were the Pashtun laborers of the North West Frontier Province, and of course the Afghans as well. Since I'd left Karachi two years ago, the violence had grown more deadly and widespread, finally reaching my parents' doorstep one morning when an enraged *muhajir* militant held Mother and a group of shoppers at gunpoint.

What Peshawar lacked in ethnic violence it made up for with almost daily car bombs planted by Soviet agents trying to destabilize Pakistan for sheltering and supporting the mujahideen. Dead bodies started turning up in Peshawar's sewage-filled canals, victims of political vendettas. The war wounded were brought daily by ambulance vans and pickup trucks, joining the growing number of amputees limping around the city. Crudely made posters of fallen commanders appeared on walls and electric poles in increasing number; clean-shaven, black-and-white faces from a time before the war stared out while a famous verse from the

Koran reminded onlookers to "never think that those who are killed in the way of God are dead. They are alive, getting succor from their Lord."

Among my friends, the game of choice was naming the top mujahideen commanders. Their faces were everywhere, plastered on mosque walls, mujahideen offices, and the front covers of mujahideen magazines. We debated their virtues and styles of fighting the way suburban American kids talk about their idols. Ahmad Shah Masood, the lanky, charismatic commander of the Panjsher Valley with his trademark *pakool* hat, was still my favorite. Ismail Khan, a former army officer with a checkered head scarf and a bushy beard, was now keeping the Soviets at bay in the Herat region. Mawlawi Haqqani, a madrassah-educated mullah with an even bushier beard and piercing black eyes, was leading the Paktia front. Abdul Haq was the suave, English-speaking commander of Kabul who had lost a foot in a mine explosion. Ustad Bashir was a former schoolteacher harrassing Soviet convoys along the strategic Salang Highway. Last but not least, there was Ismail Tareq, a distant relative leading a major mujahideen front in Laghman.

To prove how tough you were, you identified with the bravest and fiercest commander, yet you also wanted to prove your allegiance to one of the seven Peshawar-based mujahideen organizations, be it through men who had fought side by side with these commanders or direct membership. In this politically charged environment, to attack one of these commanders was akin to attacking their party. Among the friends and cousins with whom I debated commanders and parties was Mirweis, the stocky, gregarious son of Uncle Majid, Father's first cousin. A former army doctor, Uncle Majid had moved to Peshawar the year before and become a frequent guest at our house after my parents relocated from Karachi. Before he fled Kabul, two of his draft-age sons had sneaked out of the city, joined a mujahideen group, and after several months of fighting made their way to Peshawar.

Mirweis was a year or two older than I was, and though he was outgoing and well read, he looked up to me because of my supposed learning and erudition. We became fast friends, but a sharp division came from his fascination with Gulbuddin Hekmatyar, the militant leader of Hezb-I Islami, or the Islamic Party of Afghanistan. He considered Hekmatyar the best leader for Afghanistan, while I saw a fireband whose aim was to wage "war until a comprehensive Islamic system of government" was established. Like Amin, the Loyal Disciple, Hekmatyar cared nothing about the human cost of his revolutionary goal. Upon touring the Islamabad region earlier in the war and seeing some standing houses, Hekmatyar remarked to a gathering of village elders, "You have not sacrificed enough to the jihad. Your houses are intact." Like Amin, Hekmatyar ran a secret police that prowled the streets of Peshawar for suspected traitors and other critics of his party. Ironically, his speeches were littered with communist terminology like *revolution, imperialism,* and *oppression,* words whose hollow definitions were part of the reason my family fled Afghanistan in the first place.

Despite his admiration of Hekmatyar, Mirweis and his older brother Jalil were members of a splinter group led by a septuagenarian Islamic scholar named Mawlawi Muhammad Yunus Khalis. A deeply pious mullah with a henna-dyed red-orange beard and a famously wry sense of humor, Khalis, unlike Hekmatyar, was a traditionally educated religious scholar with strong tribal support. Although he wanted an Islamic government in Afghanistan, he never advocated a revolution. To him, jihad was a means to liberate Afghanistan, a way to establish the "law of God, not the law made by man." Here was a man whose message, while simple and straightforward, resonated with me deeply. I would soon learn Khalis had once been a protégé of Grandpa Agha, Sufi Sahib, and of his own chief justice cousin, both of whom funded Khalis's literary and religious undertakings in the 1950s and 1960s before Khalis fled to Pakistan to escape persecution. Always grateful for their patronage, Khalis welcomed extended family into the party. So with the help of a few affiliated members, I began frequenting the so-called political office. The name was actually a misnomer, as the office served as a cross between a hostel and a home base for logistics and operations planning. Mujahideen commanders, along with various hangers-on, were a daily sight there, as were refugees looking for letters of reference to various aid agencies.

Occasionally Khalis himself would drop in to meet with commanders and tribal leaders visiting from the front. I first met him late one afternoon, when he arrived in a two-SUV motorcade. Escorted by a couple of bodyguards, he traveled with none of the pomp and circumstance affected by other party leaders. I bowed, kissed his hand, and was introduced as the "grandson of Sufi Sahib." Khalis smiled in recognition and mumbled, "Sufi Sahib was a great man," before moving on. I bumped into Khalis several times over the course of the ensuing year and never knew if he took me for a warrior or a sycophant.

Mirweis certainly saw himself as a warrior and did his bit to drill the idea of jihad into my head. We also talked about joining his older brother in the jihad, and while my desire to take part had grown, I didn't feel ready. One day, Mirweis stopped by our house in a fatigue vest saying he'd just returned from jihad. I hadn't seen him in several months. He'd traveled to Afghanistan with Engineer Mahmoud's forces and had taken part in a hit-and-run operation on Ghanikhel, a government garrison protected by Soviet troops. They had approached within a few hundred yards of the garrison, so close "you could hear the hissing of the generators." From their entrenched position, Mirweis and his dozen comrades took aim at the only target they could find: an idle armored personnel carrier, visible under the glow of the watchtower. "Then the rockets started raining down on us. You can't imagine what it feels like to be on the battlefield, knowing that you're fighting for your country and religion," Mirweis said.

"*Naam-I khuda,*" I said—In the name of God, good for you. "May God accept your jihad." But what about me? How could Mirweis, my peer who wasn't stronger than I was, have battlefield experience already? And here he was speaking about jihad as if he were a propagandist for one of the mujahideen newspapers.

"You have to go to experience it. It's our sacred duty," he continued, despite my best efforts to steer the conversation toward another topic. "You may have fulfilled all your religious obligations, but you cannot call yourself a true Muslim if you don't do jihad. To fight," he said finally, "all you need is valor."

Was he questioning my religious credentials? Worse still, was he questioning my *ghayrat*? Gallantry, that most cherished of Afghan masculine qualities, is as essential to Afghan collective consciousness as individualism is to American self-identity. My ancestors had faced down invading British armies in the nineteenth century. Now my school-age friends were facing down the Red Army. What was I going to do? Mirweis had in effect said that if I didn't join the jihad, I was a *bay-ghayrat,* a dishonorable man who lacks the courage to fight for his land, property, and womenfolk, the most despicable insult imaginable.

Perhaps because of Mirweis's braggadocio, or perhaps because of what I had picked up at the madrassah, or even perhaps because I had nothing better to do in Peshawar, I resolved that, instead of becoming a scholar, I'd become a fighter.

I was eighteen. Still without much of a beard to show for myself, I'd nonetheless grown into a man in every other sense of the word. I could now take matters into my own hands and do what Father intended for me since I was thirteen. Father had long stopped talking about it, but I never forgot. I had sat out most of the early years of the war, too young to fight, something I long wished I could reverse. The moment of truth had arrived. It was my religious obligation and a duty to my country. The only question was whether my parents would give me their blessing. I'll cross that bridge when I come to it, I told myself.

To prepare myself, I formally joined the Hezb-I Islami Party and soon felt like a member of the family. Commiserating with the soldiers there, I began imagining myself on a mountaintop firing a rocket at a Russian tank, running through a barrage of gunfire, and throwing myself on the ground as bombs dropped all around me. Never in my life had I felt as passionately about pursuing a single goal. Over dinners on the large verandah of the political office, Mirweis always made a point of telling newly arrived commanders that I was going on the next operation with him, making it sound like an important event. But whether he was a high-ranking mujahid or a subcommander with only ten men, the response was always the same: "It's a good thought," they'd say, continue eating, and move on to more pressing concerns such as getting enough supplies for their men.

It was the fall of 1987, the seventh year of the occupation, one of the bloodiest years of the war. Under Mikhail Gorbachev, the Soviets had embraced the once inconceivable notion of ending the occupation, though no one in Peshawar actually believed this would happen. Hundreds of civilians were still being killed every day by Soviet forces. Mosques and villages were being bombed. Refugees continued to flee to Pakistan and Iran. Gorbachev may have called the Afghan war a "bleeding wound," but he didn't appear to be hurrying to stanch it. No wonder the mujahideen groups, "fundamentalist" and "moderate" alike, denounced the four-party Geneva talks between the United States, Pakistan, the Soviet Union, and the Communist Afghan government as a sham designed to install an un-Islamic government in Kabul.

Across the border in Afghanistan, the war was raging with a ferocity not seen since the mid-1980s. In the south, mechanized Soviet forces were desperately trying to penetrate a months-long siege of the strategic town of Khost led by Mawlawi Haqqani, a commander in Khalis's group. To the southwest, Communist forces were trying to fight off a mujahideen advance on the Kandahar airport. And to the east in Nangarhar province, Soviet forces were launching major offensives against mujahideen, the latest one of which was taking place in Shinwar district.

With so many fronts to choose from, one would think if you wanted to fight, it would be as easy as picking a battlefield. That's not how things worked. Throughout Afghanistan most mujahideen fronts drew their forces locally, relying on family and tribal ties. While a substantial number of these men fought full-time, most were part-time guerrillas who took part in combat then retired to their homes in Afghanistan or in Pakistani refugee camps when the fighting season gave way to winter. This was especially true on the eastern and southern fronts. Because of my location in Peshawar, it made more sense for me to fight on an eastern front instead of the northern front, which was more than a thirty-day trek across the Hindu Kush. Yet the eastern front remained quiet for several weeks.

"Something is going to come up, something big," Mirweis reassured me. "Just wait. We'll go on the biggest operation yet."

One day he stopped by my house and excitedly told me the time had come. We were to leave in a week's time. I was eager but also concerned about how Mother would react. Not only had she lost two younger brothers to the war, I was her only son. So I waited until the last minute, the day before I was to be deployed, to announce the news.

"I'm leaving for Afghanistan tomorrow," I said as casually as telling her I was going to spend a Friday night at my cousin's house.

"What are you talking about, my crazy son?" she asked. "Have you lost your mind?"

"I told you. I'm going to Afghanistan tomorrow," I repeated. Her eyes welled.

"Look at your grandma," Mother said. "She doesn't have a son and she wanders from home to home like the sonless widow that she is. What does she have? Nothing. Show mercy on your poor mother." I stared down at the concrete floor and said nothing.

"A mother without a son is like a lamp without light," she continued.

"Whatever you say, I'm going," I said coldly.

I could hear her crying in the living room, so I left the house and returned around dinnertime. While I was gone, Mother had enlisted Father in her cause.

"Is what I hear true?" he asked.

"Yes," I said.

"I cannot give you my blessing," he said. "You are our only son and under no obligation to take part in the jihad. In fact, you are obligated to stay home and look after your parents. Without our consent, participating in jihad would contradict the teachings of Islam."

It wasn't as if Father's deep-seated hatred of the Soviets had waned. He hated them every bit as much. But he felt the resistance had been hijacked by religious fanatics, and he didn't want his son to be a part of it. Perhaps something else also explained his opposition: a genuine concern for my safety. It was one thing to talk, back in Sheberghan, about shipping his twelve-year-old son to the resistance front but quite another to confront that son's actual departure. And when he invoked religion to dissuade me, it wasn't for lack of a more sophisticated argument but rather because he thought religion would speak to me.

"You are putting me ahead of our commitment to God," I said. "Isn't taking part in jihad a religious obligation?"

Father responded by trying to instill enough guilt in me to change my mind. It was no use though, and he quickly realized he was talking to a wall. After dinner I went into my room and packed a gray cotton knapsack with one change of clothes, a small towel, a bar of soap, a pocketknife, toothpaste and toothbrush, a couple of pens, a notepad, and a camera. This was all I needed for now, Mirweis told me.

The next morning Mother realized she could not stop me and reluctantly gave me her blessing. In keeping with custom, she held up a bound copy of the Koran and let me walk under it three times, kissing the holy book each time I passed. I fished into my pocket for a small bill to put inside the Koran, also per custom, but couldn't find one. Finally, as I left her house, Mother threw a glass of water on my footsteps to keep my travels safe.

Several blue Toyota pickup trucks were parked outside the political office when I arrived. A group of mujahideen chatting under a tree a few yards from the front gate saw me and my heaving backpack (a telltale sign of a novice), and acknowledged me warmly, offering a customary "May God accept your jihad." Inside the compound, close to forty men busily went over the details of our journey. There were several commanders, and supply and logistics men, along with nearly a dozen refugees looking to hitch a ride to the front.

After greeting as many men as I could, I went looking for Saboor. A distant cousin, Saboor was a logistics soldier who lived at the political office. Short, reed-thin, and frail, he was actually a tough adversary, able to stand his ground in the face of intimidation and demands made by top commanders and their fighters. Because of this, he gave the impression of having a no-nonsense personality; however, I quickly discovered his irreverent side when I discussed Khalis, the deeply pious mullah with a henna-dyed beard, and his recent marriage to a fourteen-year-old refugee girl. Saboor, who was twenty-five and well past his marriage age, gleefully remarked, "What a man, what a man," with an envy that even I shared.

When I finally tracked down Saboor, he politely brushed me aside. "No time to talk," he said, as he jotted down names, counting the soldiers each commander would lead, compiling lists of contact names in tribal areas, and keeping track of how much money would be doled out to whom. In the large first-floor drawing room, several commanders, including the Nangarhar province commander, Engineer Mahmoud, were meeting with senior party officials to discuss last-minute details of the upcoming operation. When they walked out they held bundles of money, destined not for their own pockets but for those of their men who, depending on age, experience, and term of service, would receive between fifty and two hundred dollars at the end of each mission.

Mirweis arrived bareheaded and wearing fatigue pants over combat boots, standing out amid a throng of traditionally dressed men in leather sandals and plastic flip-flops. His outfit was flashy, like mujahideen in the Panjsher Valley wore, resembling their fawning copycats on the streets of Peshawar. Didn't Mirweis know better? I walked up and embraced him anyway. He said we'd be leaving shortly, but first business needed to be taken care of. This "business" ended up taking hours, so Mirweis and I lazed about on the grass under a shady tree, killing time as we drank endless cups of tea, and eventually ate lunch.

Then, shortly after noon, it was time to depart. Our destination was Parachinar, a small, sleepy town in Pakistan's tribal zone on the Afghan border, some seven hours away. Mirweis and I hopped into one of the pickup trucks, squeezing in among eight other men. No sooner had we turned onto the main street than Mirweis shouted the battle cry *Allahu Akbar!*, punching the air with his fist. The rest of us responded as one, *Allahu Akbar! Allahu Akbar!*, as much as an act of piety as a chance to tell everyone on the streets we were headed for the front. With the exception of children and a few men, most people didn't even notice us. Still I could not help recalling from my childhood a time in Sheberghan when groups of shabby, recently conscripted villagers, loaded in the back of brilliantly painted old trucks driving around town, shouted out their allegiance to God, the Prophet, his Four Companions, and the country. Now it was my turn. After four long years of living in Pakistan, I was finally heading back to Afghanistan to realize my dream of performing my sacred duty of jihad. I was aware of the perils that lay ahead. Just a couple of months earlier, Nabeel, a pudgy, vivacious relative who lived next door with his aunt's family, was killed in a Soviet air raid. But fear had not yet set in. The bumpy ride was comforting, like rides I had taken to Grandpa Baba's house in Kabul as a kid. I was enjoying the sights of the small, bustling market towns along the road and the cool, fresh mountain air as we drove away from Peshawar's stifling heat and pollution. Yet I still had no idea what I'd be doing. All I knew was that I wanted to take part in the jihad. But what did that mean? Killing Russians and their Afghan puppets? Firing rockets and mortars? Planting landmines or conducting hit-and-run raids? I'd had no military training, and my knowledge of these activities was limited to what I had heard firsthand or read in the mujahideen newspapers.

I asked Mirweis where we were going. Tora Bora, he answered. Tora Bora? It was a strange name, one I'd never heard before. Where is that, I asked, and what does Tora Bora mean? Mirweis was stumped. I knew Tora was the feminine form of "black" in Pashto. But Bora? Was it some kind of ridge? "It means nothing," Mirweis said, "it's just a word." Tora Bora was a *markaz* (in Arabic, a "center"), the word of choice in eastern Afghanistan for a mujahideen base camp, though its name didn't conjure images of legendary mujahideen strongholds like Panjsher, Khost, Jaji, and Herat.

We arrived at Parachinar after dark. A cop manning the city's checkpoint recognized our driver and waved us in. Parachinar was the capital of Kurram Agency, one of seven federally administered tribal areas that served as key launching pads for the jihad. Dozens of mujahideen ammo dumps, safe houses, and training camps were spread around Parachinar, as were a handful of medical clinics attending to the war wounded. The town also had a large Shiite Pashtun minority. The Shiites hated the Afghans, whom they accused of siding with the Sunnis in massacring hundreds of Shiites during a standoff the year before. Both sides resorted to frequent gun battles that left dozens dead. To prevent further bloodshed, the government imposed periodic daytime and nighttime curfews on Parachinar, though the curfew clearly didn't apply to mujahideen. Not only were the police Sunni, but they were also paid to ensure the smooth flow of men and supplies through Parachinar.

We turned off the main road and drove for a mile or two until the dirt road dead-ended. Several pickup trucks had arrived ahead of us, while those that had already dropped off their passengers turned around and immediately headed back the way they had come. After climbing out of the pickups, we walked into an eerie dark valley where the only flickers of light came from a handful of houses.

Soon we arrived at the gate of a large compound where we were led to a second-floor guest room for dinner. The hosts were generous, real Pashtuns seemingly committed to the ancient code of hospitality. Back when the Russians first invaded, this kind of Afghan generosity was what sustained the war effort. By the time I arrived at this place in 1987, though, hospitality had become commercialized. Like the cop at the checkpoint, the lord of this compound was on the mujahideen payroll.

Shortly before sunrise the next day, we said our prayers, wolfed down a breakfast of bread and tea and cheese, then divided ourselves into groups of ten for the march to Spinghar—the White Mountains—that mark the Afghanistan-Pakistan border. Mostly unarmed, we followed the direct but steepest trail while our supplies were moved up a less treacherous path. The morning chill made the first hour or so of the hike easy. Mirweis told me to enjoy it while it lasted. As we straggled through dense forest, I thought about what my cousin Rooin had said to me the night before we fled to Pakistan: "So many Afghans have left the country and have come back kissing the soil with tears in their eyes."

The words had left an indelible impression on me, but much like leaving Afghanistan, returning was confounding and almost frustrating. No clearly marked border indicated where Pakistan ended and Afghanistan began. Forested mountains with snow-covered peaks soaring more than fourteen thousand feet cut between both countries. In deep, narrow valleys and on high, green slopes, isolated nomads grazed their sheep and goats, but it was hard to say whether they were Afghans or Pakistanis, not that it mattered in a region inhabited by the same Pashtun tribes. I asked the men in my group where Afghanistan was but was met with befuddled looks. "It's over the pass," one said. "It starts at the summit," said another. "We have two hours to go," offered a third. Then, some time later and much to my disbelief, I heard the words "We're in Afghanistan."

I had missed the dramatic moment I was waiting for, just as Father had missed the moment he wanted to breathe freedom when we entered Pakistan, and in truth I was too self-conscious to kneel and kiss the rocky ground in front of men who had gone down this road many times before. Instead I decided to wait until the next prayer break. There on my scarf, which doubled as my prayer mat, I quietly praised God for safely bringing us to Afghanistan.

Beyond the first pass, all was quiet, not a sound save for my own breathing and the panting of men trekking up from the opposite direction. Then, slowly, the war zone opened up like a landscape poster being unrolled. At first the edges emerged, a few armed men, then a small convoy of pack mules carrying supplies, large containers of cooking oil and sacks of rice. Then I heard the sound of gunfire in the distance. Was that fighting? I couldn't tell if it was that or boys having fun shooting at something or other they had spotted.

At the end of our fourteen-hour trek, we arrived at a ramshackle cluster of tents and mud huts built on the side of the mountain. Engineer Mahmoud and several subcommanders and aides had already taken their place in a hut while the rest of us crowded into a tent heated by a smoldering fire. Food was brought on dirty tin plates—beef stew with gummy rice and loaves of hard bread. While I washed down the meal with sweetened green tea, Mirweis told me how to secure my lodging. Once you claim a spot, don't leave it, and if you have to go outside, ask someone to save it for you. You may be with a band of brothers, he observed, but up here in the mountains the brothers dispensed with niceties. Everyone was on his own. Mirweis and I alternated guarding our spot in the corner of the tent whenever we had to go out to relieve ourselves, but the tent was so packed with men that our spot would compress each time one of us left for a few minutes. Even so, it didn't stop me from falling into a deep slumber, leaning against my knapsack, my knees folded.

The next day, we descended the pass and started down to a valley floor. There I saw rusting parts of tanks lying amid wild shrubs, remnants of a battle fought long ago. Then, as we neared a hamlet, we met a horse carrying a heavy load that turned out to be a body wrapped in a white shroud. We stepped aside and asked the old man prodding the horse what had happened. He told us the body belonged to a kid who had died during an attack on a government post. He was being paid to take the body back to the boy's family in Pakistan.

Late in the afternoon, we stopped by a tiny one-room village mosque for a quick break before finishing the last short leg of our journey. Inside two men with rifles lying by their sides sat on the straw-covered floor dipping pieces of bread into a bowl of buttermilk and munching on sticky rice. With a bandoleer tightly bound around his broad chest, the older of the two, who looked menacing, stood up and coldly greeted us in Pashto. He was from Pakistan's tribal areas, while his younger companion, not nearly as skilled in Pashto, sputtered out that he was from the Punjab province of Pakistan. I was surprised by their presence. Pakistanis fighting in Afghanistan had always sounded like Soviet propaganda to me. Speaking in Persian, I told Mirweis I didn't like what I was seeing. He said the men belonged to our group, which comforted me some, but didn't quell my trepidation completely. The men offered us the food that was still left in their bowls, but we declined and sat in silence.

We headed north from the village, toward a high mountain range no more than a couple hours' hike away. Someone pointed at several snowy peaks and said that was Tora Bora. Though the sides of my new sneakers had melted and the soles of my feet were covered with blisters, I began taking longer, steadier steps, even as the altitude rose and my breathing grew heavy. Our path gave way to a well-maintained gravel trail more than ten feet wide, large enough for a car, though there hadn't been a car or a truck for miles as the closest paved road ended at a town two hours behind us. A couple of hundred yards up the trail, I could see smoke, and several pack mules trotted through what looked like a gate but was no more than a rope tied between two poles and stretched across the path.

This didn't exactly resemble the entrance to a sprawling army and police compound, but it was well guarded. Armed men stood on both sides of the gate, their chests thick with bandoleers. To our left, by the side of the mountain, a heavy machine gun was mounted atop a stone guardhouse. A blue sign nailed to the house said IN THE NAME OF GOD, THE MERCIFUL, THE COMPASSION-ATE and underneath that TORA BORA STRONGHOLD, ISLAMIC PARTY OF AFGHANISTAN.

After greeting the guards, we stopped to say the evening prayer on the prayer ground abutting a shallow ravine. It was getting dark, and we were eager to reach the main base, a fifteen-minute hike across the valley. Straggling up a narrow trail that rose and fell across the floor of the valley, I could hear faint voices and see small shadows of men and flickers of light in the distance. Approaching the main base, we passed the smoky kitchen where several old men were hard at work stirring large pots over woodstoves. Younger men carried plates of food to the flat ground that served as an outdoor mess hall. It was dinnertime, and all I could think about was eating, drinking lots of tea, and finding a place to sleep. After dinner we were handed cotton sleeping bags and led to the medical tent, where Mirweis and I crashed. It was a clear, crisp starry night, and as I got into my sleeping bag and closed my eyes, I was relieved this part of my journey was over and was too exhausted to wonder what lay ahead.

Throughout our three-day journey from Parachinar to Tora Bora, lack of sleep hadn't been an issue. Without light for recreation or any other activity, we'd go to sleep after sundown and get up before dawn for prayers. Yet after I forced myself to get up the next morning to perform the ablution at a small brook and say my morning prayer, I quickly found myself back in my sleeping bag. Perhaps it was a desire to shelter myself from the mountain chill or perhaps exhaustion had caught up with me. All I wanted was to go back to sleep, especially since I had no clue what my new routine was going to be like.

When I woke the second time, other men were still bundled up in their sleeping bags, and some were sitting in a circle drinking tea and eating bread. After breakfast Mirweis told me that they were handing out weapons and that we should go down to the ammo dump to receive ours. I couldn't wait to get my hands on one. Mirweis and I walked along a narrow, winding trail down a steep slope from the clinic to the ammo dump. It was nearing noon and the air was warming up. Under a bright, clear sky, the sun was hidden behind a soaring mountain that towered over a shallow, rocky creek.

At the mouth of the cave that served as an ammo dump, open wooden boxes of rifles wrapped in newspapers stood on the ground beside a pile of cartridges and magazines on a greasy tarp. A line of impatient youngsters, some a couple years younger than I, stood in a semicircle around two men, one of whom handed out weapons while the other took down names in a small notebook. Although we weren't dressed in our best, we must have looked like eager little boys waiting to receive gifts of cash during the Eid holidays. Some of the men pleaded for more than the two extra magazines that each person received along with a bunch of cartridges.

After fifteen minutes in line, it was our turn. The weapons were folding-stock AK-47s and wooden fixed-stock ones. I'd heard that the Chinese copy of the Kalashnikov was the second best after the Russian original, while the Egyptian version was widely seen as the least reliable. At first glance, I liked the metal folding-stock version better than the fixed one with a knife bayonet. The metal version was compact, slick in appearance, and looked light and easy to handle. Wrapped in recent Chinese newspapers, the guns smelled of grease. I was thrilled to hold the weapon in my hands, feeling its weight, knowing that this gun was mine.

It was a good thing no one asked me if I knew how to use it, as I had never fired an AK-47 before. My experience with guns was limited. One stormy night in Sheberghan when I was about eleven, my mother's cousin, a police officer, asked me to fetch his Makarov pistol from his house. I stuck it down my pants and headed back home in the rain, loving the weight of the gun against my body. A year later I took a small pen gun Father kept in his drawer and fired a single shot into a mud-brick wall while my cousin Rooin watched in awe. I had no idea how to use an

AK-47, the weapon of choice for both sides in the war, and there was no formal training program at Tora Bora. Looking around me, it appeared everyone else knew how to fire them. Even the young boys were confidently loading and cocking their guns, and flinging them across their shoulders. I took my gun and did my best to look like I knew what I was doing.

Once we had our weapons and ammunition, Mirweis and I walked down to the creek to join the others in washing our guns. Squatting on the bank, we spent the next hour scrubbing grease off the rifles, cleaning them thoroughly. Then we dried them and rubbed the sides and the barrels until they glistened. Mirweis then said he would show me how to disassemble the rifle and put it back together, but after a clumsy display, Awalgul, a regular at the clinic and a close friend of Doctor Hamid's, stepped in and finished the lesson. A veteran fighter, Awalgul handled a gun the way an experienced jockey handles a horse. When I confessed that I did not know the first thing about firing a gun, he smiled and assured me that my inexperience was not a deficiency. I didn't need three months of training to fire an AK-47. Like many old-timers, Awalgul himself had received only rudimentary instruction in guerilla warfare and in basic military tactics and weapon use, at a training camp in Pakistan. He had learned useful things, such as how to pick up an unexploded hand grenade and throw it back at the enemy, but years later he still laughed at the absurdity of being made to jump through a fiery loop, a skill he never found occasion to put to use. The Pakistani instructors, men with little or no war experience of their own, were teaching guerrilla warfare essentially out of a textbook.

Sitting by my side, Awalgul patiently explained what each part of the gun was for, how to properly handle the rifle in various situations, how to sling it across my shoulder, how to keep the safety on, and how to hold it while creeping across open ground. I was like a child learning to play with a new toy, and I was determined to get at least as good as Mirweis at handling my toy. By evening, after a day of practice, I could disassemble my gun and put it back together in under ten minutes.

I spent the next several days with Mirweis and a few other enthusiastic new arrivals at target practice. After initially being thrown off balance by the gun's kickback, I quickly got the hang of it. I was a poor shot, but after several magazines, on both selective fire and automatic, I felt I could put my new skill to use if need be, but I wasn't prepared to teach what I had just learned. While there were several new arrivals who had never fired a gun, including a boy whose complete lack of facial hair made me look grown-up, shooting was not something I wanted to demonstrate in front of veterans. I wanted to continue target practice, but because it was considered a waste of ammo, it wasn't encouraged.

In the absence of formal training, I had to rely on the expertise of veterans like Awalgul and wait for my turn in the field to learn the basics. Much of what I needed to know to survive was common sense; some of it sounded counterintuitive at the time. When you come under a rocket attack, for example, the worst thing you can do is to follow your instinct and run for cover. It is safer to be lying on the ground next to an exploding bomb or mortar shell than getting up and running away, because shrapnel tends to fly up from the point of impact. When you are running under fire across open ground, you should constantly zigzag, never move in a straight line. This makes you more difficult to hit. If you are standing a solitary guard at a crossroads, the worst thing you can do is to focus on an oncoming target. If it is an enemy, more likely than not it is a distraction for someone who will attack you from the rear.

Shortly after our arrival, I had a chance to explore the surroundings. This was easy to do because, for the most part, we set our own schedules. Tora Bora was less an army camp than a mountain stronghold. There was no marching in lockstep on the parade grounds every morning, no halting and coming to attention to salute officers. In fact, there was no hierarchy of officers among us at all, only commanders and subcommanders, and the rest of us under them.

Before the war Tora Bora was a network of tall, intertwined, rugged, and sparsely forested mountains with numerous caves where goats and sheep and occasionally nomads took shelter in cold weather. During the war the caves served as safe sleeping areas for the mujahideen. Here at Tora Bora, caves honeycombed the valley, some primitive and untouched, others fortified and expanded. A narrow man-made hole in the mountain by the southern entrance served as a cell for local prisoners. A larger one up a high slope across the jagged ravine held a dozen or so recently captured Communist army soldiers. Near the bottom of the valley, two long, triangle-shaped caves had been enlarged to hold hundreds of rifles, machine guns, rocket launchers, and boxes of ammunition. The fact that Tora Bora was a well-established mujahideen base was also well known to the Soviets, who made several serious attempts to put it out of business.

Large enough to house over five hundred people at a time, the base was also well organized by the standards of the day. The clinic at Tora Bora was not only run by highly skilled paramedics, whom we called doctors, but was also well stocked with first aid kits, morphine ampoules, and antimalarial pills. In those days not every mujahideen base had a clinic, which was one reason for the high rate of fatalities. As it happened, I soon found myself spending much of my time with Engineer Mahmoud's inner circle.

Doctor Hamid was a fast-talking, hazel-eyed medic and mortar gunner who served as an aide to the commander. My older cousin Jalil, who had served a couple of years at Tora Bora, was another aide and mortar gunner. Finally there was Qari Nazeef, a Stinger gunner who was among the first mujahideen selected by the Pakistanis to be trained in using the American-made shoulder-launched missiles. Once an aspiring *qari*, or professional reciter of the Koran, Nazeef's career was upended by the outbreak of war. He was a practical joker and never passed up an opportunity to make fun of

nomads who occasionally stopped by the base in search of medicine. Putting on a pair of radio headphones as if they were a
stethoscope, he would "examine" these illiterate nomads and try
to extract embarrassing sexual confessions from them. "So how
many times a week do you make love to your wife?" he would ask
a mystified nomad, assuring him that the stethoscope could detect
lies. "If you don't tell the truth, you don't get the medicine."

Watching him sit and tell obscene jokes, it was hard to picture him zeroing in on a Soviet jet with a deadly Stinger missile,
to say nothing of chanting the Koran before a somber audience.
That was how a lot of the men behaved, though: jocular on the
outside but deadly serious when it came to fighting. Nazeef was
an expert with the Stinger, having shot down more than half a
dozen Soviet jets. That didn't mean the Soviets didn't still send
sorties our way; it only meant that the jets flew high enough to
stay out of range, thus losing their bombing accuracy. In my
first week, just as I was lulled into thinking it was an abode of
tranquillity and not a war zone, I heard the sound of jets approaching the valley. The next thing I knew, I, along with everyone else in sight, was running into a nearby bunker. Several
bombs went off in rapid, thunderous succession. The impacts
felt so close I was afraid shrapnel would worm its way into the
bunker and rip us to pieces. I began murmuring the customary
Islamic declaration of faith along with the rest of my cave mates:
I bear witness that there is no god but God and Muhammad is
his *servant* and Prophet. When it was quiet outside, I emerged to
find Engineer Mahmoud calmly rummaging through the trees
and Mirweis walking toward me with a triumphant smile on his
face and a ten-pound chunk of warm shrapnel cradled in his
arms. I was too shaken to feel a sense of triumph; nonetheless I
smiled back to let him know I was okay.

In addition to the clinic, there were several bomb shelters, including one about twenty yards from the clinic. The two outdoor
roofed kitchens—one in the upper half of the base, and one in the

lower half—were large and equipped with several stoves and samovars. The upper base kitchen, which prepared tea and meals for most of the camp, looked as if it had been recently built, as it was better equipped than kitchens in most large Afghan households or those run by professional cooks. There were outhouses about a hundred yards from the kitchen; however most men preferred to "go for a walk in the desert." The eating grounds, about thirty by twenty meters wide, would be covered with tarps during meals. The food was tasteless. Lunch was often a dish of vegetable stew with a piece of bread, while dinner consisted of boiled rice and, three or four times a week, rice with boiled meat. Thanks to our proximity to Engineer Mahmoud, we'd occasionally get a few luxuries. One morning someone brought us a large metal vat of honey. It was crude, yellowish, and not honey-colored, but dipping pieces of bread into it was a delight.

A few yards below was a small mosque, a flattened area that had foot-high walls on all sides except the front where a niche had been built. During all hours of the day, you could see men, including some young, white, skull-capped madrassah students visiting from Pakistan, reading the Koran or praying under the shade of several tall trees that surrounded the prayer ground.

Sometimes I went up to the antiaircraft positions situated on mountaintops around the valley. The men stationed in these positions were the loneliest in camp. They would trek down to pick up food and water only once a day, then it was back to their positions for the remainder of the day and night, waiting for airplanes that rarely came. Even if they did, they would fly too high for the DShK-38 heavy machine gun to be of any use. Our position had come under attack, to be sure, but with Nazeef's Stinger, the jets were as vulnerable as we were.

In the absence of combat, all we did was wait. Sometimes during the day Mirweis and I would go down to the ammo dump and help unload supply mules. At night we pulled hour-long shifts of guard duty around the upper base. That was largely the extent of our activity. A few times some of us in the clinic managed to sneak in a nap after dawn prayers. One day Engineer Mahmoud walked in wielding a large tree branch and shouting, "Get up! Get up!" and before anyone could scramble out of his sleeping bag, he went around the tent striking everyone. "No more naps after prayers," he barked. "Read the Koran, do something, but no naps." He left in a huff after we all got up and sheepishly folded our sleeping bags. That became the new base rule. After that no one dared to sleep or even lie down after morning prayers. If we didn't read the Koran, we just sat on the floor of the tent, wrapping ourselves in *patoos* until the day got warm, which usually didn't happen until ten or eleven in the morning.

Napping mujahideen wasn't what I had envisioned the camp would be like when I arrived. Reading the mujahideen publications in Peshawar, I thought many mujahideen would be emulators of the pious early warriors of Islam, fasting and fighting in the name of God by day, and praying and reading the Koran by night. While you would regularly find a few boys, mostly madrassah students or Arab and Pakistani volunteers, reading the Koran on the prayer grounds, the base was far from an extremist breeding ground. Everyone felt he was here to carry out jihad in defense of his faith and country, but no one spent every waking minute in worship. Engineer Mahmoud's suggestion that we read the Koran had been just that—a suggestion. I didn't see him reciting the Koran more than once or twice, and those close to him did not display excessive piousness, let alone fanaticism.

This may have been attributable, in part, to Engineer Mahmoud's own easygoing personality and leadership style. In other fronts things were different. In southwestern Paktia province, for example, Mawlawi Jalaluddin Haqqani had surrounded himself with his fellow mullahs, and his ranks were filled with madrassah students. At Tora Bora there were a fairly large number of madrassah students, but no mullahs were in the upper ranks.

Almost every senior aide had received some form of secular education before the war. Educated men on the frontlines were by no means uncommon in Afghanistan. In fact most mujahideen commanders had some religious or secular education. A few mullahs were scattered around the camp, but many more were high school and college graduates. Engineer Mahmoud himself had been a student at Jalalabad University's engineering school when the war broke out. His given name was Shaistagul; he adopted Mahmoud (after the great eleventh-century Afghan warrior-king and conquerer of India) as a nom de guerre. Doctor Hamid, who ran the clinic, had graduated from high school, while Nazeef had fallen one year short of obtaining his diploma.

Like many mujahideen commanders, Mahmoud encouraged a relaxed atmosphere at Tora Bora. I had expected his subordinates to be deferential, bowing and prostrating and uttering "yes, sir" and "no, sir" when spoken to. While we sometimes rose when he showed up, no one was especially demonstrative, despite the fact he was not only the top commander at Tora Bora but also the second highest ranking commander for Nangarhar province, second only to Hajji Qadir, who served as the military chief of the party and had his own front in Shinwar. Mahmoud's subcommanders were expected to keep him apprised of what was happening, but in fact most of them ran their own groups, ranging in number from a few dozen to several hundred men.

This laid-back atmosphere may also have developed because Tora Bora wasn't the hub of action it had once been. With Soviet casualties mounting and the Stingers neutralizing their air power, the tide of war was shifting in our favor. Increasingly, Soviet and government forces were assuming a defensive stance, concerned more with protecting major towns than with driving away mujahideen forces. The last major Soviet incursion into Tora Bora had happened the previous winter. As those who witnessed it recalled, the Soviets landed hundreds of paratroopers atop the high points surrounding Tora Bora. The mujahideen, under heavy artillery fire, were forced to abandon the base, running for days from mountaintop to mountaintop, spending nights in caves. The attack was fierce and relentless. After less than a week of controlling the valley, the Soviets departed, laying landmines and leaving behind empty cans of food, cellophane wrappers of cigarette packs, steel rods that looked like tent pegs, and thousands of spent shell casings that could still be easily found on the ground. The attackers never returned.

Much to my disappointment, I soon learned there was no major operation to prepare for. The larger offensives had been postponed until next spring and summer. As it turned out, the demoralized Communists had abandoned their nearest outpost without a fight just before our arrival. One afternoon we visited the village where it had been. Perched atop a hill and surrounded by a minefield, it looked large enough to house fifty soldiers or so. The place had been thoroughly ransacked by villagers. I don't know if the soldiers had left anything behind, but nothing was left when we arrived. I was eager to see the place anyway. With nothing else to do, we spent the afternoon throwing rocks at antipersonnel trip-wire mines that dotted the ground around the post.

The villagers were elated by the Communists' departure—it meant the village would no longer be the target of regular mujahideen attacks—and they joined us throwing rocks into the minefield, shouting and cheering every time one went off. Even though the Russians were gone, it was important to establish good relations with villagers. They not only provided you with food and shelter, but more importantly intelligence. Good relations included patrolling their houses, spending nights in their mosques, and establishing enough of a presence to give them a sense of security. The village then became your turf. When one group controlled a large swath of land there was a greater feeling of security, but when several groups competed for control of a single district, the area degenerated into a war zone with villagers living in constant fear. Infighting between mujahideen groups had been going on for years. Around Kandahar, for example, daily exchanges of gunfire between two groups had become commonplace. Even worse, in Laghman after the initial Soviet attacks in the early 1980s, the province fell into a series of bloody internecine fights among various mujahideen groups, which contributed to the flight of many Afghans into Pakistan. The Soviets, of course, encouraged this behavior whenever possible.

Meanwhile, life at Tora Bora took on a familiar routine. Other than target practice up on the mountain slopes and the occasional rattle of the antiaircraft machine guns in response to incoming jets, I hardly heard the sound of war. When we weren't drinking tea or being entertained by Nazeef, we adjourned to a flat area down from the outhouses and played volleyball over a rope tied between two poles.

Toward the end of the month, word went around the base that Mawlawi Khalis, the party leader, was touring the region and planned to visit Tora Bora. Engineer Mahmoud must have known about it all along, but we didn't find out until the day before Khalis arrived at Chaparhar, a small town that had recently been abandoned by the Communist forces. Engineer Mahmoud wanted to take an escort party to Chaparhar, about six hours away, to accompany the great leader to Tora Bora. Nearly everyone at the clinic was invited, mostly for practical reasons. Nazeef shouldered his Stinger, while Doctor Hamid carried a submachine gun and a small first aid kit. Engineer Mahmoud also asked Mirweis and me to tag along. It was a privilege to escort the party elder, a man who had put his men ahead of both himself and politics; such a leader was a rarity in Afghanistan.

Shortly after dawn prayers, we headed out through the northern gate up a peak, carrying little more than rifles, canteens, and of course Nazeef's Stinger. During the several hour walk, the faint sound of distant jets put Nazeef on alert, but they never came close. There was little to worry about on the ground, as we were the only mujahideen group that operated in this newly liberated territory. Just before noon we stopped at a small village where Doctor Hamid asked a young boy to lead us to a certain land-owner's house. As soon as we arrived there, the family arranged to feed us. A child brought a tarp and spread it out on some shady ground by a brook under some trees. A couple of other boys brought pots of tea and glasses. Then bowls of buttermilk and two big plates of sticky white rice arrived.

Sated and refueled, we left the village and within an hour or two arrived at the center of Chaparhar district and headed to a sprawling mud compound not far from the marketplace. A green oasis surrounded by barren desert and rocky hills, Chaparhar's densely planted trees kept it cool during the summer and gave the town the appearance of a large orchard that had been littered with mud huts built too close to each other. As in many other villages in this province, the houses had their guest quarters outside where there was little privacy.

Engineer Mahmoud, Qari Nazeef, and Doctor Hamid went straight to the compound where Khalis was meeting with the village elders. The rest of us stayed outside on a verandah shaded by tall birch trees. There was a brook nearby, and large tarps had been spread on the ground. More than two dozen armed men had converged on the tarps. Some had just arrived and were welcoming each other. I went around and greeted everyone. More men began arriving, filling up the space. While they all belonged to the Islamic Party, they were led by various commanders and operated independently in the Chaparhar region. Some were there to escort Khalis to Tora Bora, while others just wanted to catch a glimpse of the old man. The men relished the opportunity to freely sit around the center of a formerly Communist-controlled town they had tried for years to capture. The whole gathering had a festive air. This was the first liberated town of its size I'd visited, and while most of the men there were strangers to me, we acted more like guests at a wedding than soldiers.

The food too, when it was finally brought out on large tin platters, looked enough for a wedding. There were large platters of well-cooked rice and lamb, small plates of beef stew and spinach, loaves of freshly baked bread, and plastic jugs of water. The food was placed on several long serving cloths spread across the ground. We sat around them and began to eat. Some of the men wolfed down the food as if they had not eaten for days.

After lunch Mirweis and I went to the bazaar and had our first ice cream in Afghanistan. When we got back to the compound, the place was packed with several dozen village elders sitting on the ground. Flanked by Engineer Mahmoud and other commanders, Khalis was sitting on a cot near the assembled crowd, mumbling words into a large microphone that was connected to a public address system tied to a tree. The old men in the audience, wearing their best silk turbans, listened with rapt attention. These were the same men who had supported his call for a jihad eight years earlier. This was the territory of the Khogyani, Khalis's tribe and one of the largest and most powerful in eastern Afghanistan, and while Khalis was not a tribal leader himself, he had built a large following among these tribesmen. Now, after eight years of jihad, their sacrifices and support had paid off. The Communists had left the town in defeat, and the Red Army was being brought to its knees.

It was a moving sight, but I decided to leave as it was a private meeting between Khalis and the tribal elders. I went back to the eating ground and took off my shoes. I laid down on the ground next to a tree intending to take a nap. The villagers had started cleaning up the place, and several mujahideen were napping on the ground, including Mirweis, his hat pulled down over his head. Unable to sleep, I decided to wash my socks and shoes in the brook. The next thing I remember, a man in his twenties, of medium height and build, walked up to the middle of the verandah where a group of four or five men were sitting in a circle. He greeted them, and one of the men, apparently a commander judging from the pistol he wore, stood up. As the commander reached out to hug the man, the stranger took a step back, raised his rifle, and pulled the trigger, pumping what sounded like half a magazine into the commander's stomach.

The commander let out a muffled cry and held his stomach, looking dazed. The assassin took off, running into the trees, all the while trying to change magazines. No more than ten people actually saw the shooting but panic ensued. I grabbed my rifle and jumped behind the closest tree, while Mirweis crouched on the ground.

Someone shouted, "Hit him!" I don't know if most people knew what had happened or where the target was moving, but now nearly everyone was shooting toward the trees where the killer was running. I fired several bursts of automatic fire. In the chaos of shouting and yelling that overtook the place, it was hard to aim or to know if I'd hit him. Then I saw the man fall to the ground, get up, fall back, get up again, and start staggering away until he finally collapsed a hundred yards away, his body riddled with bullets.

It was over in a couple of minutes, but it took much longer for the pandemonium to die down. My first assumption was that the shooter had been a Communist agent. Soon a crowd formed around the commander. He was lying on his back, groaning quietly as he held his shattered hands—white, mangled joints jutting through scraps of flesh—over his blood-soaked stomach. Some of the men were shooing away children and others who were rushing toward the scene.

Doctor Hamid ran up to the commander and pulled a knife from his pocket and started cutting off the wounded man's waistcoat. He then pulled out his first aid kit and asked the man to lift up his body so he could remove the vest and shirt entirely. Opening his terrified eyes, the commander made a feeble attempt to rise, then fell back. After a second try, Doctor Hamid removed the coat and tore off the shirt. While he tried to stanch the bleeding, the commander's younger brother rushed to the grounds. Seeing his brother in a pool of blood, he threw his rifle to the ground and broke down in tears. He asked the commander to name the shooter. The commander responded by mumbling his last will and testament.

It had now been ten minutes since the shooting, and men who knew both the killer and the victim explained that the shooting had been a personal vendetta. Khalis's faint voice could once again be heard on the public address system and things were starting to get back to normal. But just as Doctor Hamid started closing the dying man's wounds, I heard the unmistakable whoosh of incoming rockets. There was no place to take cover. Everywhere you looked were trees. I had been taught that taking cover under a tree is the worst thing you could do in a rocket attack, but what if you found yourself in a forest? Did you hide under a big tree or a small one? There was no time to think. Men were dashing around and throwing themselves on the ground wherever they happened to be. I followed several men running toward a garden and ducked behind a short wall. The Katyusha rockets whooshed overhead, past the compound Khalis was staying at, and exploded a hundred yards away in a field.

We got up and ran back to the grounds where Doctor Hamid was still working on the wounded man. I was wondering if we were in for more rockets. The nervous expressions on the other men's faces said they expected we were. The Communists must have learned of Khalis's presence in the town, along with nearly a hundred armed mujahideen, not to mention dozens of village elders and tribal leaders. The attack, I later learned, had been mounted from a Communist position some fifteen kilometers away. We were within easy missile range. Engineer Mahmoud sent a couple of men to the grounds ordering an immediate withdrawal. Doctor Hamid decided to stay behind and do what he could to save the commander's life.

At the compound, we waited outside while Khalis and his entourage prepared to leave. As a calm Khalis strode out, someone held the reins and helped him get on a white horse that was furnished for him. A dozen men walked in front of Khalis as he rode down the alley, while the rest of us followed behind. A sense of nervousness filled the air, and I was still shaken by the events of the last half hour, but for the first time I was thinking about Khalis and his safety, not about my own.

As we wound down a narrow alley that was hardly wide enough to allow more than one man on each side of Khalis, and walked out into a wider dirt road, the procession stopped. Several boys of five and six were shooting marbles in the middle of the road. The men ahead shouted at the boys to move away. Barefoot and wearing clothes as soiled as their hands, they reluctantly withdrew to the sides of the road, looking annoyed. They couldn't care less about this large group of armed men and the man on the horse right in front of them.

I began walking fast to catch up with Khalis. Mirweis followed me. By this time there were five or six men on each side of Khalis. In the sweltering afternoon sun, he was breathing hard and sweating profusely, occasionally wiping his forehead with the back of his hand. Yet he looked calm and determined, his blank eyes fixed on the ground ahead of him. I wondered what he was thinking, what he was feeling. If it was fear, he didn't let on.

By sundown, we arrived at a village. Khalis was taken to a large house. There we joined him in dinner, prayed, and then split into small groups to stay at village mosques and houses. Doctor Hamid arrived later and reported that he had been unable to save the commander. After prayers Khalis sat on a cot, receiving village elders and tribal leaders. I joined the assembled villagers to pay my respects to the old man. I held his right hand in both my hands and kissed it. Looking tired and distracted, he nodded and mumbled so quietly that I couldn't understand what he said. I left him and walked to the mosque, my lodging for the night.

Early the next day, we heard the sound of approaching jets. Someone shouted at me to get out of the mosque. I dashed into the field in front of the mosque, looking up at the sky. I couldn't see anything, but I had no doubt that someone had been feeding the Communists intelligence about Khalis's movements. We were going to be attacked again. But then the sound of the jets died away. I don't remember if Khalis had been planning to spend more time in this region, but we immediately convened at the compound and headed back toward Tora Bora, where he and we would be safe.

Later that morning, the planes followed us to Tora Bora. When we arrived at the center, Khalis stopped to rest at the upper base. After lunch and prayers, he went down to the lower base to talk to the men there, and twenty of us accompanied him. About half an hour after we arrived, we heard the bombers again. The guards led Khalis and his aides into a bunker. When the explosions died away, we went outside and saw that bombs had landed within a few hundred feet of the bunker's entrance. I was astonished at how close they had come. Engineer Mahmoud was clearly worried about Khalis's safety, but he didn't appear to think that there was a rat in our midst, and, as far as I could tell, there was no immediate investigation. Yet it was not hard to conclude that we were being watched by two sets of eyes: those of the enemy who wanted Khalis dead and those of God who wanted to protect him.

The next day Khalis and his entourage left Tora Bora to continue their tour of the region, and Mirweis and I decided to head back to Peshawar. I'd enjoyed my introduction to jihad and wanted to stay longer, but there was nothing for us to do. No operation to take part in. No supplies to unload. In fact, no frontlines to ferry them to. Several men who had arrived before we had were thinking the same thoughts, and we decided to go together. Others would follow us soon, including Qari Nazeef, Doctor Hamid, Jalil, and Engineer Mahmoud. Within a few weeks November would bring the first snowfall, and the crowd at Tora Bora would dwindle to a handful of hardy local guards.

Chapter Six

Winter 1987–1988—Back in Peshawar, I felt proud to have taken part in jihad, even if I had little to show for it. I'd learned how to fire an AK-47, picked up basic guerrilla tactics, stood guard duty at Tora Bora, escorted Khalis out of harm's way, shot at a fleeing assassin, and been under fire of rockets and bombs. What I couldn't say was that I'd taken part in a raging battle. I had had it easy.

Mirweis proudly told my mother that he "made Masood a mujahid," but she was just happy I was back in one piece and had gotten it out of my system. Little did she know that, although I took a receptionist's job at another aid organization, I longed to go back.

In March, I once again set out for Afghanistan, leaving Mother in tears and Father making a halfhearted attempt to stop me. This time we were headed for Ghanikhel, a government garrison and the center of Shinwar district across the border, the same military outpost Mirweis had helped to attack the year before.

"We're going to stick it to the *murdah-gows*" (the pimps), he said, pumped up and gesturing obscenely with his hand. "The pimps, you know, they're probably drinking woodka, but their days are numbered. Two days, three days at the most." The pimps were Communist soldiers, militiamen, their Red Army friends, the Khalqis, the Parchamis, and the Khadis, who were the secret police. "Woodka" was vodka. Mirweis called them pimps as he was too polite to utter the slang term for female genitalia instead.

The offensive was unusual for being a daytime attack on a large, conventional enemy target. That we could plan such a brazen attack underscored how far the mujahideen had come from the early days of the war. While not completely abandoning small-scale hit-and-run attacks on military convoys and outposts, the mujahideen were increasingly moving on the offensive by employing conventional warfare tactics and more sophisticated weapons. Along with the CIA-supplied Stingers, which effectively neutralized Soviet air superiority, the 120-millimeter Spanish mortar using Israeli-supplied shells proved a devastating medium-range weapon, one we were going to employ against the enemy at Ghanikhel.

I was itching to take part in a major operation, not to mention helping test our new toy. Veterans who were trained to use the mortar, Commander Khalid and Subcommander Shafiq, had already left along with their crews. Climbing into the back of a pickup truck, we left Peshawar late in the afternoon and drove to Landi Kotal, a decrepit border town on the Pakistani side of the Khyber Pass, and another gateway into Afghanistan.

On the surface Landi Kotal looked like another Pakistani border town: one cramped main road flanked on either side by nondescript storefronts selling smuggled electronics, hashish, and guns; buggies and trucks fighting for room on its narrow side streets; armed, turbaned tribesmen with thick black mustaches crowding the marketplace. Nothing remarkable. I would soon discover, though, that behind the high walls of some of the larger compounds was a different world. Many had been rented by the Pakistani Intelligence Service, known as ISI, to serve as safe houses and ammo dumps for the mujahideen. Unmarked trucks carrying weapons and supplies from Karachi and Rawalpindi, Pakistan's military headquarters, rolled in, dumping their large cargos into warehouses from which mule riders ferried them for destinations across the border. More than a quarter of the weapons destined for Afghanistan passed through Landi Kotal.

As one of the largest resistance organizations in Nangarhar province, the Khalis Party operated a vast compound with several warehouses and spacious guest rooms. Two trucks stood in the driveway, their cargo concealed by tarps. Inside we found Commander Khalid, who walked with a limp thanks to a mine explosion three years earlier that had cost him his left foot. Mirweis tried to engage him in conversation, but Commander Khalid was uninterested in making small talk. Turning on his handheld radio, he contacted one of his deputies to make sure the supplies were on their way to the front. Affirmative was the reply.

Making further radio contact with other commanders, Commander Khalid sketched the outline of our operation. Together with forces from two other mujahideen groups—Hekmatyar's Islamic Party and Sayyaf's Islamic Unity of Afghanistan—he was going to launch a massive mortar attack on Ghanikhel. It was a tall order, but Khalid had faith in our new mortar.

The next afternoon we crossed the border and walked for several hours through the hot desert until we reached the launch site. It was much easier than the trek I'd taken to Tora Bora. There were no snowy mountains to climb, only an endless expanse of sandy desert. As night fell and we continued walking, I felt, for the first time, that I was on a guerrilla mission. Mirweis couldn't contain his excitement. Courage may have been all we needed to fight, but he was now convinced that the Spanish mortar would deliver the lethal blow that he and his comrades had failed to deliver the year before. Along the way we stopped several times to drink water and to let the heavily loaded mules that had joined us rehydrate.

Shortly before dawn we arrived in a desolate glen. From there we followed a narrow path leading into a small valley from which we were going to launch the attack. The landscape was barren, but in the twilight I could see fresh footprints in the sand left by the men ahead of us in the caravan.

"Excellent position," Awalgul declared jubilantly as he surveyed the area. "Safe from enemy fire, several open reinforcement routes, and plenty of water."

After saying the obligatory morning prayers, Mirweis and I joined several men from Commander Shafiq's crew to unpack the shells and dig in the weapons. Holding binoculars, Awalgul and his four-man spotting team scrambled up to the top of the hill for range and direction finding. They were Commander Shafiq's eyes and ears. Without a spotter, you might as well be blind.

Ghanikhel lay five miles to the northeast. For years Ghanikhel had housed some thousand men and been a major offensive unit of the Communist army in the province, but a Communist deserter had informed commanders that it had been partially evacuated, with the soldiers shipped south to Kandahar. Only three or four hundred men were left behind. Knocking out the garrison would deal Communist forces in the region a lethal blow.

Commander Khalid had set up his base several miles south, where, besides overseeing the operation, he commanded a Katyusha battery. Having picked up bits and pieces of the operation plan from Commander Khalid in Landi Kotal and other men along the way, I knew that the Katyusha team's goal was to block enemy reinforcement and supply routes. Small-arms attack groups were deployed to surround the three Communist outposts about five hundred yards away and were to advance once we launched heavy artillery fire.

As the sun started to shine, I took a swig from my canteen. Springs were nearby but they wouldn't be easy to get to once the firing started. A cool breeze arose. I took that as a good omen, though I was growing nervous—how big, loud, and frightening was the firefight going to be? The mortar would be deafening. The equipment even came with several sets of fancy-looking sound-suppressing earmuffs. A few crew members put them on, but the rest of the men didn't bother.

With the tubes dug in, the shells unpacked, and two triggermen in position, I climbed up the hill to join Awalgul and his crew. Without binoculars I couldn't see much, though it was scary being out in the open, feeling that someone across the desert might be watching me through his own binoculars.

The operation started with a round from the smaller caliber, 82-millimeter mortar in Naziyan. The gunner fired several more rounds in rapid succession. Then a volley of Katyushas flew from Commander Khalid's position en route to a Communist garrison toward Jalalabad. The two military units and security posts nearby responded but were taken by surprise, unable to react decisively. An exchange of artillery fire erupted, and looking back, we could hear and see the rounds fly and explode in the distance raising tiny patches of smoke and dust.

Several mortar rounds whistled over us and landed just behind our launch site. Lowering myself down the hill, I could see Commander Shafiq calmly walking around as he talked into his radio. While rockets whooshed and mortars whistled overhead, I could hear men in the valley shouting and laughing as they carried fresh rounds to the launchpads.

Looking at his watch and apparently receiving orders from Commander Khalid, Shafiq opened fire. Both mortars were loaded, and two men with earmuffs grabbed eight-foot-long nylon ropes. The rest of us put our fingers in our ears and braced ourselves for the first shot.

The chant of *Allahu Akbar!* rose as the men pulled the ropes attached to the triggers. It was the most deafening sound I'd ever heard, even with my fingers in my ears. For a minute or two I couldn't hear anything at all, and I thought the sound had ruptured my eardrums. Releasing his fingers from his ears, Awalgul picked up his binoculars and peered at Ghanikhel.

"This time," he said as if to himself, "we will hit it, *inshallah*." God willing.

He radioed in a one-hundred-meter drop in elevation. The gunners made the necessary adjustment, and the mortars were reloaded. At Shafiq's order the mortars boomed again. This time my ears suffered less from the sound. I could hear the explosions and smelled the pungent odor of gunpowder drifting in the air.

An hour passed after the Katyusha first launched a round. More mortar rounds landed on the target. I was amazed at the accuracy of Awalgul's spotting, along with how the gunners were able to follow his directions.

Then we saw a large explosion. "The tank is blown up," someone said. Several men at the launch site started running up the hill to look. A tank identified by Awalgul as a T-62 was in flames. A crowd of gawkers surrounded us, each reaching for the binoculars to get a closer look. Awalgul ordered them to stay down but the sight of a burning Russian tank was too good to miss.

Suddenly a volley of heavy Soviet machine gun fire strafed the area.

"Down! Run! Scatter!" Awalgul screamed. While we held our ground, the gawkers crawled their way back to the launch site.

From our perch, I could see the destruction caused by our mortar rounds. The buildings were caving in; smoke, fire, and dust were everywhere. Trees that had been previously hidden by the buildings and a watchtower were now visible.

The incoming artillery rounds grew more sporadic, coming from directions other than Ghanikhel. One exploded about twenty yards from Commander Shafiq, throwing everyone on the ground and loosening one of the tubes.

Amid a lull, I scrambled down to the launch site to join Mirweis, who was bursting with energy, and the crew carrying more mortar rounds. Mirweis could hardly be recognized, his face blackened with dust and grease, looking like an Army Ranger in a Hollywood movie.

Awalgul walked down triumphantly and radioed Commander Khalid to report what he had seen. Scouts planted near the garrison had apparently given Khalid similar accounts of destruction. Shortly thereafter, Commander Khalid's voice crackled over Shafiq's radio. Pack the weapons and withdraw at once. Several loud cries of *Allahu Akbar!* went up in the air. Mission accomplished.

As occasional enemy rounds fell nearby, we cheered and sang while we withdrew. After half an hour we stopped near a spring. It was time to say late afternoon prayers. Still under sporadic fire, we scattered throughout the valley to relieve ourselves, perform ablution, and prepare for prayers. We then assembled near a cluster of trees to pray and were just finishing when Commander Khalid's voice came through on Commander Shafiq's radio: "Head toward Dorbaba where all the mujahideen will gather for the evening."

By the time we arrived at Dorbaba a couple of hours later, the sun was setting. Commander Khalid and his men had already arrived. To celebrate the victory, he had ordered a sheep slaughtered.

The next day a Communist army deserter was brought into the large compound where we had congregated. The frightened conscript told Commander Khalid that more than a hundred Communist soldiers had been killed and many more injured during our attack on Ghanikhel. The Soviets tried to bring reinforcements but were turned back by heavy fire from us and from other mujahideen groups taking part in the operation. Overwhelmed by the devastation of the mortar, the surviving soldiers fled after the first rounds hit the garrison.

I couldn't believe what we had accomplished, nor did I stop to think about who the dead men had been, whether they were KGB agents, Afghan Communist soldiers, or merely illiterate farmers conscripted into the Communist army. They were men in uniform, targets that needed to be eliminated, not human beings to have any feeling for. When they died, we celebrated. It is a common combat experience, dehumanizing the enemy. It is the only way you can rationalize taking another human life.

I turned to Mirweis.

"We got the pimps," he gloated.

Meanwhile, Father and Mother were hatching plans to keep me in Peshawar. Through an aquaintance, Father learned about a job opportunity at the Afghan Media Resource Center, an organization created and funded by the U.S. government to train Afghan mujahideen as journalists to counter Soviet propaganda with their own photographs, film, and news dispatches.

At Father's request, I met the friend, the former president of the Public Library and currently an editor at the Afghan Media Resource Center. The AMRC was looking for a translator. To qualify, I had an on-the-spot test, reading aloud and translating into Persian a poorly written story in a local English language newspaper. Then I was asked to translate a slightly more polished article from a Persian-language newspaper into English. I turned the English story into presentable Persian prose, while butchering the Persian story into choppy English. Surprisingly, the eminent journalist liked what he heard and, after talking to his boss at the Afghan Media Resource Center, offered me the job, which I reluctantly took.

As I found out later, the AMRC was one of the most controversial media programs the U.S. government had ever funded. Its genesis was rooted in good enough intentions. The goal was to train Afghan mujahideen as print reporters, video journalists, and photographers, and send them as "journalists" into Afghanistan to cover the war. Unlike Vietnam, the Afghan jihad was often described as a "closed war," with the Soviet ambassador to Pakistan publicly threatening to kill any journalist captured traveling with the mujahideen. As a result, few Western journalists ventured inside Afghanistan. The AMRC's founders hoped that Afghan freedom fighters passing themselves off as journalists would help fill the void in coverage. Instead they came to be seen by Western critics as propagandists for the U.S. government.

By the time I joined the center, it had trained more than three dozen members of the resistance organizations as "photographers," "cameramen," and "reporters," and they had already brought back some extraordinary photos and video footage. Occasionally, print journalists would be sent to Afghanistan, and my job was to help translate their stories into English. Having taken two English classes at the IRC school, I could string together a sentence or two without grammatical errors. The work was so monotonous that within weeks I was able to master the art of writing such elegant summations of combat as "Mujahideen attacked a Soviet convoy, killing five soldiers and wounding ten others. One mujahid was martyred during the offensive and two others suffered injuries." This proved to be a skill that, as I was to find out years later, was not unlike writing commentaries about the daily ups and downs of the financial markets.

The American journalists sent in succession to supervise the center's work often took issue with word choices. Two common words of disagreement were *mujahideen* and *martyred*. These words, they said, were not "objective." *Rebels* and *killed* were more appropriate substitutes. This kind of revision didn't always sit well with Afghan editors, some of whom appeared to have been sent to the center specifically to keep tabs on the flow of information and on the Americans themselves. For instance, the sullen news editor with a salt-and-pepper beard and piercing black eyes was also a member of the extremist faction of the Islamic Party of Afghanistan. In retrospect, hiring a person with such ties may sound absurd, but there was a certain logic to it at the time, as the Islamic Party received the lion's share of U.S. military aid and was considered the most important mujahideen group.

"We're mujahideen, not rebels," the news editor said each time a journalist insisted on using the word *rebel* in copy. I too found *rebel* offensive. It was the Soviets' word of choice for us, along with *counterrevolutionaries, insurgents,* and *bandits.* The Islamic Party man further argued that not using *martyr* would be disrespectful to the million-odd Afghans who had lost their lives in the war. "We are a nation of martyrs," he would say as he crossed out *rebel* and replaced it with *mujahideen.*

I was tired of all the bickering and longed to go back to Afghanistan. To get an assignment, I convinced the head of AMRC that I was uniquely suited to cover mujahideen operations in eastern Afghanistan. I was a member of the Islamic Party of Khalis, the largest group operating in the area, and I knew its Nangarhar province commander, Engineer Mahmoud. Armed with a small tape recorder and a couple of notebooks, I was assigned to cover an upcoming operation.

I caught up with Engineer Mahmoud in early summer. He was in town to discuss the operation with his commanders and party officials, as well as with Pakistani military strategists. The Soviets had started pulling out their troops from Jalalabad in compliance with the Geneva accords signed earlier in the year. Abandoning a strategic city near the Pakistani border was an odd choice, but the Soviets bent over backward to allay doubts about their commitment to the accords. With the Soviets leaving Jalalabad and the Afghan Communist army demoralized, an opportunity had been created to seize a major city, and Engineer Mahmoud wanted to do it. This was to be the first big offensive on the city and my first participation in an operation involving several mujahideen groups.

In early July, accompanied by Mirweis and Jalil, I left for Tora Bora. The trail leading there had become as familiar as the stretch of Grand Trunk Road that ran through Peshawar. On our second day inside Afghanistan, we arrived after sundown at the familiar smoky tent and mud-hut "hotel" built in the side of the White Mountains. At more than ten thousand feet, the temperature was dropping fast, so we quickly headed inside a tent where there was a small fire and a group of men cloaked in shadows, coughing and huddling together for warmth.

A tall, bearded man in an army fatigue vest over traditional *shalwar kameez* then walked inside. His complexion was a shade lighter than mine, but at first glance he looked like another Afghan. As he went around the tent greeting everyone in Pashto, I noticed he had a slight accent, and a blade was sticking out of one of his overstuffed vest pockets. I asked Mirweis if he knew the stranger.

"He is an English Muslim," Mirweis answered.

"I hope he's not a spy," I whispered, uneasy at the thought of an armed English spy posing as a convert.

"No, no, he's a Muslim," Mirweis insisted.

"How do you know?"

Mirweis said he'd already learned that a veteran British convert was coming along on this mission. I then remembered a certain "British Afghan" by the name of Karimullah who had participated in the Ghanikhel operation. I had heard his name in passing, and while I was curious to meet him, we were assigned to different units and I didn't give him much thought after that.

Having shaken hands with everyone in the tent, the man sat down next to me and started a conversation with someone. In an effort to get his attention, maybe even surprise him, I said "hello" in English. He smiled, taken aback that someone here spoke English.

"*Tah englisee pohighee?*" he asked—You know English?

"A little," I replied in English. At other times, I would never have passed up an opportunity to practice my English with a foreign journalist or aid worker. This time I was more interested in finding out who this "English Muslim" fighter was, and as I was convinced he was a spy, I thought I'd try to draw out some conversation. To my disappointment, the man tersely replied "very good," then turned back to his new friend.

Before long, he turned back to me. I asked him in English what his name was.

"Zimaa noom Karimullah day. Staa noom sih day?" My name is Karimullah. What is your name?

"Zimaa noom Masood day," I said.

Again his attention shifted elsewhere. I got the message, so I moved into one corner of the tent, wedged myself between two men, and, putting my head on my knapsack and shoes, went to sleep. I didn't see Karimullah again until late the next day when we arrived at Tora Bora. There he was more willing to talk to me in English. He had befriended Engineer Mahmoud, as well as Awalgul, and spent most of his time within the close circle of the commander's aides in the medical tent.

Karimullah did not mind my insistence that we speak in English. Engineer Mahmoud, who'd picked up some English at engineering school, listened to our conversations, impressed by my linguistic skills. When Karimullah reported to him, with more than a hint of exaggeration, that my English was "superb," Mahmoud beamed with delight.

The more I talked to Karimullah, the more I was intrigued by him. I wanted to learn about his background. Most Afghans go by only one name, but I knew that foreigners had surnames, so I asked him what his was.

"Nooristani," he offered. "Karimullah Nooristani."

"Are you from Nooristan?" I asked him.

He hesitated before explaining that while he was British born his family hailed from Afghanistan. His father, a rice merchant from Nooristan (the infidel valley that the Iron Amir had conquered at the end of the nineteenth century), had moved to England many years back and married a British Muslim woman. Karimullah said he had three brothers. He rattled off their names: Nasser after Gamal Nasser, the pan-Arab champion, Luke after the Koranic character Lukman, and Yahyaa after the Biblical prophet. I later told Mirweis about Karimullah's upbringing, and we both marveled that, despite having grown up in England, he had returned to Afghanistan to join the jihad. From then on I saw Karimullah not only as a fellow mujahid, but also as a fellow Afghan.

Over the next several weeks, while lazing around the medical tent before the Jalalabad operation, I convinced Karimullah that we should spend half our time speaking in Pashto and the other half in English. His Pashto was good enough to carry on simple conversations, but he said he needed help with his writing. I offered to help and even promised to teach him some Persian if he agreed to teach me English in exchange. He agreed, and so our special linguistic arrangement was born.

Impressed by my English, Karimullah asked me where I had learned it. I told him that I had attended mujahideen schools and an English language course in Peshawar but that my studies had been disrupted because of the war. The thought of resuming my education had never really crossed my mind, not that opportunities were screaming at me. Perhaps because I wanted to impress him with my scholarly interests, I told him I wanted to continue my studies. He told me a lot of Afghans lived in America and many of them went to school.

"If all these Afghan students can attend university in America, I don't see why you would not be able to," he said, speaking with such conviction that by the time he was finished, I had no doubt of the outcome to the plan he then proposed. He said he had studied political science—he used the word *hoqooq*—at Harvard University, and considering the many languages I spoke, he said there was no reason I too wouldn't be able to attend a good American school. Karimullah then said he'd try to help me get to America and study there. Thanking him for his kindness, I told him he could help me only if it was not "a trouble" for him. I had long given up the idea of more study, but Karimullah's passion made it sound like a real possibility, if only for a moment.

While our language barrier occasionally got in the way of a good joke and complicated serious conversation, Karimullah never lost his ability to charm or make us laugh. Once a group of us, including Engineer Mahmoud, had stopped by a village near Tora Bora. As we sat down to eat bowls of sticky rice submerged in cold buttermilk, Karimullah looked at Engineer Mahmoud and smiled. "I feel like a martyr," he said with a broad smile.

Engineer Mahmoud was puzzled by the comment. "What are you talking about, Karimullah?" he mumbled through a mouthful. "You're alive."

"No, just sitting here in the cool shade by a little brook hearing the birds sing and eating the food next to my best friends makes me feel like I'm in heaven," Karimullah said. "This is how martyrs must live in heaven." Engineer Mahmoud chuckled, amused like the rest of us by Karimullah's innocent comparison of our wartime peasant's meal to heavenly bliss.

My growing friendship with Karimullah didn't make me lose track of the reason I'd come to Tora Bora. The operation was coming up. No group had previously attempted a direct assault on Jalalabad. It was simply too big a target for our primitive weapons. This time around, however, we were equipped with an Egyptian-made 122-millimeter multiple rocket launcher (MRL) called the Sakr-18 (Falcon, in Arabic). It had a bigger warhead and a range of eighteen miles, longer than anything we had previously been given. More than a dozen men from our group had been hand-picked by Engineer Mahmoud and sent off to Pakistan for training in using the rocket launcher. Every day mule teams arrived carrying Sakr rockets, ammunition, and other weapons. Word about our plan spread to other refugee camps, and before long Tora Bora filled up with hundreds of refugees who arrived in small groups several times a week.

Among the many madrassah students who came to offer their support were a pair of former classmates I had not seen in a couple of years. They seemed surprised to find me at Tora Bora, and more so by the depth of my immersion in life there. While they said they had traveled to various fronts, they didn't look like diehards. Religious learning was their main preoccupation. I would see them daily on the eating and prayer grounds and make small talk but for the most part avoided them.

And for good reason. Watching my former classmates and their fellow students hunched over their Korans or fingering their prayer beads, I couldn't help but feel how much I'd changed since leaving them. Still pious, I no longer spent every waking moment of my life ostentatiously murmuring prayers. And while I took jihad to be an important religious duty, I wasn't striving to reap heavenly rewards but to defend my country against invaders.

Within days Engineer Mahmoud arrived at Tora Bora, followed by a half dozen senior commanders who were taking part in the operation. Mahmoud spent long hours meeting with the commanders in his cramped room, communicating by radio with other commanders, poring over maps, and reporting to Pakistani army planners who were attempting to enlist other mujahideen groups into the operation (ultimately no other significant force agreed to join). With nearly five hundred men at Tora Bora, about half of them volunteers from refugee camps, Mahmoud had every reason to be confident.

On the day of the operation, Engineer Mahmoud left the base shortly after dawn prayers to personally check the troops on the front lines. Most of the men had already gone with their commanders to positions closer to Jalalabad. The hundred or so of us who remained were to attack isolated enemy positions some twenty miles east of Jalalabad. I wasn't privy to the battle plan, but I knew several Sakr rocket launchers would hit the city from the east, followed by a large force from the Black Mountains swooping down on the city from the west, leaving us to surprise isolated government military posts. I was assigned to Doctor Hamid's mortar team, along with Mirweis and Hashmat, Doctor Hamid's teenage brother-in-law who had shown up just before the operation.

Men assigned to the forward attack groups, including Karimullah, had their bandoleers bulging with ammo and had even stuffed cartridges into the pockets of their waistcoats and shirts. While I felt no need for extra ammo, I grabbed a few more cartridges anyway. I was more concerned about the mortars. I had witnessed the high-caliber mortar's awesome destructive force at Ghanikhel, but I had never fired one. I didn't even know how it worked. The mortars were notoriously unreliable; numerous times faulty rounds had exploded and killed the gunners. Rumor had it that certain serial numbers were "bad," and only experienced gunners could tell the difference.

When we marched out of Tora Bora and followed a supply train of mules to the launch site, I felt the same way I did when I left Peshawar the first time for the front. The thrill I felt walking through lush, green cornfields and mud-hut villages was not unlike the way I felt riding in the back of the pickup truck on my way to Parachinar. Soon I realized this feeling wasn't excitement, but more of a chill that ran through my body. I felt sick and thought I had a fever, maybe even malaria, which I feared would take me out of the operation. Doctor Hamid took my temperature and said there was nothing wrong with me, even ruling out malaria because he had given me an antimalarial pill the day before.

I ignored the ill feeling and pushed on to the launch site, which was concealed behind a series of small rocky hills that stretched across the desert. By the time we got to our position, the mule drivers had already dropped off their cargo in a dry, narrow irrigation ditch that ran along the bottom of a hill. Our targets were military posts on hills a couple of miles away. Heavy machine guns were mounted atop a hill five hundred meters to our left. Attack groups would sneak up another hill to our right, swoop down under cover of fire, and storm the posts.

On a flat, rocky site strewn with spent shells, Doctor Hamid began setting up the bipod and launcher. Mirweis, Hashmat, and I began uncrating the shells and placing them in the ditch. Next we formed a line to carry the shells to the launch site. I stood in the trench, Mirweis at its edge, and Hashmat near the mortar. For the next hour we carried the shells to the launch site, tossing them from one to another. This unskilled labor reminded me of throwing bricks up a high wall to a mason when I was a kid, but it was an integral part of the team effort.

Compared with the larger plan to strike the city of Jalalabad with Falcon rockets, our outpost attack might have seemed insignificant. Yet Engineer Mahmoud attached importance to it, showing up personally with Qari Nazeef to oversee its commencement. Doctor Hamid checked the sights on the mortar while Mahmoud talked on the radio. We gathered around him as Mahmoud walked up to the launch site, ready to give the order to fire. Then someone pointed at a trail of villagers—old men, women, and children—walking down a path a hundred yards or so behind us. Mahmoud had met with village elders around the area so they could inform the residents of the upcoming operation.

Doctor Hamid yelled at them to hurry, fighting was about to start, but they were traveling with a slow donkey overburdened with goods. Irritated though he was, Mahmoud had no choice but to wait until the villagers finally cleared out, leaving behind a long trail of dust. He gave the order to fire.

Doctor Hamid shouted *Allahu Akbar!,* and we responded in kind. Then he fired the first round. Another shout of *Allahu Akbar!* was followed by a second round. Then he waited. A two-man observation team with binoculars at the top of a hill reported the point of impact to Doctor Hamid. As the men cried "left!" or "right!," "front!" or "back!," Hamid adjusted the sights, fired another round, then waited. After several rounds, the spotter reported that he was right on target.

Suddenly a mortar round whistled toward us. I knelt in the ditch, covering my head as it exploded close behind us. The incoming shot confirmed the target, and Doctor Hamid fired a rapid succession of rounds. A volley of enemy fire came back at us. Now each round Hamid fired drew an equal response of enemy fire. Between crouching for cover in the ditch next to Hashmat and Mirweis, I got up and tossed shells to Doctor Hamid. Incoming rounds were landing all over the place—fifty yards to the left, a hundred yards behind, twenty yards to the right—yet they all missed our position like darts thrown by a drunk at a board, hitting everything but the center. The erratic assault made me imagine the enemy gunner as a scared young conscript being forced by his commander to fire rounds and then running for his foxhole.

Then the Sakr went into action. Several launchers had been placed around the area to overwhelm the enemy with heavy firepower. The closest one was about a mile to our right. When the long rockets lofted into the air, people in our group let out a loud shout. Then one of our smaller multiple rocket launchers commenced firing. I was mesmerized by the sound of the MRL-11s booming over our heads toward the enemy.

The response was a barrage of heavy artillery that made our mortars seem benign. Enemy fire rained down from every direction, sending us hurtling to the bottom of the ditch. I felt that chill again, that sick feeling all over my body, as my temperature rose while the rocket explosions crept closer and closer. I was scared to death. Yet I realized I could do little except pray.

Doctor Hamid shouted for more rounds and resumed firing. When I got up from my shelter, I saw him steadily loading the mortar, undistracted by the enemy fire. We formed a line and began feeding him new rounds. He ducked once or twice when a round came in particularly close, but he didn't look afraid. It was almost as if he had a sense, by sound or by second sight, of whether an incoming shot posed any danger to him. I wished I felt his calm, instead of feeling an angry impatience over not being able to silence the enemy guns.

The firefight continued for hours. I grew accustomed to the sound of artillery and would occasionally get up from the trench to watch explosions on the rocky ground or in the village behind us, sending up big plumes of smoke and dust and fire. If you mastered the trick of knowing whether the rounds would land at a safe distance or not, you could witness a lovely sight. The outgoing rockets from the Sakr were even more spectacular, lighting up the late afternoon sky in red and blue. It was an inspiring feeling—until a mortar round or a rocket exploded nearby and shook the earth under my feet, and I hit the ground. Then it was time to say again the declaration of faith. In these moments I did not think I had dodged a badly aimed shot or that the enemy was teasing us or that the wind must have blown it astray; I thought that God had just saved my ass.

Toward sundown, the barrage slowed to a trickle. The Sakr continued but the smaller MRL had stopped. Fewer enemy rounds were coming in. "Sometimes the Communists let you pray," someone said, which surprised me because I knew that Communists didn't pray. After consulting Engineer Mahmoud, Doctor Hamid ceased fire and we all adjourned to pray. We had missed midafternoon prayer and wanted to take advantage of the lull to say the sunset prayers. We walked about a hundred yards from the launch site and gathered under trees on the bank of the ditch. Several haggard members of another attack group had already assembled there. A man who looked like a mullah spread his chador on the ground and prepared to serve as prayer leader. Without taking off our shoes, we formed a line behind him.

Under Islamic law, you can skip a prayer and even deny allegiance to God (in word, though not in your heart) if your life is in peril. But being under fire is not an excuse for missing a prayer. We prayed for no more than two minutes, leaned down, and stood back up to complete the requisite cycle. As the prayer leader finished chanting the opening *surah* and moved on to other verses, I heard the distinct sound of an approaching mortar round. By now I had developed a vague sense of when a round was likely to hit our position and when it would go astray. This one would be close. My ears perked up and my heart pounded, but I kept looking ahead, my right hand over my left, trying to concentrate on the words of the prayer. Just then the prayer leader, still chanting, tilted his head slightly in the direction from which the round was coming and suddenly dropped flat on the ground.

There was no time for the required left turn and right turn—*Assalamu alaikum wa Rahmatullahi*—to break off a prayer. Everyone threw himself on the ground. The shell landed within fifty feet, spraying shrapnel over us. As soon as the explosion ebbed away, we rose to complete our prayers, but another mortar shell approached, sending us all back to the ground, and the prayer leader decided it was too dangerous to continue, telling us to say our "missed prayers" afterward.

Night had fallen. Sporadic artillery fire continued in the distance. We left the unused shells in the ditch and settled for the evening in a fairly large mosque in a nearby village. More than fifty men from various attack groups had congregated there. The house of God was our sanctuary for the night, even though the enemy did not care about its sanctity. The mood was somber as men spoke in tired voices. We hadn't completed our objective, and what was more, one of the men in the attack group that was to storm the post we had been shelling had been killed and another had been seriously wounded. We had no way of knowing what casualties the other mujahideen groups taking part in the operation had suffered or what magnitude of damage the Sakr had inflicted. That intelligence would have to wait until morning, when scouts placed near the city would report back their findings. Meanwhile, the chill that had been with me since we left Tora Bora developed into a fever, but I didn't want to disturb Doctor Hamid, who was busy planning with Engineer Mahmoud on the radio for the next day.

I was worse the next morning. I had been throwing up and felt weak. I finally told Doctor Hamid I had a fever, and he gave me malaria pills. He said I could stay at the mosque if I wanted to, but I insisted on returning. Around midday we resumed fire. The preliminary damage assessment of the Sakr strikes had been less than encouraging. There had been some damage, but more strikes were necessary to knock out the posts. The Sakr and the MRL went into action again, but the Communists were putting up tough resistance, and the attack was going nowhere. Doctor Hamid was hitting the right target, but it wasn't causing significant damage. Our attack group had come under heavy fire at the bottom of the hill that housed one of the Communist posts and had sustained a casualty. There was no way they could advance.

Around two in the afternoon more than a hundred of us gathered in a nearby village, where a makeshift mess hall had been set up. I was retching continuously, unable to walk or even carry my own gun. I approached Engineer Mahmoud who was, as usual, talking on his radio. He looked at me and asked what was wrong. I told him I was fine, that I could carry my gun.

"You shouldn't be carrying a gun," Engineer Mahmoud said, and grabbed my rifle from me, slinging it across his shoulder. I hadn't ever seen him carry a rifle before and now he was carrying mine. Never had I felt more worthless or guilty than that moment when I weakly turned over my gun to a man I'd come to admire as a commander. After lunch I went to the mosque and spent the next three days and nights lying in a corner, hearing the sound of war in the distance and watching with anguished guilt as swarms of exhausted mujahideen came in at night to rest and, if there was any food, to refuel.

By the fifth day, the supply of Sakr rockets was depleted. Hundreds of shells had been fired, and scant significant damage had been inflicted on enemy positions. Most of the rockets had missed their targets by a long shot, and nearly three dozen civilians had been killed. Engineer Mahmoud called off the attack, and within days everyone headed back to Tora Bora. I was exhausted from the illness and with no new operation planned was unsure what to do.

Karimullah was certainly eager to get back to Peshawar, saying he had been away from home for too long and he feared that his family would be worried. We returned to Tora Bora where we picked up our knapsacks, then headed back toward the border using the same route we'd taken into Afghanistan. After our first day's trek, we camped at the same "hotel" where we had first met. After two more days of hiking through the mountains, with a brief layover to make "ice cream" with snow and sugar at a sixteen-thousand-foot-high pass, we arrived in Parachinar. At an Afghan restaurant we wolfed down our first proper meal in more than two months, then walked to the bus station to catch a ride to Peshawar.

As we pulled out of the station, Karimullah suddenly switched to English. He said he was going to write a letter of recommendation to one of his professors at Harvard and that he would sign the letter under a different name. He then took out his passport from the inside pocket of his vest, and handed it to me opened to the photo page. It was a picture of a clean-shaved man with short hair. I looked at the photo and then at Karimullah, and for a second, I couldn't believe my eyes.

"Carlos Mavroleon," he said, pronouncing each name slowly. "It's a Spanish Greek name," he continued. "My mother is Mexican. Mexico is a Spanish-speaking country. My father is Greek. In Greek, Mavroleon means 'black lion.' *Toor zmaray*," he said, which was "black lion" in Pashto.

During the trip, he acknowledged that his tale about being the son of a rice merchant from Nooristan had been a cover to assuage suspicions about him. He had confided the truth to only three or four people in the party. Whenever anyone else asked who he was, he gave them his cock-and-bull story.

In reality Karimullah, as I continued to call him, had lived a privileged life in London. He had attended Eton, the English public school, but dropped out in his final year to travel through Afghanistan and Pakistan, where he converted to Islam, was adopted by a Pashtun family, and took up his name, which means "noble of God." After a year in the tribal areas, he went on to Harvard before moving to New York City, where he worked as a bond trader and got involved with a group advocating support for the Afghan jihad. When Khalis and other mujahideen leaders visited in 1986, he met them in New York and later accompanied them to the White House. The same year he quit his job and, at Khalis's invitation, moved to Peshawar to join the jihad.

In Peshawar, we shared a rickshaw to Arbab Road, where he dropped me off before continuing on to the political office. I saw Karimullah several times over the next weeks, and before he left for London, he promised to get in touch with his friends in America to get me a Harvard application. However, weeks went by with no word from Karimullah. Finally I asked Saboor at the political office if he had heard from him. He said he had but that Karimullah had mentioned nothing about any applications.

Early November in Afghanistan. Snow blanketed much of the country. Temperatures dropped well below freezing. Tora Bora had virtually shut down, guarded by a skeleton crew of a dozen bored and lonely men who would endure a harsh winter of snow and isolation in dark caves and bunkers. Yet on the snowless lowland plains and deserts that surround Jalalabad, where the temperature rarely drops below forty degrees during the day and the night chill nips but doesn't bite, the fighting continued, and that was where I desperately wanted to be.

Four long months had passed since I was at the front. When I ran into Engineer Mahmoud at the political office, I could tell he was as eager to fight as I was. The inconclusive Sakr-18 operation had left him with an even greater urgency to strike at the enemy. This time, though, Pakistani planners were suggesting a more modest target: the border post of Torkham, on the Afghan side of the Afghanistan-Pakistan border, along with a larger military garrison a few miles down the road. Throughout the war Soviet and Afghan Communist forces had tenaciously hung on to a handful of Afghanistan's international border crossings while being unable to close up the porous border itself. Now, the Soviets

having abandoned Jalalabad, Torkham had become an oppor-
tune target.

The afternoon air in the Khyber Pass was crisp when we arrived
at Landi Kotal. The minibus dropped us off at a bustling station
near a market of storefronts and food vendors about half a mile
from the border. On the Pakistani side, tribal Khyber riflemen
armed with ancient British Lee-Enfields kept watch, while on the
Afghani side, Communist forces controlled Torkham with their
Russian AK-47s. Only nomads, traders, and women with children
could cross the checkpoint. While we walked to the safe house
where we would spend the night, I was excited by the prospect that
once we controlled Torkham, Communists wouldn't be able to
stop Afghans from crossing into their own country.

The safe house was nondescript and smack in the middle of
Landi Kotal's mud compounds. Once inside, though, I realized I
was in a sprawling compound. A stable had been turned into a
makeshift ammo dump. Weapons lay everywhere, in the court-
yards and packed into the rooms. On the wall of the verandah
hung a framed color photo of Khalis. An antiaircraft gun was
mounted on top of a guardhouse. This was a "secret" mujahideen
warehouse, one of hundreds scattered along the Afghan-Pakistani
border, though its existence was hardly a secret in Landi Kotal.
Almost every week, trucks from as far away as Rawalpindi, the
Pakistani garrison town, came here and dropped off weapons, ammunition, and other supplies. Then the material was ferried into
Afghanistan on the backs of mules and donkeys.

The next day, we headed for the border. Our pickup truck took
a country road that wound around the town of Landi Kotal and
dropped us off about ten miles away from a cluster of hamlets.
Not far from there was our route, an unguarded road that Afghan
smugglers used to transport electronics into Pakistan. With our
group were three Arabs, two of whom were disguised in traditional Afghan clothing. The third wore a U.S. Army winter coat

and expensive-looking hiking shoes. His face was clean and he smelled of perfume. I tried out a few of the useful Arabic sentences I remembered from my days at the madrassah.

"*Kaifal haal?*" I asked—How are you?

"*Alhamdulillah*," he replied with a smile—Praise be to God.

His name was Abu someone. Arabs often introduced themselves by their honorific names, as in *abu* or *umm*, father or mother of such and such a person, though I knew many Arabs who came to Afghanistan adopted noms de guerre, in part to disguise their identity in case of capture. Abu was friendly yet I quickly exhausted my store of intelligible Arabic phrases. To keep the conversation going, I resorted to individual words. Some words puzzled Abu, such as *shajar* and *sahraa* (tree and desert). Others such as *safinat al-sahraa* ("the desert ship," one of hundreds of Arabic terms for camel) brought smiles of recognition. Then I recited the opening lines of a Persian martyrdom song I had heard Arab fighters sing at Tora Bora:

> *I am a martyr, I am a martyr.*
> *I have realized my wish.*
> *For I'm swimming in a pool of blood.*

Abu didn't know the song, though he recognized *martyr* despite my accent. The word *martyr* deepened the smile on his face. He then began speaking about martyrdom. My poor Arabic allowed me to pick out only individual words but I pieced together what he was saying. He was describing the postmortem experience of the martyr. With the first drop of blood that left the martyr's body, he was lifted by angels to the gates of heaven. Abu gestured at his wrist as if he was slitting it, indicating dripping blood. With the second drop, Abu continued, the martyr entered the garden of heaven. Finally, with the third drop of blood, he was greeted by *houris*, the heavenly virgins of the Koran.

I nodded, though Abu's desire to attain martyrdom so he could meet heavenly virgins struck me as licentious, almost comical. I knew from the Koran how favorably God looks upon martyrs but had never encountered this account of the martyr's journey to heaven. Where did Abu learn this? I was tempted to ask him what happened with the fourth drop of blood, but before I could, he asked me to translate his vision of martyrdom to the others. I gave my friends a rough version of it, knowing full well their reaction: complete bewilderment.

Abu was hardly alone in his desire for martyrdom. Arab and other Muslim volunteers had joined the jihad caravan since the early days of the war. Throughout the world of Islam, the war in Afghanistan was seen as the first perfect jihad of the twentieth century, a conflict that pitted a small, impoverished Islamic nation against a vast infidel superpower. It could not get more perfect. The battle called for collective action by the Muslim community. There were other Muslim wars, of course, such as the Algerian war of independence, and even more recent ones such as the Iran-Iraq conflict, which was called a jihad by both Iraqis and Iranians. Yet never before in the twentieth century had a Muslim nation been so suddenly and savagely brutalized, nor had one responded with such fierce resistance. The jihad inflamed religious passions, and many answered the call.

At the beginning of the war, though, their number was small. The country was too remote, too dangerous, and, despite being Islamic, too culturally alien to Arabs. There was no organized effort to transport jihad enthusiasts from their mosques in Cairo and Mecca and Medina to the battlefields of Afghanistan. By the time I arrived in Peshawar in the mid-1980s, though, Saudi Arabia was bankrolling the war, Egypt was supplying weapons, and offices and hostels in Peshawar and recruitment centers around the world (often under the disguise of refugee charity), attracted thousands to Pakistan and Afghanistan.

Saudi Arabia's ardent support of the jihad, along with the Egyptian government's aid with weapons, was common knowledge. What was less known was that many Egyptian "volunteers" were actually political prisoners the government wanted to dispose of. I remember seeing pictures of Khalid Islambouli, the militant Islamist who assassinated Egyptian President Anwar Sadat in 1981, in several mujahideen magazines. He was included in a "caravan of martyrs" collage that showed images of long-dead Afghan activists, some of whom had cut their ideological teeth while studying and mingling with Muslim Brotherhood members in Egypt during the 1960s. Islambouli's brother, Muhammad Shawqi Islambouli, and al-Qaeda's number two man Ayman al-Zawahiri had been among the first prisoners the Egyptian government sent to Afghanistan. It was a win-win situation for Egypt. They conveniently rid themselves of troublemakers while currying favor with the religious establishment and the sympathetic public. It was an equally ideal arrangement for radical Islamists, as Afghanistan provided a safe and remote haven for their leaders to gain military experience that would prove useful when they would try to topple the Egyptian government.

Contrary to conventional wisdom, the Arab volunteer program never gained significant critical mass. The Arabs operated one small, semi-independent unit in Paktia province, only miles from the Pakistani border, yet they had to attach themselves to a mujahideen group if they wanted to fight in Afghanistan. Even at the height of Arab participation in the jihad in the late 1980s, there were no more than a thousand Arab volunteers fighting on the ground at any given time. They were poor fighters, but they had money, and money carried clout with our leaders in Pakistan. Saudi Arabia poured hundreds of millions of dollars into the war effort. Meanwhile, an estimated two hundred thousand Afghans fought on the battlefield at any given time, so while some Peshawar-based Islamist leaders welcomed Arab participation, the inbred Afghan suspicion of foreigners kept their numbers relatively small.

When I first met a group of Arab fighters at Tora Bora in 1988, I was not opposed to their participation in the jihad, but I shared most Afghans' suspicion of their intentions. Young, quiet, and sincere, many of them believed that it was their religious duty to help fellow Muslims in time of need. Yet dressed in their brand new clothes, army jackets, and hiking boots, I also remember the confused looks on their faces. I saw few of the older Arab veterans, as they were either at the Paktia front fighting or in Peshawar sending neophytes our way.

Whether young or old, the Arabs had a burning desire to attain martyrdom, something that I had not personally wanted even in my most feverish moments of religious zealotry. Once at the end of a high-pitched rendition of the martyrdom song "I am a martyr, I am martyr," a young, pale-faced Saudi named Abdullah said, "I am here to become a martyr, if God wills." He explained he and his friends were prepared to serve as human shields, to hug falling Soviet bombs as they fell from the air, even to throw themselves in front of tanks. To them what mattered most was the attainment of martyrdom. They continually prepared themselves for it, lest they enter paradise ritually unclean. They frequently brushed their teeth with the religious *miswak* tree root and applied generous amounts of perfume to their bodies (often an oil-based musk carried in slim bottles). While the use of perfume is an Islamic tradition, they acted more concerned with how their bodies would be received after death than with the fact that martyrdom is a choice, not a necessity. I myself had performed no great acts of courage, but I could not comprehend the desire to embrace death. Having taken part in a few battles, for me war boiled down to one word: survival. Without perseverance and a desire to survive, you cannot hope to win.

When we arrived at Pati Jawarah the following afternoon, the atmosphere at the base brimmed with the kind of nervous excitement that always preceded an operation we thought was sure to succeed. It looked almost like a Friday open market. Men were arriving by the hour at the base—a knot of gray tents and several thatch-roofed stone huts that housed the base commander. After securing a sleeping bag and a spot, I met the base commander, a tall, soft-spoken man who bore an eerie resemblance to Engineer Mahmoud. He greeted me warmly and said I would be assigned to an MRL team.

On the second or third day, I was target practicing down in a ravine when I met Lieutenant Qadir. A serious, sturdily built man with a dark complexion, he had graduated from the army academy and was serving as a junior officer at a distant outpost in western Afghanistan when the Soviets invaded. After deserting and fleeing to Pakistan, he joined the Islamic Party and began fighting around the Pati Jawarah mountains. Professional military men like Lieutenant Qadir were highly valued by mujahideen groups because of their scarcity, and I noted a sizable age difference between us. Lieutenant Qadir belonged to the generation of men who were in their early twenties at the time of the Soviet invasion, while I, at nineteen, was a late arriver on the scene. However, Qadir and I hailed from the same part of the country, and once he discovered I had some education, he treated me as an equal.

I spent most of the time in Qadir's quarters. Lonely and eager to talk, Qadir and I discussed our pasts and the war, and reminisced about friends we had lost. He was looking forward to the operation, but was focused more on the end of the war, so he could return to Pakistan to get married. Many men his age would long since have been married, war or no war, yet Qadir had devoted his entire life to jihad. Now, with the Soviets leaving Afghanistan, and victory seemingly at hand, it was time for him to start a new life.

"This time we're going to take Jalalabad, if God wills," he said. Because of the friendship we formed so quickly, I asked if I could take his picture. Qadir had never had his picture taken at the base, so he grabbed a rifle and posed next to a small, handwritten sign that simply read PATI JAWARAH BASE CAMP. I promised to send him a copy.

On a crisp afternoon a week later, about fifty men, including most of the Arabs, gathered on the prayer grounds to hear the base preacher's weekly sermon. There was not a cloud in the sky but it was chilly, and like most men in the congregation, I had wrapped myself in my *patoo*. The preacher delivered his usual war-time sermon. Sprinkled with oft-quoted passages from the Koran and the Hadith, the address was essentially a reminder that we were engaged in a holy act for which we'd be lavishly and generously rewarded by a beneficent and just God. Then he wrapped up the sermon by saying in Pashto, "The battlefield may be behind those mountains," pointing at the mountains to his left and at the Black Mountains in the far distance, "but we can always start our jihad right here." Angry at what he claimed was an attempt by Arabs at Pati Jawarah to convert the Afghans, he urged us to beware of the "corrupting religious influence" of the Arabs in our midst and to cling to our own form of Islamic worship.

It was a shocking statement, akin to putting a bounty on the Arabs' heads. We were puzzled, while the Arabs, who didn't understand any of the preacher's words, prayed on silently. After standing in prayer behind the preacher, our rifles on the floor beside us, the congregation dispersed. While we milled around in conversation, I saw three Arabs running toward the base commander's headquarters. Someone in our midst must have tipped them off to the preacher's sermon. A crowd gathered outside the commander's tent. Through an interpreter the commander spoke to the furious and frightened Arabs.

"We came here to do jihad, not to be killed by Afghans," the Arabs said. They also threatened to report the matter to party officials in Peshawar and take their affront to none other than Khalis himself. Fearing bloodshed and losing crucial Arab financial support, the commander gently urged the preacher to stop threatening the Arabs. He then asked the rest of us to stay clear of them. The Arabs lodged themselves in a separate tent and kept largely to themselves.

Not long afterward, orders were issued to prepare for battle. On the day of the operation, men hurriedly prayed, ate breakfast, and wrapped loaves of bread in handkerchiefs as they dashed to the front. I'd been assigned to the Katyusha BM-21 multiple rocket launcher. The launcher had been pushed up a ridge but was not yet in position. I headed to the ammo dump along with half a dozen other men. We put our rifles down and started carrying rounds—one at a time—a hundred yards up the ridge. It took a couple of hours to move fifty rounds, which we placed in two long rows near the launcher.

Engineer Mahmoud arrived to oversee the operation from the main antiaircraft position. The plan was simple: isolate the Torkham post by striking and capturing the Landi Khyber garrison about five miles from the border. A sprawling complex just off the main Jalalabad-Torkham road, Landi Khyber housed a Communist army border guard battalion that was there to protect Torkham and the surrounding areas. A Soviet base nearby had recently been abandoned. Once Landi Khyber was captured, Torkham could be quickly overwhelmed. This was part of a larger plan to once again strike Jalalabad. The Kabul-Jalalabad road, the main supply route for the city, had been blocked by a large mujahideen force composed of men from four different groups. Strike teams had been sent to attack the border post from both the northern and southern sides of the road.

The operation began with BM-21 volleys followed by advance mortar attacks from Lieutenant Qadir's team. Small arms groups were poised to swoop down on the garrison. After the rocket volleys, we waited for the damage assessment reports. We were well out of mortar range, but we knew the Communists had truck-mounted Katyushas of their own. I went up to the antiaircraft position to join Engineer Mahmoud. He was looking at a puff of smoke in the far distance, less than fifteen kilometers away. He handed me the binoculars to look, but I couldn't see anything except clouds of dust. Around noon word finally came over the radio from one of the frontline commanders that the Communists were on the run. One of the posts, the commander reported jubilantly, had been overrun and they were advancing on the rest.

"*Allahu Akbar!*" one of the antiaircraft gunners shouted. "*Allahu Akbar!*" we all shouted in unison, save for Engineer Mahmoud, who was never much for outward displays. Instead he told the commander to watch for mines, and immediately started heading down off the ridge. It took only five hours for victory. Apparently the Communists had orders to evacuate as soon as they came under attack, putting up no resistance whatsoever. We left Pati Jawarah at once and headed for the abandoned garrison a mile across the Jalalabad-Torkham road. Just then I heard jets approaching. We were in an open field with nowhere to take cover and nowhere to hide. I ran as the jets dropped their payloads, but the bombs exploded several hundred yards away—too far to be a mistake. Someone declared it was a friendly incident; we'd heard a rumor that many pilots were deliberately missing their targets.

At the garrison on the other side of the Jalalabad-Torkham road, celebratory gunfire rang in the air. The compound had already been ransacked. Left behind by the retreating Communist soldiers were books, propaganda literature, and some helmets and belts and worn-out uniforms. The only items of value I found were a steel helmet, a belt, and a book of poetry. I shoved the book and the belt into my knapsack, put on the helmet, and walked out into the afternoon sun with my first and only spoils of war.

Little happened during the next weeks. With the fall of the Communist border post, a steady flow of traffic had begun from Pakistan, mostly mujahideen-operated pickup trucks coming into Afghanistan and a trail of refugees headed in the opposite direction. I spent my days at an overcrowded former Communist barracks, drinking tea, tending to occasional supply trucks, and spending nights with the overflow crowd in nearby village huts. The frontline had by then moved several miles closer to Jalalabad, but it was still five or ten kilometers from the city, and there was no plan to advance just yet.

One day I was standing by the side of the road to Jalalabad talking with two men who had also waited for what seemed like an hour to catch a ride to the state farm, the site of the new command center fifteen kilometers down the road. Not really very far from the smoky horizon, the war seemed distant. I was a safe distance from the frontline. Every trip I took away from the battlefield reminded me of how much I missed being there.

A mud-splattered Toyota pickup finally arrived. "Where are you headed?" the driver cried out.

"Farm Number Six!" I shouted back.

"Get in."

We hopped in the back of the overloaded Toyota and rode down the potholed road toward Farm Number Six. For a short distance the driver went fast, but then had to slow as he kept hitting deep holes and bumps. Squeezed into a corner and leaning against the back window, I held my AK-47 between my knees. My two companions squatted in front of me. Before long it was dark and the shelling and gunfire had died down. Or had the roar of the truck muffled the sound of war? Suddenly the driver slowed down. Turning to look, I saw the glare of a flashlight ahead. Recognizing it as a friendly signal, the driver pulled over to the side of the road. Three men emerged from behind the ruins of a house and hurried toward us.

"Where are you headed?" one of the men asked the driver.

"Jalalabad. But first I have to drop off these three at Farm Number Six."

"We have a *shaheed*." In Afghanistan the word is used only for a martyr who dies in combat. Clearly this man felt the martyr was someone important. "The body is at Farm Number Seven," he continued. "It has to be taken to Peshawar immediately."

"Who is it?" the driver asked casually, the way one inquired about the model of a downed helicopter.

"Zabit Qadir," was the reply. Lieutenant Qadir.

I was speechless. All I could see in my mind was an image of Lieutenant Qadir's mutilated face.

"Why are you going to Farm Number Six?" the man asked. "To see Engineer Mahmoud? He's not there. He's gone to Jalalabad to oversee the operation. We need someone to take the body to Peshawar." He then asked if my companions and I would go to Farm Number Seven to pick up the body. He assured us the border guards wouldn't give us any trouble.

We all agreed but I was in a daze. Suddenly I didn't want to go to the front. I felt terrible about Lieutenant Qadir, and for the first time I now feared for my own life. Qadir died first, I would be next. It was simplistic thinking, but I was overwhelmed with dread and anger. This was a new experience for me. From the day I joined the resistance, I dismissed fear as a fact of life, but now I was as frightened as a child. I had been taught that fear and skepticism had no place in a holy war and to feel either was akin to treason. I was committing both crimes at once.

When we arrived at Farm Number Seven, we found Lieutenant Qadir's body wrapped in a large woolen blanket and lying next to a tall pine tree. He had been struck in the stomach by shrapnel while operating a recoilless rifle some ten miles from Jalalabad. He bled profusely before a medic could come to him and died shortly afterward. Near Qadir's body was a charred tree that somehow made me realize where I was. It was an orange orchard, the same orchard I'd walked through as a child during a family vacation before the war. I had climbed on my father's back to pick ripe oranges. The air had been filled with the cool, crisp smell of citrus. Now it exuded death. I stood in front of Qadir's body and hummed the Koranic verse recited on the occasion of someone's death: "We belong to God and to Him shall we return."

The driver backed up close to the body. He got out of the truck and opened the tailgate, removing sacks of wheat. We lifted the body and placed it on a felt mat and carefully laid it in the back of the truck. The two men who had come this far with us paid their respects and went on their separate way. I got in with the body and stretched my right arm over it to hold it in place. Then we headed for Peshawar, me holding the body of my friend who I'd met only two months ago. As we drove, I became aware of a strong musky scent. In Afghanistan people apply perfume to the bodies of the dead to mask decomposition. It is not applied to the bodies of martyrs, though, as it is said their bodies exude a natural scent, the scent of heaven. A martyr, the Koran says, is not dead but alive and being fed by God in heaven. This musk was clearly the scent of a true martyr.

Forty grueling kilometers across the Pakistan border, we arrived at Nasirbagh, a ramshackle refugee camp on the outskirts of Peshawar. With the help of a few men from the house, we carried the body inside, placing it on a cot. I spent the night in the only room available, with Lieutenant Qadir, his body resting on one cot and I on another.

In January, Karimullah returned from London with two white South African filmmakers. One was a soundman, the other a cameraman. Karimullah was on a new mission, and he wanted me to be a part of it: to make a documentary about the defeat of the Soviet army. The problem was that Soviet troops had already withdrawn from eastern Afghanistan ahead of a mid-February deadline. So we traveled to Kunar province, one of the fronts from which a long-rumored multipronged attack on Jalalabad was to be staged.

To Karimullah's delight I informed him that I'd filled out and mailed the application to Harvard he'd sent me a couple of months earlier. An Afghanistan-bound Harvard graduate, Richard Murphy, whom Karimullah had met in London, had brought the application to me. It came in a fat envelope, which included a copy of the recommendation letter Karimullah had written to one of his former Harvard professors. When I opened the package I thought that I'd already gotten in. In it, writing in his "capacity as a journalist," Karimullah went out of his way to sing my praises. (He later said he didn't want to frighten Harvard by writing about our combat experience.) The application itself, while tailored for international students, hardly suited my background. It asked for a transcript (nonexistent), two letters of recommendation from teachers (difficult to impossible to find), a list of extracurricular activities (I had no idea what that even meant, not that we participated in any such thing in Peshawar), and finally SAT and TOEFL (Test of English as a Foreign Language) test scores. With the help of Karimullah's friend and considerable ingenuity, I nonetheless managed to complete the application: I wrote an essay about my family's flight to Pakistan and my work with the AMRC; I drew up an official-looking transcript and had one of my teachers at the Islamic Unity of Afghanistan school sign and certify it; I had another teacher at the IRC English language school write a letter of recommendation.

On the evening of February 15, the BBC reported that the Soviets had completed military withdrawal from Afghanistan on schedule, with General Boris Gromov, the leader of the Red Army in Afghanistan, becoming the last soldier to cross the Friendship Bridge over the Amu Darya River into Soviet Uzbekistan. There were celebrations at refugee camps in Pakistan, we were told. I wondered if these were pep rallies organized by the Peshawar-based mujahideen rather than spontaneous outbursts of mass euphoria. Such celebrations had happened the year before, after the Soviets first agreed to withdraw, and I could not imagine my friends and relatives again taking to the streets of Peshawar and chanting, "Death to the Soviet Union! Death to Gorbachev!" In

Kunar too, February 15 was just another day on the calendar. The Soviets had left the province nearly a year earlier, followed by the Communist army. Thus the mood in Kunar was anything but jubilant. Still busy patching their lives together, the-war weary residents hardly had interest in greeting the last Soviet soldier with song and dance. In the absence of public celebrations, we concocted our own, joining bored but jovial men from our group in a dynamite-fishing expedition outside Asadabad, the capital of Kunar province. It made for good film footage.

We eventually visited the frontlines, and found it was all quiet there too. The war had stalled. With the battle of Jalalabad still weeks away, I headed back to Peshawar in late February, leaving Karimullah and his film crew behind. I spent the next month and a half in Peshawar preparing for the SAT and TOEFL, memorizing quaint and uncommon entries in the English dictionary and brushing up on my Pythagorean theorems, among other things.

I took my TOEFL test in Peshawar, and a week later, armed with No. 2 pencils, took a Flying Coach minibus to Islamabad, the Pakistani capital, where I joined a gaggle of nervous-looking students at a local college to take the SAT. As far as I could tell, I was the only Afghan among the fifty or so test takers—and proud of myself too. The results, when they arrived, were mixed: I had aced the TOEFL, and done well on the math part of the SAT, but apparently had missed too many questions in the verbal part. Having learned from Richard Murphy that my admission to Harvard depended on more than a glowing letter from Karimullah, I began to see Harvard as elusive and hurried to get back to the front.

By the time I returned to Afghanistan in April, the battle of Jalalabad was in its second week, and things weren't going according to plan. In Peshawar, there was hope that Jalalabad would fall within days, and news services continued to trumpet the "best organized mujahideen offensive." Across the border, however, on the busy, potholed road to Jalalabad, there was anything but order. Men from our group had abandoned their barracks near the border, eager to be among the first liberators of Jalalabad, but when I got to the front, I found that many of them were dug in far from the city, resigned to a war of attrition. The airport, contrary to rumors, was firmly in enemy hands, defended by the Jowzjani militias. And after an initial wave of desertions, Communist soldiers had stopped coming our way.

During this time, a two-week tour of the frontline in the heat of battle, I ran into the Arab youth chained to a tree. Though I heard about similar sightings from other mujahideen, I never did see another Arab in chains. When we got to the farm, men from our group were burying a fallen Arab under a tree. It was unusual —burying a "martyr" so close to the frontline. Usually we carried our dead, when we could, to their villages or to their families.

The fallen Arab had neither option, but thanks to the camaraderie he'd cultivated with the men, he'd been brought to the farm and was receiving a proper Muslim burial. As I walked over to the site, two men shoveled dirt into the grave. I could see nothing of the body. A musky smell hung in the air. We offered a little prayer as the men kept filling the grave. I don't know about the others, but my prayer was not heartfelt. I had come to see these would-be martyrs as misguided and even dangerous foreigners who did not belong in our midst. But standing there as a believer, I could not help but ritually pray to God to forgive him and send him to heaven.

After the burial, it started raining. It came out of the blue—one minute the thick orange grove looked heavenly shaded; the next, it darkened like a windowless basement. Then it started pouring, a deluge of a kind I'd never seen before—thunderous, pelting, ominous. Initially Saboor, the driver, and I ran into the truck to seek shelter but after an hour we left to join the fifty or so mujahideen cramming into the dank, bombed-out offices of the farm.

It poured through the night and into the next morning, making the room stuffy and rancid. But the rain had one positive effect: it put a stop to the morning government bombing. The SCUD missiles (thought to be fired by Soviets) had become less threatening than before. Initially their mass and shriek frightened us, but now, after a few weeks of it, we had gotten used to them. Since the start of the battle of Jalalabad, the attacks had become sporadic and inaccurate.

In the afternoon we got even better news: a major government base had been abandoned. Almost without thinking we were off to Jalalabad, lest another group seize control of the prize.

Leaving Saboor behind, we took off in three pickup trucks and drove at a steady pace. The ride was uneventful, without need for the usual hit-the-gas and slam-the-breaks evasive maneuvers. The bombs and artillery rounds that usually dogged us on the road had ceased. The only evasive measures Ihsanullah, our happy-go-lucky driver, had to take were against potholes and speeding trucks trying to wedge into our convoy and an occasional truck or minibus loaded with refugees bound for the border. Farmhouses stood here and there on either side of the road—some had been damaged and others abandoned—but no one was in sight. Surprisingly, when we got closer to the city, I saw farmers working the fields—right in the middle of the war zone. Only five miles from Jalalabad two men were so busy working that they didn't even bother to stop and look at us. Tough, reckless, or greedy, it was hard to say which they were.

It was still raining when we got to the base. The sprawling former headquarters of a Communist army division was under attack—like a dead cockroach being devoured by an army of ants. A hundred men from various groups with a dozen trucks furiously picked the place apart while teenage boys from another group were on top of the only abandoned tank, fooling around with the machine gun. Everyone was carting weapons, ammo, canteens, and other gear to their trucks.

When we got down to the base, Commander Amanullah, the steely-eyed commander of the unit traveling ahead of us, ordered us to join a dozen other men in seizing the southwest corner of the base. A watchtower was there and men were moving down a heavy machine gun. It was then that I heard the sound of fighter jets. They came in pairs, six of them or the same pair making three sorties. No sooner did their hum become audible than we started looking for cover. Men standing by the gate rushed outside, but everyone else ran inside the barracks or crawled under the trucks. I joined Ihsanullah under his truck as we declared the *kalimah*.

The bombs fell every ten minutes or so, and when they stopped, we stood up. Miraculously no one had been hurt. But as we started loading the truck, the projectiles rained down again. Katyushas, howitzers, mortars. Amid a lull, Commander Amanullah led us in a retreat to the farm. With no heavy weapons at our disposal, there was no reason to stay. We spent the night at the farm. Engineer Mahmoud was there along with his aides and a radio man. The news from the front was not good. A dozen men from other groups had been killed as they withdrew from the Jalalabad base, about one in ten. But there was worse news: the radios were reporting that as many as two hundred Communist prisoners of war had been executed and their bodies dumped a mile from the road near the border. The culprit: our group.

"They're talking rubbish," Engineer Mahmoud fumed when we heard the news on the radio. "They're exaggerating, turning two into two hundred."

Rumors had it that the Arabs had been the perpetrators. Nevertheless, I could not come to terms with the fact that our group might have committed such an act. But the alleged atrocity consumed the news for the next several days. Western journalists documented it with photographs of body bags carrying the remains of dead Communist soldiers.

Engineer Mahmoud left for the border the next day to investigate. Expressing guilt and defeat, his face was ashen, and he had his brown *patoo* wrapped around him. He must have known something that I didn't know, and would never know. I spent the rest of the day in the relative safety of the farm. The news from the front got worse. The Communists had retaken the base we tried to seize the day before. We also found that another group of mujahideen had been forced to retreat from their latest attempt to take the airport. Further, the Communists had breached the blockade around the city, moving in reinforcements from Kabul.

It was hard not to feel defeated and demoralized. Our second attempt in nine months to take Jalalabad was floundering before our eyes. Devised by Pakistanis, the battle plan did not anticipate the tough resistance put up by the Communists and failed to take into account the central fact of war in Afghanistan: cities and towns are rarely taken by force.

Jalalabad was clearly not ready to surrender—not for another two years, even as pitched battles continued. There was little reason for me to stay. I had been at the front for two weeks, a lot longer than I'd promised the AMRC. While jihad came first, I did need to leave. Dropping off my weapon at a post near the border the next day, I headed back to Peshawar to report on the failed battle.

Karimullah had returned from the front the night before and had just taken his first bath in two months. He looked fresh and well rested in his ironed *shalwar kameez*. I'm not sure if I ever did, certainly not on this particular day. We were sitting on the carpeted verandah of the political office, drinking green tea from china cups. Karimullah and I would ordinarily have a celebratory meal and ice cream in Peshawar's Khyber Bazaar whenever we returned from Afghanistan.

Whatever dramatic insider's account he had planned to portray in his film about the mujahideen triumph over the Red Army never materialized. In the chaotic first few days of the Jalalabad operation, his film crew had become separated from him, lost valuable footage, and run out of film. Finally, when one of them managed to get himself wounded, Karimullah had them evacuated to Peshawar.

Karimullah fought on for several weeks, cheering like everyone else at the rapid fall of several government posts outside the city, only to see the battle draw to a stalemate.

Something was wrong with Karimullah. He looked distracted, his upbeat disposition gone. Disappointed by the turn of events, he said he was looking to get on the next flight to London. I didn't ask him why, but I sensed he, like I, felt the battle was going nowhere. Nevertheless, I managed to cheer him with the news of my test results, however mixed they were.

"Fantastic," he said, genuinely happy for me. "I'm so proud of you, Masood Jaana."

I hadn't heard from Harvard, however, and I told him I was worried they might not have received the application.

"Have absolutely no worry," he said. "God will take care of everything. *Inshallah,* everything will go well. And sooner or later we will have something to celebrate."

Inshallah. God willing. Afghans used the word so frequently and casually that it diminished its power and meaning. Yet Karimullah uttered it with such sincerity and passion, I could not help but feel inspired. *God will take care of it. In God's hands, everything is possible.*

Later that day I was even more encouraged when he called a former girlfriend outside Boston and told her that the "Afghan freedom fighter" she'd obtained the application for was sitting right next to him. If God willed, I'd be arriving in Cambridge in "a matter of months." He handed me the phone to say hello to her, but I couldn't get past "Hello, how are you?" Within a week Karimullah left for London, promising to call if he had any news and to visit me in America later in the year. But I had a feeling I'd never see him again.

A couple of weeks later I got a call from the director of the United States Information Service. As the foreign propaganda arm of the U.S. government, the USIS ran the AMRC and the director had agreed to write a letter of recommendation to Harvard. USIS had received a telegram from an Afghanistan specialist named Whitney Azoy, who taught religion and anthropology at the Lawrenceville School in New Jersey. In his telegram, Azoy wrote that Harvard liked my application but was unable to admit me because they didn't know what to make of my academic credentials. Harvard had contacted a number of prep schools, including Lawrenceville, in hopes of finding one that would admit me. Although I'd missed the application deadline, Lawrenceville was considering admitting me for the fall and was looking for funding. I knew that being considered for enrollment at Lawrenceville was an honor, but I was disappointed by Harvard's decision. I had little time to dwell on that, though, as several telegram exchanges later USIS confirmed Lawrenceville's acceptance. Harvard also agreed to reconsider my application for admission the following year if I did well at Lawrenceville. It seemed like a consolation prize, but I was still getting the chance to study in America. I called Karimullah right away with the news.

"Fantastic," he said. "I'm so proud of you, Masood Jaanah. You're going to one of the elite schools in America, one of the best."

I had no idea what he was talking about. Going to school with what I thought would be a bunch of young kids didn't exactly inspire me, even if it meant a chance to spend a year in America. Karimullah explained that it was only a matter of spending nine months at Lawrenceville before I'd get into Harvard, which he said was practically a given. That encouraged me to put aside my reservations and commit to a year at Lawrenceville.

Over the next month I received information booklets and brochures from Lawrenceville, including a postcard of the school's vast, idyllic campus. My parents were overjoyed. Mother proudly informed everyone in the extended family that I'd won a scholarship to study in America. Yet while preparing to leave Pakistan, an image of America as a morally corrupt society began to form in my mind. A close friend had just returned from a visit to the United States and proudly presented me with a souvenir pen emblazoned with the picture of a woman who shed her bikini when the pen was turned upside down. "America is about two things: sex and alcohol," my friend said. "On Friday nights, after the work week is over, all Americans do is get drunk and fuck."

This wasn't an entirely foreign concept. In Afghanistan, married men engaged in frequent, supposedly for-procreation-only "activities" on Thursday nights. You would see them on Friday mornings crowding the hammams, or public baths, washing up before heading to mosque with enormous grins on their faces. My friend was talking about something else, however: the prevalence and widespread acceptance of premarital sex and alcohol. While he was a member of the Islamic Party of Afghanistan, he also didn't fail to engage in sexually charged conversations about his time in America. For instance, when he was in New York, he had visited more than one peep-show parlor and, by his own admission, did more than take a quick peek. He had no regrets about it.

While I enjoyed his account of how Americans imbibed alcohol and copulated like animals, I was offended by his suggestion that I was headed for a life of sin. Anyone who knew me should have known I disapproved of such things. I had to dispel any notion in his head that I was vulnerable.

"Yes, they are animals," I said, turning serious. "I'm sure a lot of Afghans living there are no better."

Feeling guilty, he dropped his voice to an apologetic pitch. "I didn't mean you would be doing those things," he said. "I know you are a person of high morals."

Meanwhile, politically and militarily, little had changed in Afghanistan since the start of the battle of Jalalabad in March. In the months since the Soviet withdrawal, Communist forces had abandoned strategically insignificant small towns and villages, allowing various mujahideen groups to claim control over them. Yet the mujahideen government-in-exile remained in Peshawar, as the mujahideen had concluded Jalalabad would not fall anytime soon. Meanwhile, Hekmatyar's faction, never an enthusiastic participant in the battle of Jalalabad, turned its attention to

Kabul, pounding the capital city with the Egyptian-made Sakr-20 rockets we had first test-fired the year before. The result was a fresh influx of refugees from Kabul. Among them were many of my relatives. I was delighted to see them after so many years, but like everyone else in Peshawar, referred to them derisively as "Sakr-20 refugees," implying that these were Kabul residents who willingly lived under Soviet occupation, and tacitly condoned it, only to flee under threat of Sakr-20 bombardment. Even if they weren't members of the Communist Party, they'd lived on the wrong side of the jihad.

By late July, with just a few weeks left till my flight to America, men I'd come to call brothers—Engineer Mahmoud, Qari Nazeef, Doctor Hamid, and Doctor Jalil—were still fighting in the Jalalabad area. Occasionally I'd run into one of them in Peshawar. Their faces spoke volumes about the battle. Even Nazeef, the resident joker at Tora Bora, brushed off my attempts at humor. While the war wasn't over for them, I knew it was over for me. So why did I still long for the battlefield? In the year and a half since I'd joined the resistance, I hadn't spent more than three consecutive months in Peshawar. I was always trying to get back and presently found the urge difficult to overcome. War junkies compare the urge to drug addiction. While not a war junkie, I feel the term comes close to capturing the experience for me. You remember the adrenaline rush, your brushes with mortality, the false omnipotence a simple rifle endows you with, and above all the camaraderie—feelings that never go away.

The opportunity to return came in the form of an irresistible offer from Mirweis: a chance to visit with Commander Ahmad Masood. Having ended his jihad to work as a translator and fixer for foreign journalists, Mirweis offered his services to three journalists traveling north to visit Masood and invited me to tag along.

"You can work for AMRC and make money on the side," he said invitingly. "And you'll meet Masood. Didn't you always want to fight under him?" Here was the man who had persuaded me to join

the jihad with tales of gallantry, now making money off his experiences. A true Laghmani, I thought, both shrewd and industrious.
It was hard to hold it against him, though, even if his visit included
a trip to Masood's northern front (Mirweis had frequently railed
against Masood for agreeing to several cease-fires with the Russians
instead of fighting them). While I didn't share Mirweis's views in
the matter, my opinion of Masood had cooled considerably since
the time I worshipped him as my hero. I felt much of what Masood
said and did these days was for the benefit of the now ever-present
British and French camera crews that followed him around like a
pop star. This type of behavior almost certainly inspired some of
Peshawar's Panjsheris, acolytes from Masood's native Panjsher Valley who strutted around in Masood's trademark army fatigue jackets and pants, acting as if the only legitimate jihad was the one
fought on their home turf. The men I'd fought alongside, with their
simple clothes and dedicated vision of jihad, didn't have to emulate
anyone to prove their worth and mettle.

Unfulfilled childhood fantasies die hard. To simply shake the
hand of the man regarded as the greatest Afghan guerrilla leader,
to hear him speak, perhaps even tell him about my father's plans
for his own Masood—it was too good an opportunity to pass up,
especially now when his longtime rivalry with Gulbuddin Hekmatyar's Hezb faction was once again heating up. Just a few weeks
earlier, one of Hekmatyar's northern commanders had staged a
daring daytime ambush against a convoy of commanders loyal
to Masood, killing more than two dozen of them. Posters of the
"martyrs" soon sprang up around Peshawar. The mass killing
decimated Masood's ranks of northern commanders, and rumor
had it that Masood was planning a spectacular counterattack of
his own to finally end the Hekmatyar menace once and for all.

The AMRC, resigned to my departure for America, needed little
persuasion before agreeing to send me along with a cameraman to
cover the operation and get an interview with Masood. My parents proved a tougher obstacle. I had only five weeks left before

my flight to New York, and they worried that given the long distance to the north, I wouldn't make it back in time. Father specifically told me I did not have his permission to go, which was ironic given my plan to meet the man he wanted me to fight under as a thirteen-year-old boy. Mother threw a crying fit to no avail.

"I'll be back before my flight," I said. "I promise."

The next day I joined Mirweis and his friends and boarded a small Pakistan International Airlines plane headed for Chitral, a border town and gateway to northern Afghanistan. It was my first flight, and as I sat nervously in my small window seat, I looked to the three journalists I was traveling with for reassurance. Peter was a cameraman for the BBC. John was a lanky, redheaded former United States Marine trying to break into war journalism. Patrice was a chain-smoking correspondent for the French weekly *Libération* and grandnephew of the legendary French aviator and writer Antoine de Saint-Exupéry.

From Chitral we set out with a supply caravan for the five-day journey to Taloqan, a recently captured town where Masood had temporarily moved his command base. From the moment we crossed the border and began our trek across the jagged, soaring mountains, the donkey and mule drivers, many of them wearing combat fatigues, spoke endlessly about Masood and his battlefield exploits. They berated members of Hekmatyar's Party in an Afghan hillbilly northern accent, confidently saying that "Aamir Sahib"—Mister Director, which was Masood's title since assuming leadership of a new war council—was going to teach them a lesson the same way he taught the Russians one.

Along the way we met several Pakistan-bound foreign journalists coming back from meeting Masood. They spoke worshipfully of the Great Commander, using words like "greatest," "legendary," and "incredible." Some of the veteran journalists complained that Masood didn't "delegate" enough. I didn't yet know what that word meant but gathered from the context that it was a mild criticism.

Masood clearly delegated when it came to his security. Aware how badly the Soviets wanted him dead, he had created a large network of spies for his personal safety. Legend had it that while Masood was based in the Panjsher Valley, would-be assassins were discovered and eliminated miles before getting close to the commander.

Peter, who had met Masood on several occasions, helped us get past the first checkpoint at the mouth of the Farkhar Valley. Climbing into two old Soviet military jeeps, we drove through the night to a former summer royal resort that had recently fallen into the hands of Masood's forces. Located on the bank of a river, the resort consisted of a large mansion, several guesthouses, a volleyball court, a soccer field, bike paths, and large picnic areas under tall evergreens with swings hanging from them.

A day or two after our arrival, a jet dropped bombs that missed the main compound. As the bomber flew away, I wondered if it had been lured to the area by false intelligence on Masood's whereabouts spread by Masood's own agents. Except for the brief bombing, the place was quiet, broken only by the occasional convoy of military trucks laden with uniformed mujahideen that roared up the road to the frontlines. I took this as a good sign. The rumors of an upcoming operation had apparently not been exaggerated.

Not surprisingly, Masood's aides gave vague answers to inquiries about where he was. He might drop by the resort "tomorrow" or "after the operation is over," and we even heard that "he rarely visits" the resort. In the drawing room of the mansion, I befriended some of the commander's aides, including a young Afghan-American from California who was translating American military textbooks on modern conventional warfare into Persian.

"Aamir Sahib," he said, "has bigger plans than this operation. The mujahideen's failure at Jalalabad was the result of their inability to adopt conventional tactics. Aamir Sahib is preparing his forces for an operation that can succeed. We've already established a conventional army."

Nice textbook analysis, I thought. But what about the operation Aamir Sahib was planning right now against the Hezb forces? No one would talk about it. Almost all mujahideen groups fought one another but no one wanted to be blamed for infighting.

On the third or fourth day, word came that Masood was on his way. Having heard this before, we dismissed it. Several hours went by with no sign of the commander. Then in the early afternoon military jeeps pulled into the driveway carrying uniformed fighters, apparently members of Masood's security detail. Later in the afternoon two more Soviet military jeeps pulled up. As Mirweis and I watched from the verandah, out came the man himself along with a posse of bodyguards and commanders, looking thinner, paler, and shorter than I had imagined. He had his trademark wool *pakool* on his head, worn beret style, and a checkered *kaffiyeh* thrown over his shoulders. For a moment, standing twenty feet away from him, I felt overwhelmed by the sight of my childhood hero, but I reminded myself I was looking at a larger-than-life figure who was very much life-size in person.

I followed a group of aides to greet him, struck as I got closer by his bony face and thin beard, which his enemies described as a "goat's beard." The throng of aides, fighters, and well-wishers grew, and as he embraced them I heard his distinct, lilting Panjsheri twang and high-pitched voice. Waiting in line, I thought about how I would greet him. In Afghanistan strangers rarely introduce themselves by name, but I thought I could make an impression on him by offering my name. Masood wasn't a common name in Afghanistan, although in recent years sympathetic parents had started naming their sons after the commander. Finally I nervously approached him, shook his hand softly, and, putting my left hand over his bony, vest-covered shoulder, gave him a traditional hug.

"*Assalamu alaikum,* Aamir Sahib," I said, calling him by his new title. "I'm Masood."

He gave me a mischievous smile, which I took as something he did whenever he met one of his namesakes. "I came here with Peter, one of your great admirers," I said, "and I'd like to sit down and interview you about post-Soviet Afghanistan."

"Very good," he said, reaching out to Peter to give him a quick hug. Peter mumbled a couple of the Persian phrases he'd picked up.

I stepped aside to let Mirweis and the others greet the commander. When he was finished receiving everyone and ready to retire to a corner guest room, I approached him again and said, "Aamir Sahib, I'd be honored if you sat down with me for an interview."

"If I have time, I will not hesitate to spare it," he responded. "Let's talk tomorrow."

That evening we joined him for tea in a large guest room packed with his top commanders and a group of petitioners. Having learned the meaning of the word *delegate* years later, I now realize what the journalists we met on the road were referring to. As a line of admirers and petitioners grew to the far end of the room, Masood talked to each person individually, reading each scrap of paper on which a petitioner had scribbled his request and asking one of his aides to take care of whatever problem the petitioner had brought him. It was an old-fashioned, hands-on, in-touch-with-the-masses style of leadership.

Shortly after noon prayers the next day, Masood dispatched a guard to our room to bring us for the interview. The cameraman and I met him in a small room adjacent to a makeshift ammo dump. Sitting across from me, he looked straight into the camera. Seated on a taller stool than he, I felt I was at an advantage until I remembered I was sitting across from one of the greatest guerrilla leaders of the twentieth century. "It's been six months since the Soviets completed their troop withdrawal," I said in a shaky voice. "Could you tell us what plans you have for post-Soviet Afghanistan?"

Masood launched into a short monologue, dashing off one-liners about the "wishes of the valiant Muslim nation of Afghanistan" for a "truly Islamic government" and the "importance of unity among the mujahideen groups."

I then quizzed him on the upcoming operation and whether he suspected Hekmatyar had personally engineered the assassination of his commanders. Like an expert politician, Masood dodged my question and instead launched into a tirade about those "who sow the seeds of discord" among the "brave mujahideen" and how the "people of Afghanistan have grown tired of war."

Listening to his performance, I wondered how he really felt about Hekmatyar, the Hezbis, and the future of Afghanistan. He and Hekmatyar had been militant student activists at Kabul University in the early 1970s before fleeing to Pakistan to escape imprisonment. While not as radical or brutal as Hekmatyar, he shared Hekmatyar's aspiration to lead Afghanistan to becoming an Islamic state. Of course, both men wanted personally to establish the Islamic state. What else explained the much-trumpeted operation to get rid of Hezb forces in the north? It was about more than simply revenge.

By the end of our first week in Farkhar, the operation against the Hezb was off to a spectacular start. Masood's forces had launched a multipronged attack on every major Hezb base across two northern provinces. Faced with overwhelming firepower, most of the bases surrendered without a fight. The ringleader of the operation against Masood's commanders had been tracked down in Taloqan by the second day, so we packed ourselves in the back of a large truck and headed there.

We met the ringleader in a compound down the street from Taloqan's marketplace. He was in bad shape. His legs were shackled at the toes, and he was limping to an outhouse, escorted by two armed guards. His pant legs were pulled up above his shins, the way macho men in northern Afghanistan did, the only remaining shred of dignity he used to have. Here was the man who had orchestrated the killing of more than thirty of Masood's top commanders, reduced to a loathsome creature waiting to die.

We caught up with Masood in an unkempt, sprawling public garden on the edge of town. He had overseen the operation from the garden and looked pleased with the results. He was standing next to his jeep, surrounded by his loyal lieutenants, greeting well-wishers. Mirweis and I joined the line to greet him. I walked up to him and, bowing slightly, shook his hand.

He blinked in recognition. I inquired about his health and managed to say, "The operation was successful."

"May you be well," he said as he turned to Mirweis before getting into his jeep and driving off.

It was now the last week of August, less than two weeks until my flight. A seven-day journey back to Peshawar lay ahead. We learned that we could catch a caravan bound for Pakistan within two days. I was cutting it close, but before we left for Farkhar I walked around Taloqan, the town where the Evangelist had once served as a judge. Except for a few bullet-pocked walls and rocket craters, the town was pretty much intact. Tough old men pulled carts laden with goods. Buggies carried children and veiled women. The marketplace was teeming. I spent a good hour looking for souvenirs for my family. I couldn't find anything suitable for Lachi, but I decided to buy Mother a couple kilos of Badakhshan cumin, the most flavorful cumin in Afghanistan, used in cooking rice. Perhaps I would get to taste it before I left for America.

I made it back to Peshawar in the nick of time. Just a couple of days to pack, get my travel documents in order, confirm my flight, change a few thousand rupees into dollars, and say good-bye to friends and family.

The night before I left, Mother threw a party and invited forty close relatives, including several newly arrived cousins. Many of these cousins had recently moved to Peshawar with their families. My cousin Doctor Jalil, however, could not make it to the feast because he was at the front in Jalalabad.

This was a strictly family affair so I could not invite friends, not even close ones, whom I'd already bid farewell. Nevertheless, the boys and I crammed into our guest room while the women, children, and older men gathered on the verandah. After dinner, one newly arrived cousin sat at his harmonium and crooned old Ahmad Zahir standards, love songs we'd grown up with. Frozan had a good voice and could imitate Ahmad Zahir's vocal range. Listening to him, it was easy to get nostalgic but I kept checking the time. Nine, ten, eleven. Eighteen, seventeen, sixteen hours till my flight and a day or two to America.

Once or twice I walked out onto the verandah to find Mother, in her new long black dress, laying out desserts and fruit and telling my sisters to make sure no teacup was left unfilled. Mother was fidgety. She wouldn't listen to anyone who told her to sit down. She couldn't. If she sat down, her legs would shake uncontrollably. We hadn't spoken much all evening, but I caught up with her outside the kitchen. She was carrying a large nickel teapot.

"Look, it's your last night, my son," she said. She drew me close and kissed me, and I could see her eyes welling up. I kissed her hand.

At the far end of the verandah, Father was leaning on a pillow and engrossed in an animated conversation with the male relatives. When they spotted me, they stopped and cast proud looks my way. I acknowledged them with a slight bow and turned back to Mother.

"Why don't you sit down?" I asked Mother. "You should be happy tonight. It's not as if I'm going to Afghanistan. I'm going to America."

"I don't know when I'm going to see my son again," she said.

"Next summer," I said and walked back to my room.

It was time to turn over the harmonium to another cousin, whose clumsy performance soon drew yawns from everyone. It was getting late. Even so, my cousin was asked to do an encore: "May God Be Your Friend, May the Koran Be Your Guardian, May Ali Be Your Benefactor," another Ahmad Zahir classic.

The guests left around midnight. Only Aunt Nasreen, Mother's younger sister, stayed behind to help with the dishes. We went over my luggage—two big leather suitcases tightly packed with everything from dried mulberries and nuts to a prayer rug, a copy of the Koran, and an old paperback edition of Hafez I'd found in an Afghan market the week before. In addition Mother had gotten me a nice Afghan rug for my dorm room.

The next morning I woke up early to say my prayers. In recent months I'd grown lazy and missed one or two of my dawn prayers, but I didn't want to miss this one. It was the first prayer of my journey to America. When I was finished, I walked out onto the verandah. Mother was still saying her own prayers. After half an hour she got up and folded her rug.

"What are you in the mood for?" she asked. Her eyes were bloodshot with sleeplessness.

"Everything," I said without meaning it.

Her eyes brightened and she walked into the kitchen. Aunt Nasreen soon joined her. Mother spent the next couple of hours preparing a grand breakfast of pastries, chai, qaymaq cream, fried eggs, and fresh bread.

Mirweis and another cousin showed up around noon in two big rickshaws and a car driven by a friend of theirs. They carried my bags to the car while, in keeping with custom, I walked under a bound copy of the Koran. As we left the house I said good-bye to Aunt Nasreen, who stayed behind to do the final honors: throwing a glass of water behind me—May your footpath grow verdant —a symbol of life.

Mother sat beside me in the car and held up well until we got to the airport where she broke down in tears. Some of my friends had shown up, and I said good-bye to them before turning back to Mother. As she held me in her arms and showered me with kisses I couldn't help but cry. But soon I stopped myself.

Father tried to calm her in his brusque way. "Stop it," he said. "He's your son, and he'll come back to you." As usual, Father showed no emotion. I walked up to him, kissed his hand, and matter-of-factly said, "May you forgive me." It is a phrase commonly said when someone moves away from friends and family. It was the closest I'd ever come to expressing a personal sentiment.

His blue eyes twinkled. He gave me a cold kiss on the head and said, "Don't forget your mother and father. Write and call when you can."

As I walked to the check-in counter, I didn't realize how much I'd miss them and my country. It was not the first time I'd left my parents for a different city. But I was moving to a faraway and strange land, and I had no idea how long it would be before I returned, or where I'd see them the next summer, in Pakistan or a newly liberated Afghanistan.

Chapter Seven

September 1989—The flight to New York took more than twenty-four hours, with a four-hour layover in Karachi and a longer one in London. En route to London, I delved into my book of Hafez to see what fortune had in store for me but couldn't get past the familiar poems about love and wine, images that I couldn't help but associate with sex and alcohol, the twin sins my colleague at AMRC had warned me about. Putting away the book, I pulled out some Lawrenceville materials, including a brochure from the school with a picture of girls playing field hockey in tiny skirts, and a postcard with an aerial view of the sprawling, green campus. Would all of America look this way? From what I'd seen in movies, along with conversations I'd had with others who'd visited the country, I imagined New York as a city of soaring skyscrapers with distinguished-looking white men in dark suits and fedora hats walking down sparkling clean sidewalks.

When we landed at JFK, I grabbed my two big, overstuffed Afghan leather bags and hauled them into the noisy arrival area. Amid the sea of people waiting for their loved ones, several men held up name placards, but I didn't see one for me. Then I heard my name.

"Masood Jaan," someone said in an American accent. A tall, slender, middle-aged man with a clipped graying beard waved me over. Whitney Azoy, the anthropologist and teacher at Lawrenceville, didn't need to look at the picture I'd stapled to my application form to spot me. I was the only bearded man in *shalwar kameez* within eyesight. He gave me a big Afghan-style hug and introduced me to a fellow teacher who had come along for the ride.

Dr. Azoy explained that we had to wait for two other students who were arriving within the half hour. One was a jovial, dark-haired Irish student named Matthew, whose English I could barely understand, the other a bubbly six-foot-tall English girl named Cinnamon. I awkwardly shook her hand, a little embarrassed. I never had female classmates before, and I didn't know if we could be friends.

Walking out to the parking garage, Dr. Azoy gently placed his hand on my shoulder. Touched by the friendly gesture, I instinctively responded by holding his other hand. When we approached the van, he slowly released his hand from mine. "In America," Dr. Azoy said in Farsi, "if you hold another man's hand like this, people will think you are a homosexual." I was shocked. In Afghanistan, men holding hands were as common as couples holding hands in America and didn't reflect on one's sexuality.

We left the airport and drove through dilapidated neighborhoods: boarded-up houses and storefronts; overpasses vandalized with bright graffiti; overflowing garbage cans at street corners; and the biggest surprise of all, slovenly men and women, the majority of whom weren't white. There were even a few Pakistanis among them. The formally dressed men of my imagination were nowhere to be seen. Where were the soaring skyscrapers and fast moving cars on clean boulevards?

Then I caught a fleeting glimpse of them. "New York City," Dr. Azoy announced grandly as the Manhattan skyline appeared in the distance. It wasn't as striking as the pictures of New York I'd seen at the American Center in Peshawar. Having dreamed about walking amid the tall buildings in New York City, I was unimpressed. Then we got to the New Jersey Turnpike, where we passed a large garbage dump whose stink, even with the windows closed, was overpowering. The endless rows of Dumpsters reminded me of burning Dumpsters I saw in my old Karachi neighborhood and were not a sight I expected to see in America.

Soon we passed farmhouses and barns, with cows and horses grazing in the afternoon sun. We exited the turnpike and drove down several windy back roads to the Lawrenceville campus, which, as we passed through the wide, wrought iron gates, I was surprised wasn't guarded. We dropped off Cinnamon and Matthew at their dorms then drove to the headmaster's office. Dr. Azoy wanted me to pay my respects to what he called in Farsi, the *rayis-I Lawrenceville* (literally, "the president of Lawrenceville"), though he was actually the headmaster. He explained that the headmaster personally admitted me over the objection of the admissions officer. Headmaster Josiah Bunting III had written me a personal note in one of the brochures I'd received, although I didn't know how to pronounce his strange first name. Was it Juiciah? Juisaayah? Jaaciah? Dr. Azoy described Headmaster Bunting as "incredibly brilliant" and "a fascinating character." "You'll like him," he added.

I imagined a dour old man with a furrowed forehead and a stick to punish unruly pupils. In fact Mr. Bunting was tall and athletic, casually dressed in a T-shirt and running shorts, and playing animatedly with his dog—the opposite of what I was expecting. I'd never seen a man dressed so immodestly off a soccer field or a volleyball court, and it had never occurred to me I'd be meeting a headmaster wearing *naykar,* the Afghan word for "knickers and shorts."

Dr. Azoy introduced me as "our Afghan scholar." Understanding the word *scholar* to mean an *aalim,* or "man of great learning," I was concerned about Dr. Azoy embellishing my unimpressive academic credentials. Mr. Bunting's credentials, by contrast, were stellar: West Point graduate, Rhodes scholar, Vietnam veteran, history professor at Columbia University, author of a critically acclaimed novel, and former president of two small liberal arts colleges. He was now in his third year as Lawrenceville's headmaster, having taken the helm in 1987 when the 170-year-old boys' school started admitting girls.

Sitting down in his office, I nervously expected him to quiz the "Afghan scholar" on topics I would surely fail. To my relief, he talked about how thrilled Lawrenceville was that I had come. "You're attending one of the best schools in America," Mr. Bunting said. "You should be proud of yourself. This is the best of America."

The comment stuck in my head. We left his office to pick up registration papers and brochures at an office down the hall. Dr. Azoy then suggested we attend a cookout in a nearby field. A group of scantily clad girls greeted us. Dressed in my light blue *piran tunban* and my *pakool,* I couldn't spot a single fully clothed person. It was a sea of naked arms and legs, male and female. Even the adults were in shorts, eating hot dogs and hamburgers and sipping soda from Styrofoam cups. Some were throwing Frisbees, others were trading jokes and holding hands. It was a festive atmosphere, but for my first day in America, I found it downright licentious.

A pair of girls walked up to us, one Indian, the other half Muslim Arab. "Daaktar Athoy," the pretty Arab girl exclaimed, hugging him. After the other girl embraced Dr. Azoy, he introduced "the scholar." My heart was pounding as I nervously thought of ways to turn down an offer to embrace without offending them. I took a step back, quietly cursing Satan and asking God for strength. Much to my relief they simply held out their hands, which I shook.

Dr. Azoy and I headed back to the van and drove to Kinnan House, the "jock house" that I would call home for the next nine months. Unaware that Lawrenceville's dorms had been modeled on the British house system, I had a hard time grasping why the buildings were called houses. Azoy later explained he'd picked Kinnan for me because he thought I'd benefit from living with its house master, *Aaghaa-I Besselink*—Mr. Besselink—whom he described as a "history master" and one of Lawrenceville's most intellectually sophisticated teachers.

On the second floor of Kinnan, Mr. Besselink greeted us through the open door of his suite. He was a portly man with lapis blue eyes and a double chin that made him look older than his age, which I guessed to be around fifty. He was dressed in crisp pleated slacks, a blue short-sleeved shirt, and a striped tie. Speaking with a soft Germanic accent, Mr. Besselink invited us into his apartment. Newspapers were piled next to his sofa. Strewed around were unopened shoe boxes, shopping bags, dry-cleaned shirts in translucent plastic covers. The kitchen, at the other end of the room, looked untouched. I was disappointed he didn't offer us tea, but I was realizing Americans simply didn't do certain things.

We made small talk. Dr. Azoy offered that "perhaps Masood can start Lawrenceville's first *buzkashee* team."

"And what is *buzkashee*, Whit?" Mr. Besselink inquired.

Laughing, Dr. Azoy described *buzkashee* as "the Afghan equestrian game" in which men drag a headless calf across a football-size field. Mr. Besselink was either puzzled or annoyed, though Dr. Azoy didn't appear bothered at all when he asked Mr. Besselink to show me my room. Handing me a key, Mr. Besselink pointed to a room at the end of a brightly lit hallway.

Walking me to my room, Dr. Azoy asked if I needed anything.

I thought a while and said, "A *qutbnuma*."

"A *qutub-numa*," he repeated. "Tell me, my boy, what is a *qutub-numa*?"

Not knowing the English equivalent, I explained I was looking for a small round object with a hand that indicated which direction Mecca was in. I needed to know which way to face when praying.

"A compass," he proclaimed triumphantly. "*Qutub-numa*." He said he'd look for one. In the meantime, we walked outside and figured out roughly which way Mecca was: southeast of New Jersey.

Having always faced west when I prayed, facing east felt strange, so I reminded myself of the Koran's teaching: whichever direction you face, you will find God's face.

I went back to Mr. Besselink's apartment for a longer chat. He was kind and gracious, asking me about my trip, before telling me about himself. He was from an old Dutch family, Calvinist in faith and philosophy, and had started teaching economics and American history at Lawrenceville in the mid-1960s after dropping out of a PhD program at the University of Chicago. He loved sports—American football was his passion—and recruited the school's top athletes for his dorm. I'd soon learn Mr. Besselink, or Mr. B. as he was called, was revered by his "boys," all of whom lived on the first floor. The rest of us, two postgraduates named Todd and Eric, my "big brother" Josh, and another senior, lived down the hall from Mr. B.'s suite.

Mr. Besselink handed me some school literature, including the Lawrenceville hand book, reminding me that attending one of America's top schools entailed abiding by a set of rules. In my broken but passable English, I told Mr. Besselink I'd already read the book but didn't understand what a lot of them meant. He explained the main ones: no drinking, no smoking, check in on time, when lights-out was, coed visitation only with his approval, a rule I didn't have to worry about. He then handed me a bag of toiletries, most of which I had never used in my life: sticks of deodorant, Q-tips, dental floss, soap, shampoo, a toothbrush and toothpaste.

Lights-out was coming up, but all I wanted was to shower, pray, and sleep. Grabbing a change of clothes from my bag, I walked into the bathroom. One of my floormates emerged naked from a shower stall with a towel around his shoulders. I hadn't seen the naked body of a man or a woman since I was nine when I stopped going to the public bath with Father. Revealing or seeing a person's private parts is considered a sin in Islam. I tried to walk out, but my new floormate apparently mistook the terror on my face for a foreigner's eagerness to talk in a new language and began a conversation. I kept looking him straight in the eye, blocking out the rest of his body, while he casually dried himself off with his towel.

When he finally left, I took my first American-style shower. The powerful jets of hot water beating against my back and face rejuvenated me. I wanted to stay longer but was afraid I'd have to confront another naked floormate, so I dried myself and put on my clean *shalwar kameez* in the shower. Walking back to my room, I felt fresh and clean when I ran into Todd, a tall blond Texan who lived across the hall from me. Later Todd told me that I "reeked" when he first met me, holding his hand over his nose for emphasis.

I felt humiliated, hating myself for exuding foul body odor like an unkempt poor villager. "Personal hygiene," the Prophet said, according to a famous hadith, "is part of the faith," and even during the course of long treks across Afghanistan, we always performed the ritual ablution, as many as five times a day.

The next day Mr. Besselink summoned me to his suite. As usual, he was dressed immaculately in dark pants and a blue short-sleeved oxford shirt. Remote control in hand, he was watching a game of football on television. He hit the mute button and asked me to sit down.

"How did you like your first day in America?" he asked.

"I liked it," I said to be polite.

Then, perhaps detecting the smell of tobacco on my clothes, he asked me if I smoked.

"I do. Sometimes," I said, without feeling the need to lie.

He rolled his eyes. "It's a reprehensible habit," he said.

"I understand," I said, guessing "reprehensible" meant something bad.

"We have a rule here," he added. "Students are not allowed to smoke on campus. I don't care if you're nineteen, twenty, or twenty-one. You're considered a minor at this school. And minors are not allowed to smoke on campus."

I had read the booklet of rules and policies, many of which made me feel like I was back in Sheberghan, being sent off to bed by Father after listening to the BBC nightly news. I had nothing against the ban on drinking and sexual contact, but I decided that if I wanted to smoke, I'd simply hide it.

A week or so later my efforts to circumvent the rules caught up with me. I was walking down a quiet, empty street behind the pharmacy across campus and smoking a cigarette. About halfway down the block, I looked over my shoulder and saw Dr. Azoy outside the post office. He saw me and started walking toward me. I'd hastily smoked about half of the cigarette, but he was too close for me to flick it away. Finally, as he walked up to me, I squished the burning cigarette in my hand.

"*Salam alaikum,*" Dr. Azoy said. "Don't burn yourself, my boy," he said, realizing what I'd done. Embarrassed, I dropped the cigarette on the pavement.

"You know," he said, turning serious, "You shouldn't be smoking, and there are three reasons why. First, it is against school policy, and you could get in trouble if the school finds out. Second, it's bad for your health. And third, and most important, as a representative of your culture and your religion, you are sending the wrong signal by smoking."

I told him I was sorry but didn't say that I'd never do it again, hoping that I could be more discreet next time, or not smoke at all. We walked up the street and turned toward Kinnan.

"Now, do you agree?" he asked.

I said I did. As we parted, I couldn't tell if he found my answer convincing.

One night shortly after my arrival, I had a strange dream. I was back in Peshawar visiting my parents. Mother was in a maternity dress in her bedroom nursing a baby. Surprised, I asked her what was going on. "We missed you so much that we had to have a son and name him Masood," she giggled. "I missed my Masood so much."

I was homesick and experiencing "culture shock" at the same time—I kept hearing the odd phrase from eager and sympathetic teachers and others on campus. After consulting more than one dictionary, I formed only a vague sense of what it meant. If it meant things like naively holding Dr. Azoy's hand at the airport or experiencing horror at the sight of my naked floormate, I had all the classic symptoms and more.

Language proved the biggest source of culture shock. My English was deceptively fluent. I could read books and newspapers and magazines with the help of a dictionary. My conversational English, though, was limited to everyday small talk: "How are you?" "I am fine, thank you very much." "How do you do?" "Pleased to meet you." I'd compose simple, grammatically correct sentences then carefully pronounce them to people, thinking I'd accomplished a great feat. More often than not their response was a look of "What the hell are you trying to say?"

Sometimes the language barrier provoked unintended consequences, as I found out after I met Claudia, a tall redhead with a freckled face and infectious smile. I bumped into her and a friend outside Kinnan. I was ready to avoid them when she stopped and introduced me to her friend.

"Nice sneakers," Claudia said.

I blushed. I was proud of the sneakers Dr. Azoy had bought me, but I didn't yet know how to respond to a compliment. In Persian, "thank you" is not a typical response to a compliment. So I tried something we'd say on such an occasion in Afghanistan.

"Your eyes are beautiful," I said.

"Oh, thank you, Mossad," she said, butchering my name.

She was probably wondering what in the world I was trying to say, but I was proud to have used an Afghan line to good effect. As Claudia and her friend walked away, I decided to go further and said something that I'd clearly mistranslated from Persian. I hoped Claudia had heard me.

She had. Looking over her shoulder, she said, "Fuck you."

I was shocked. What on earth was she thinking? How was it possible for a woman to actually fuck a man? Wasn't she physiologically incapable of performing the very act she just mentioned? I knew what the vulgar expression meant but had never thought a girl could use it. To use a word I'd learned from Karimullah, it was the most "preposterous" thing I'd heard in my life.

Mr. Besselink's boys were no easier to decipher. They always said hi when they saw me, but I couldn't make sense of much else they said. "Awesome," "cool," and "psyched," to name some the polite words, were foreign to me. And while my housemates were all friendly, occasionally I got the feeling they talked about me behind my back. Once I heard one of the boys mumble to another that I was a "badass." I thought "badass" meant "stupid donkey" —an insult in Afghanistan.

Others were eager to pepper me with questions about my background, but I found this earnestness as exhausting as trying to navigate my way through the sea of prep-school slang. The more I was asked about Afghanistan, the more I missed it. At the end of each day, while students were still playing sports outside, I'd retire to my room well before our house prefect checked everyone in by ten o'clock.

Soon it was time to enroll in classes. Early one morning I went to Dr. Azoy's cluttered but airy classroom on the second floor of Pop Hall. Large maps and posters of Afghanistan and the Middle East decorated the walls. Sporting a cream-colored Nehru vest, Dr. Azoy began browsing the books I'd bought for my classes: American History, English Composition, Advanced Algebra, and Art Foundation. I wanted to take more impressive-sounding courses—Revolutionary China, Chaucer, Calculus I, AP American History—but Dr. Azoy said those had to wait. I should only take required classes, which happened to be among the easiest the school offered, so that I could do well enough to satisfy Harvard.

"You need As and Bs to get into Harvard," Dr. Azoy said flatly. "In fact, you should aim for nothing less than an A." Harvard's promise to reconsider my application was contingent upon my getting good grades at Lawrenceville.

"You'll do well," Dr. Azoy said. "I have faith in you, my boy."

I opened up to Dr. Azoy, whom I started calling Kaka (Uncle) Whitney. In turn, he wisecracked using a combination of English and Persian.

"Don't waste your time with the *dookhtarhaa-I Lawrenceville* [the girls of Lawrenceville]," he said in Farsi. It was the first of many English-Farsi phrases we coined that no one but the two of us understood. "The boys here are better at talking than getting anything from the *dookhtarhaa*," he said. "All they know is talk." There was no confusion about this topic as Afghan boys are the same way. There's even a phrase in Farsi for it: *shaytaan baazee,* or "satanic deceptions." More pressing an issue for me was the fact that I still couldn't think of Persian equivalents for *fun, cool,* and *awesome.*

Taking the easier classes turned out to be a good idea. They were for the most part taken by first and second formers, PGs, and foreign students. Mrs. Garber's English Composition was essentially English as a Second Language for the handful of foreign students attending their senior year. Mr. Daniel's introductory art course had half a dozen bubbly thirteen- and fourteen-year-old first and second formers along with a couple of older science geeks who had put off taking the required course. My favorite class turned out to be Ms. Schulte's American History. A recent Princeton graduate, she seemed excited in particular to teach the foreign students in her class, which included a Venezuelan, a Swede, a recent Russian Jewish immigrant, a Spaniard, a German, and myself.

In Afghanistan only mediocre university students major in history. Yet shortly after my arrival, Karimullah called from London and urged me to pay special attention in this class. "History," he said, "explains why Americans believe what they believe and behave the way they behave." I'd never considered history to be an expositor of human behavior, and I had more than a few questions about Americans I wanted an answer to. Could reading history unravel the mystery of why American men don't like holding hands?

I plunged into Ms. Schulte's American history class with the same enthusiasm I'd felt in Ustad Fazil's Arabic grammar class back in Peshawar. I asked questions, offered unsolicited answers, and, encouraged by Mr. B., debated both other students and Ms. Schulte herself. I was a congenital intellectual combatant and an adolescent know-it-all, trying to dominate classroom debate. Eventually Ms. Schulte had to stop me so others would have a chance to speak.

If I was impressed by Lawrenceville's academic offerings, I was overwhelmed by the extracurricular activities. There were few sports you couldn't participate in, few passions you couldn't pursue: lacrosse, fencing, water polo, even Kaka Whitney's popular Kayaking Club. Then there were student clubs: the Drama Club, Debate Club, Chess Club. While many were passionate about their extracurricular activities, clubs and sports were also used as bullet points in college applications. The more activities you participated in, the better your chances of getting into a good college. This was a far cry from Afghanistan's system of college admission where students would take a national "Conquer" test and then be assigned to a college according to their scores. The top-scoring students went to the Kabul medical school and engineering school. The worst-performing students were banished to teachers' colleges.

I decided I'd try as many extracurricular activities as I could, signing up for more clubs than could fit on an entire yearbook page. I quickly realized I'd overextended myself. My piano lessons with the school's kindly, silver-haired musical director didn't go beyond transcribing Beethoven's "Ode to Joy." Swimming lessons stopped after three sessions. I was a no-show at Kaka Whitney's Kayaking Club. I regularly showed up at the Chess Club, though, and I accompanied the Harvard Model UN team to Boston, winning the school an honorable mention for my performance as a representative of the Republic of Ireland on a General Assembly committee.

I was slowly adapting to the ways of an American education. Outside the classroom and my school activities, however, I was still an Afghan. Kaka Whitney went out of his way to make sure Lawrenceville accommodated me. Although Lawrenceville no longer required boys to wear coats and ties in class, it had recently instituted a no-hats policy in indoor areas. Although Kaka Whitney knew that I wore my *pakool* as a custom, not a religious requirement, he asked the school to waive its no-hats policy for me. Mr. Bunting, a great believer in religious freedom, had personally given his okay. Also, while students were required to wear slacks and collared shirts in class, I sometimes dressed in my traditional Afghan clothes. Aware that many religiously observant Muslims, even those with beards, were perfectly at home in Western clothes, I no longer associated these outfits with the moral decadence that flourished in Afghan cities under Soviet occupation.

I had several dress shirts that Mr. B. had given me, and two pairs of pants. One was a pair of khakis a Harvard-educated American aid worker in Peshawar had given me, the other a pair of acid-washed jeans an aunt had brought me from Canada. The khakis were too tight, while the acid-washed jeans (I called them the *patloon-I kowboy* in Farsi, or the cowboy's pantaloon) looked quite fashionable. I walked to the library in my new jeans where I bumped into Kaka Whitney and an administrator.

Looking surprised, he asked in Farsi, "*Patloon maqbool-a az kuja paydaa kadee?*" Beautiful pants. Who gave them to you?

"*Patloon-I kowboy*," I corrected him.

The administrator remarked on how quickly I had adapted. "You look very preppy," she said. I had no idea what "preppy" meant, but I took it as a compliment.

"Thank you," I said, now familiar with the correct response.

If I had taken a good look around campus, I'd have realized that finding a defective mortar shell with a special serial number in an ammo dump would have been easier than spotting a Lawrenceville student in acid-washed jeans. I simply couldn't tell the difference between my jeans and theirs. Yet I was encouraged by the administrator's compliment, so from that day I felt less awkward in jeans. Sometime I'd wear the same pair of jeans and the same shirt several days in a row until a floormate advised me not to wear the same outfit every day. Still bearded and covering my head with a hat, I nonetheless felt modern, like city judges and mullahs in Afghanistan who wore suits and ties on formal occasions.

Sometime after my arrival, Kaka Whitney arranged for the *Trenton Times*, New Jersey's largest daily newspaper, to write a profile of me. The resulting front-page story, "Afghan Fighter Arrives at Lawrenceville," turned me into something of a celebrity on campus. Young students would coyly wave at me on campus, while drivers would pull alongside to wish me good luck. Eventually I was invited to speak before community groups. Serving as a publicist, Kaka Whitney arranged for me to speak at local churches, businesses, and civic groups. Although I had no public speaking experience, I happily agreed, knowing that I could speak with authority on my country before an American audience, though it would have been a tougher challenge in front of an Afghan crowd. In early 1990, Afghanistan still occasionally made front-page news, and these groups wanted to get an "insider's view" on post-Soviet Afghanistan.

I'd arrive at these events dressed in what I considered my best outfit: the acid-washed jeans, a checkered shirt, a Russian army desert jacket, my *pakool,* and a *patoo* draped over my shoulder. Invariably someone would ask, "How long do you think the Communist regime is going to survive?" I replied that the collapse of the Communist regime was going to take time but was inevitable since our jihad had started with the Communist coup in 1978, a year and a half before the Soviet invasion. The more talks I gave, the more comfortable I became, so much so that Kaka Whitney began calling me the "roving Ambassador for Free Afghanistan."

Whitney may have seen me as a diplomat for my country, but I felt more and more like I was bridging the gap between East and West when I joined a handful of Muslim students in prayer in the basement of the Edith Memorial Chapel. Lawrenceville had about a dozen Muslim students, mostly Pakistani-Americans but also two or three acculturated Arab students in their third or fourth years at the school. At Uncle Whitney's suggestion we formed a prayer group that met, somewhat incongruously, in the basement of the chapel, where I would lead the prayer dressed in acid-washed jeans, a Brooks Brothers shirt, and a faded Russian army summer coat.

One Friday, Uncle Whitney drove us all to a congregational mosque about thirty minutes away from Lawrenceville. It was a modern mosque with a predominantly Arab congregation. With the exception of the preacher and a handful of congregants, the men sitting next to me were all wearing jeans, slacks, long-sleeved shirts, suits, even T-shirts with big logos on them. Many did not wear headgear, in violation of the Prophet's custom. While I disapproved of their bare heads and arms, I felt a bond of brotherhood with them, proud to be sitting next to fellow Muslims facing Mecca and hearing the preacher lead us in prayer for the Muslims of Palestine, Afghanistan, and Kashmir. Leaving the mosque, I remembered what Karimullah had once told me about his travels through Muslim countries. Wherever he went, he could always hear the familiar and soothing sounds of the *azan* in Arabic: *Allahu Akbar, Allahu Akbar. Ashhadu-an laa-Illahah illal-Allah*—God is Great, God is Great. I bear witness that there is no god but God.

I called Karimullah a few days later and eagerly told him about my trip to the mosque. As usual, we switched between English and Pashto.

"You must miss the sound of the *azan*," he said in English. "I certainly do whenever I visit America. Remember, America is the land of infidels. You may not like a lot of things about Americans," he said in English, "but judge them by the standards by which they judge themselves." This would prove to be very good advice.

Sometime later Uncle Latif, one of my father's second cousins, visited me from New York. I'd given Mr. B. his name as my guardian, even though Kaka Whitney for all intents and purposes actually served as my guardian and mentor. Uncle Latif was one of Father's closest friends, the son of the former chief justice of the supreme court. Father used to tutor him as a madrassah student, and Uncle Latif had followed my father's secular ways, obtaining a university degree in Kabul before immigrating to America shortly after the Soviet invasion.

I'd liked Uncle Latif as a kid. On his occasional visits to Sheberghan from Kabul, he'd bring me and my sisters and cousins expensive stationery not available in town. When I saw him now, he seemed taken aback by my beard and my mix of secular and traditional clothes. We spent an awkward afternoon in Princeton walking around town and eating lunch at a fast-food restaurant, but his curmudgeonly behavior kept me at a distance. When he dropped me off I promised to visit him the next chance I got, but wasn't sure how soon that would be.

It turned out it would be only a few weeks before I saw Uncle Latif again. My friend Richard's parents came from New York to give me a tour of the city. Richard was the Harvard grad and aspiring war correspondent who'd met Karimullah in London and delivered the Harvard application to me in Peshawar. Richard's father, Ambassador Murphy, was a veteran diplomat who had recently left the State Department. Mrs. Murphy had met her husband while a student at Radcliffe in the late 1940s.

This would be my first visit to the city, and my first weekend away from Lawrenceville. We drove to the Murphys' neighborhood on the Upper East Side. The Murphys' apartment, elegantly decorated with antiques and artifacts from around the world, was on the eleventh floor of a charming building with a magnificent view of the East River.

Mrs. Murphy gave me a New York City guidebook and asked me what I wanted to visit. After breakfast we took a cab to the World Trade Center, the first site on my list. Prior to coming to America I wasn't familiar with any of New York's landmarks except Times Square, but given its reputation, I thought I'd better skip that.

At the World Trade Center we joined a long, winding line to buy tickets. When we reached the observation deck, I hurried to the windows to look. I discovered I was scared of heights, so I held onto the railing as I walked around. Yet I was excited and proud. I was in New York City, looking out from the top of the tallest building in America. I turned to Mrs. Murphy and said, "I never thought I would stand here. Thank you for bringing me here." It was my first truly inspiring moment in America.

After a visit to the Statue of Liberty, I met Uncle Latif in the city in the afternoon. I wanted to visit the United Nations to see the famous poem of Sa'di that I'd heard was engraved on a wall there:

The children of Adam are limbs of each other
Having been created of one essence
When the calamity of time afflicts one limb
The other limbs cannot remain at rest
If thou hast no sympathy for the troubles of others
Thou art unworthy to be called by the name of a man.

Crossing Forty-second Street on Fifth Avenue, Uncle Latif explained the city's geography: Fifth Avenue divides Manhattan into east and west, while Forty-second Street divides it into north and south. Much to my relief, at the intersection of Fifth Avenue, Forty-second Street was devoid of the forbidden sights I'd been warned about. Still, I was stunned by the chaotic traffic, the presence of beggars and homeless men, and streets strewn with trash. As we walked, I kept bumping into people and walking too close to Uncle Latif. Finally he snapped at me: "In America, you don't walk too close to people. You see this distance between us?" he asked and stepped back until we were about three feet apart. "It's called personal territory. You don't violate people's territory."

"I didn't know," I said, feeling guilty and confused.

"Now you know," Uncle Latif said.

Trying my best to keep my new distance from him, I listened as Uncle Latif pointed out New York landmarks: the Empire State Building, the New York Public Library, Rockefeller Center, Central Park. Finally we made our way to the UN building. It was a disappointment because the Sa'di poem on the UN wall turned out to be a mere legend.

The next day, I went to visit Uncle Latif at his Brooklyn apartment. While he gave me directions over the phone, he said, a little annoyed, "You're a grown-up man, you shouldn't get lost."

Naturally I got lost. I called him collect from a pay phone and got directions a second time, then a third time. He lived in a brownstone in an Italian neighborhood. His apartment was small but tidy. The living room was crammed with couches and chairs, bookshelves, and a coffee table topped with a stack of magazines. He claimed to be a good cook and offered to treat me to a meal of lamb rice.

"You should get rid of your *pakool* and beard," he demanded.

"Why?"

"This is not Afghanistan," he said, clearly irritated. "This is America. You want to look proper here. I don't understand what this beard and *pakool* is all about. Your father never wore them."

I wanted to correct him and remind him of Father's bushy youthful beard, but I just nodded as I chopped onions and carrots. It was not the first time an Afghan had suggested that I remove my hat and facial hair. On the evening before leaving Pakistan, I had to fight my cousins who urged me to shave before I left. But Uncle Latif was a sophisticated, worldly man, and I expected more from him. While Americans respected me for keeping my identity, one of my own was urging me to change. I wanted to get away from him before his misguided ways rubbed off on me.

If it hadn't been for the warm reception from the Murphys, my trip to New York would have been a disappointment. They showed me hospitality I didn't know existed in America. Having lived in the Islamic world, they didn't treat me like a stranger or an outcast but treated me with respect and generosity. If there is one thing about their culture Afghans are most proud of, it is their code of hospitality. Rich or poor, they go beyond their means to take care of guests. The Murphys, who had never met me before and knew me only through their son, demonstrated what Americans and America itself was capable of.

When I got back to Lawrenceville, I started meeting regularly with a college counselor to fix on a strategy for getting into Harvard. Though pleased with my better than average grades—an A, a couple of B-pluses, and a B—and with my solid score on the math section of the SAT, the counselor said I should apply to at least a dozen colleges "just to be on the safe side." I had never been thrilled about having to reapply to Harvard, and I assumed applying to other colleges meant it was less likely I'd get into Harvard, but Kaka Whitney assured me that I would get in if I maintained my good academic standing. To boost my application, he even assigned me the title of "co-teacher" of his class on Islam and wrote me a letter of recommendation.

It wasn't long before the response letters from colleges started arriving. I got a handful of acceptances—Princeton, Duke, Swarthmore, the University of Utah—but the only one that mattered to me was Harvard's. When that fat envelope finally arrived, a few days later, I was elated and proudly pasted it on the wall of the TV room in Kinnan next to everyone else's acceptance and rejection letters.

A few weeks before graduation, Kaka Whitney asked what I wanted to do during the summer. My parents had advised me not to return to Pakistan. It was too dangerous, they said. I couldn't tell if things had really gotten worse. I knew the war wasn't over and that the mujahideen weren't making headway in trying to overthrow the Communist regime in Kabul. I had read newspaper stories about several major car bombs in Pakistan, but an occasional car bomb was hardly unusual. Perhaps Mother and Father feared I would want to rejoin the fighting in Afghanistan if I returned. Then one day Kaka Whitney excitedly approached me with a job idea.

"Why don't you go out west and work as a cowboy?" he asked. He knew someone who could get me a job. I thought it was a perfect idea. I knew cowboys rode horses, carried guns, and wore jeans. I was excited about carrying a gun on the western prairie, but unfortunately the job fell through. Sometime after that Mrs. Murphy called to see how I was doing and asked me what I was planning to do in the summer. I told her I wanted to work as a cowboy.

"Why?" she asked.

"I don't know. Dr. Azoy suggested it to me. But I'm not sure if he can get me a job," I said.

"We have a friend in Texas who owns a ranch," she replied. "Let me make some calls, and I'll get back to you in the morning."

The next day she called to say that a job could be lined up for me on a large working ranch in West Texas. "They will treat you like everyone else, like a real cowboy," Mrs. Murphy said.

I was thrilled. In my American history class we'd touched on the subject of the frontier experience, but I didn't fully grasp its significance in America's collective self-consciousness. I had no idea the west was the place where Americans proved their manhood, their spirit of independence, and their self-reliance.

A week after graduation, I flew to Harlingen, the closest southern Texas town to the eighty-thousand-acre Yturria Ranch. Mr. Yturria, the owner, came to pick me up. A prominent Mexican-American businessman in South Texas and a Korean War veteran, he had graying hair, a tanned face, and wore a tweed jacket and tie. On our drive to the ranch, he pointed at the green cornfields on both sides of the road and offered a little lesson on early American economic history. Most people in America, he said, used to be farmers or cattle herders, but they learned and adopted modern farming techniques to improve their productivity. They were mostly poor and led hardscrabble lives. They worked the land, and when there was rain they did well, and when there was drought their lives were devastated. Then something happened that changed their lives. With science and technology, they learned to vastly increase their productivity.

"So much so," he said without looking at me, "that today less than five percent of the population can feed the whole country and produce enough to export to the rest of the world." This was one of the most amazing statistics I had heard about America. In Afghanistan, I told him, most farmers still used cattle to plow the land. A handful of farmers had access to tractors, but the war had destroyed their livelihoods, and much of the land had been mined, rendered useless for cultivation.

When we drove through the gate of the ranch, Mr. Yturria decided to stop by a corral. "Let me introduce you to our foreman," he said. Inside the corral, a couple of guys were holding a calf down on the ground. Mr. Yturria called out to the foreman, a sturdily built, dark-skinned man with a big mustache, wearing a short-sleeved checkered shirt and a black cowboy hat with a red feather.

"This is our Afghan friend, Masood," Mr. Yturria said. "He is a Harvard boy. Wants to become a cowboy. Do you think you can make a cowboy out of him?"

The foreman, whose name was Johnnie Posas, smiled and shook my hand over the fence. I asked Mr. Yturria what the men were doing.

"They're castrating calves," he said.

"Do you want to learn to castrate?" Johnnie asked me.

"Sure," I said.

"Come on in."

With a single throw of his lasso, Johnnie roped a calf and threw him to the ground.

"You have to do it with your teeth," Johnnie said. "That's how we do it down here."

I wasn't sure if he was serious. When I agreed and began to kneel, he smiled and handed me a gelding knife. Holding the calf's sac in his hands, Johnnie told me to make an incision. I drew blood and the calf started mooing in pain. Following Johnnie's directions, I held the scrotum, which kept slipping out of my hand. Finally I put down the knife, pulled out the scrotum, and with Johnnie holding it, I castrated my first calf.

Mr. Yturria and I then continued up the dirt driveway until we came to a stop in front of the ranch house. It was large, with a dozen rooms, an entertainment area, and a spacious living room decorated with antique furniture and a gun collection. In front of the house was a polo field where Mr. Yturria, himself an amateur polo player, entertained guests. After introducing me to the housemaid and showing me my room and private bathroom, he wished me good luck and left.

I spent the next two weeks in the house. Johnnie would come every day around seven o'clock to pick me up, and we would go around the ranch to work. Every day when I came back, the maid had tidied up. The pantry was fully stocked. It was a luxurious life, but I was lonely. The cowhands' cottages were a mile up the road, and after dark the place turned quiet. When Mr. Murphy called to see how I was doing, I told him I felt too isolated from everyone else.

He suggested I ask Mr. Yturria if I could relocate. When I did, he happily agreed, asking Johnnie to come by and pick me up. Later that evening, Johnnie drove me to my next abode: a run-down, mouse-infested cottage adjacent to his trailer house. Bathroom floor tiles were missing and the ceiling was caving in. It was a far cry from my room at the mansion, but I liked being near Johnnie and able to participate in the cowboys' social life.

The summer passed quickly, and I was looking forward to Harvard. In the year I spent at Lawrenceville and on the Yturria Ranch, I realized that I was becoming more comfortable living in America than I would have been in Pakistan. My parents didn't understand the application and admission process, nor did they grasp the significance of attending Harvard, but they wrote to say how proud of me they were and prayed for my success. When I wrote Uncle Jaan Agha about what I'd learned at Lawrenceville, at one point defining culture as "a geographic concept," a phrase I'd picked up in Lawrenceville, he wrote back a ten-page critique of Western imperialism and worried that I was becoming too Westernized. I didn't place as much faith in Uncle Jaan Agha's beliefs as when I was younger, so instead of writing back assuring him I would always remain Afghan, I ignored his letter. I knew I wasn't Westernized; I still wore a beard, said my daily prayers, observed the fast during Ramadan, and, even though I now occasionally imbibed, I still considered myself pious.

Harvard would bring changes both small and large. I traded my acid-washed jeans for Levis, but I also knew my course load would dwarf anything I experienced at Lawrenceville. An admissions officer told me during my "pre-frosh weekend" visit that I was the first Afghan to attend Harvard in more than twenty-five years. I felt enormous pressure to succeed and had one clear goal: finish Harvard and return to serve Afghanistan.

I had been assigned to what was called a "psycho single," a first-floor private room with a shared bathroom. In my housing application I had emphasized my need for privacy. I liked my room at Lawrenceville and didn't want to share a room where I would disturb anyone by getting up early to pray. Canaday Hall, the only modern dorm in Harvard Yard, was also one of the few with single rooms. I'd learned many American slang words over the course of the past year, but it wasn't until much later that I figured out why they were called "psycho singles."

On the second day of freshman orientation week, I joined more than fifteen hundred proud freshmen and their parents at a welcoming ceremony in front of Memorial Church. Unable to find an empty chair, I stood by a tree and listened to an address by Dean Moses. The speech was crisp and eloquent and full of everything anxious, confused, insecure Harvard freshmen (and their parents) might want to hear. Only toward the end did he strike a note of caution.

"You have all been stars in your schools and communities," he said, "but here at Harvard, you are one another's peers. You're equals. Study hard, be competitive, and respect your peers."

I wasn't sure his words about academic stardom applied to me, but I joined in the applause anyway. We walked to Radcliffe Quad for an afternoon cookout, after which I headed to Harvard Square. I had seen a fiery street-corner preacher there during my pre-frosh weekend visit, and I wanted to see if he was still there. Sure enough he was—Bible in hand, shouting at the top of his lungs about Jesus and salvation. A small crowd had gathered around him as he said AIDS was a curse by God on those who had abandoned Jesus. I was less interested in what the preacher had to say than in how those who heard him responded. When he told a heckler that "only Jesus could save" him, the young man shouted back: "Give us condoms!" Soon more onlookers ganged up on the preacher demanding condoms. Such a display would be unthinkable in Afghanistan, but in America, the most religious country in the West, insulting preachers was practically a sport.

In Canaday and other freshman dorms, conversations were more earnest. A favorite topic was who had not received perfect SAT scores. Apparently Dean Moses's speech hadn't made much of an impression. I hadn't received perfect SAT scores, nor had I been the valedictorian of my school. What was I doing here? I realized how out of my league I was when I failed every test required of incoming freshmen: writing, quantitative reasoning, and computer literacy.

Shortly after my arrival, Karimullah called from London. He'd started a documentary film company and was anxious to get back to Afghanistan.

"You've made us all very proud, Masood Jaanah," he said. "You've fought in the lesser jihad, now prepare yourself for the greater jihad. This is going to be a real test of your faith."

"I know very well what you mean," I said, and recited the Prophet's famous saying about the need to wage a greater jihad to overcome our "human passions and desires." One can fight a jihad to restrain oneself, which is more important than fighting a holy war against infidels.

I was committed to fighting the greater jihad. I soon met Hakim, a scraggly eighteen-year-old Saudi Arabian student. Soft-spoken and polite, Hakim took my beard as a sign of religious devotion and began calling me daily so we could pray together. When I didn't answer my phone, he'd show up at my door and announce it was time to pray in my room. Initially I liked having a praying partner, but after many late nights of studying, I stopped answering his early morning calls of "Brother Masood" and his knocks on my door at four in the morning. Eventually he stopped coming, though I'd still run into him at the Muslim student center in the basement of Sanders Theatre. I attended Friday congregational prayers at the mosque and occasionally attended evening prayer sessions, and sometimes I'd be asked to lead the prayers, but more often than not I preferred to pray in the privacy of my room.

My desire to adhere to my religion got a boost from another unexpected source. While leaving the administration building in Harvard Yard one day, I met a friendly, blond football player named Scott. He casually invited me to watch *The Simpsons* with him and his friends over some ice cream, and I happily accepted his invitation. I went to the graduate housing apartment of one of his friends where a half-dozen people had gathered. We watched *The Simpsons* and as we started eating our ice cream, someone took out a Bible and started reading from it. There was a prayer at the end of the meeting. I felt duped. I ran into Scott once or twice after that, but I politely declined his invitations. It turned out, though, that Scott had friends working around the campus, members of a nationwide campus organization called Christian Impact. They used to congregate in the smoking section of the Union, an area accessible to people without university IDs. Because I smoked and preferred to eat in the smoking section of the Union, I invariably ran into members of Christian Impact and found myself in a position to defend my faith.

I told them I was a devout Muslim and if they were looking for a convert, that they should try to persuade me Christianity was superior to Islam. I asked them about the Trinity, a doctrine Islam regards as heretical. The standard response was well rehearsed: Trinity does not mean there is more than one God; it is simply God manifesting himself in three different forms, just as water can manifest itself in liquid, solid, and gas forms. In a way, this was a very Sufi idea, but as a Muslim I could not accept the Trinity of God and pressed further. What about salvation? I asked. Isn't it presumptuous to believe that by merely accepting Jesus as my savior I can go to heaven? Doesn't going to heaven presuppose good works in addition to divine grace? Islam urges its followers to believe in God and to perform good deeds, but this alone does not guarantee entry to heaven, which is granted by the grace of God. My arguments with Christian Impact members would grow heated. On more than one occasion they asked me in vain to get on my knees and accept Jesus as my savior. The arguments, however, made good material for papers. In my expository writing class, we were asked to write a final paper about a campus group. I chose Christian Impact and earned my first A.

I didn't shun all student groups. One group I was drawn to was the Republican Students Club. Although I never formally joined (since I was not a citizen, I wasn't sure if I could), I did attend meetings, drawn in part by a desire to pay tribute to Ronald Reagan's steadfast support of the Afghan jihad. Ideology also played a role. Temperamentally conservative, I was drawn to the party's platform of family values and strong defense. The campus Republicans were notoriously disunited, though they rallied together in support of the impending Gulf War. Student members were encouraged to show their support for the troops in every possible way. I supported the war from the moment Saddam Hussein invaded Kuwait, not simply because I thought Saddam had illegally occupied a small neighboring country, but because during the 1980s, Baathist Iraq was one of a handful of Muslim countries (along with Syria and Libya) to condone the Soviet occupation of Afghanistan.

I went to Harvard intending to study political science and international affairs. I enjoyed my three political science classes during my freshman year, but decided I wanted something more challenging. At Harvard, political science was popular among the academically challenged "gov jocks." A government major himself, Karimullah had nonetheless encouraged me to study history in order to understand Americans, and an older Har-vard grad I had met at a dinner party in New York told me that "history is everything. It's politics, economics, philosophy, sociology all thrown into one. Study history, and you'll learn everything."

Besides government courses, I took classes in early Islamic history, Ottoman history, Islamic philosophy and mysticism with the foremost Western scholars in these fields. I had long been fascinated by Islamic history, having read traditional biographies of the Prophet Muhammad and pious stories of the caliphs, along with hagiographical accounts of great men in Islamic history. Taught by an eminent scholar, medieval Islamic history became an early passion. While my familiarity with Islamic history and the expectation I'd do well was a key consideration in taking the class, I was equally interested to see how my history was taught in the West.

The professor was a brilliant scholar, ill at ease in public, but with a wry sense of humor. In class, he displayed occasional flashes of inarticulateness that belied his erudition and literary gifts. One of the early topics we discussed in his class was the concept of jihad, for which we read long passages from *The Venture of Islam,* a scholarly work by the late orientalist Marshall Hodgson. Jihad, Hodgson argued, was essentially an extension of a long-standing tradition among pre-Islamic Arab tribes fighting for plunder. Another book said that it was "the prospect of tangible gain" that attracted many to join Muhammad's army, not, as I had learned, a sincere desire to fight for God and go to heaven. Some of these early leaders, described as men of great piety, lived luxurious lives and amassed great wealth during the early military expeditions. For example, Osman, the third of the Four Righteous Caliphs who succeeded Muhammad, was accused of nepotism and elitism and was hated by many. By contrast, in traditional Islamic history Osman is revered by Sunni Muslims as the man who, around AD 650, commissioned the "collection" of what has remained the canonical text of the Koran. These conceits would easily offend an Islamic sensibility. However, as a professor of Islamic history once told me, it is not what happened, but what Muslims believe to have happened, that matters.

During my sophomore year, I received an invitation from the Spee Club, one of nine all-male final clubs at Harvard, to join club members for drinks at the French Library in Boston. The printed invitation came in a handsome envelope engraved with the club's mascot—a bear. I had been "punched" for membership at the invitation of an Iranian-Swiss member.

Established in the nineteenth century for the crème de la crème of Harvard society, the men's clubs based in large houses around Harvard Square were the "final stop"—hence the term final clubs —for cultivating lifelong networks of friends. While at Harvard, students from the right families and prep schools were expected to join the right clubs, socialize with the right people, and network with the right men before graduating into the world and becoming members of the right country club. At Harvard, each final club boasted famous alumni. Spee's most famous alumnus was President John F. Kennedy, whose portrait hung on the wall of the club's library. Club lore had it that, although Jack had been one of the most popular punchees, when his name came up for a formal vote one member objected, "But he's a Catholic."

By the time I arrived at Harvard, it was the era of blind admission and need-based financial aid. Like the larger institution, Spee and the other clubs went out of their way to nod to multiculturalism. In truth I did not consider myself a member of a minority. I wasn't an immigrant; I was an international student who aspired to return to Afghanistan when I finished college, and I felt Spee, with its large number of international members, would be a good fit for me. Still the final clubs were among the last vestiges of elitism at Harvard. Because they allowed only male members, they were seen as sexist institutions. Under pressure from campus feminist groups, Harvard severed official ties with the clubs in the mid-1980s. To outsiders the clubs were places of decadence and debauchery, where drugs and booze flowed freely. Reports of strippers hired for parties and charges of sexual harassment abounded. Initiation rites involved excessive drinking and sometimes running naked through the Yard in the dead of winter.

The Fall Punch got off to a good start. I had already met several Spee members and found them bright, articulate, and cosmopolitan, decadent intellectuals who were the type of men with whom I'd eventually form lifelong friendships. While the punch events were essentially about consuming copious amounts of alcohol, the Spee members who were aware of my religious beliefs never made me drink to excess. When a member insisted I have another drink, one who understood my situation would intervene on my behalf.

As part of the punch process, prospective members attended cocktail parties, lunches, and dinners with members and alumni over the course of several months. Getting "punched" was an invitation, not a guarantee of membership; most punches were eliminated before the end of the season. Every other week or so, you got a call from a club member inviting you to a more important event with a smaller number of students. I was eventually elected a member, and because the Spee house was just down the street from Canaday Hall, it became my after-hours hangout. For the rest of the academic year, I spent most of my free time at Spee, sometimes partying until three or four in the morning. With the stereo blasting we would shoot pool, smoke, and polish off the seemingly bottomless keg of beer in the club barroom. Sometimes late at night, when we had no beer in our dorm, I'd simply walk over to the club, fill large empty Coke bottles with beer from the keg, and bring it back to the dorm to drink with female classmates.

Since I was now drinking freely, I didn't want to convey a false impression that I was still a practicing Muslim. That would mean I'd have to shave off my beard. My new friends encouraged me to shave, telling me that people—including girls—would treat me less as a foreigner, and more like an American. I had resisted their exhortations from the time I arrived at Lawrence-ville, but I finally broke down in a dingy little barbershop in El Paso, Texas, where I was checking out Tex-Mex restaurants and cheap motels as part of my job as a researcher and writer for the Harvard Student Association's Let's Go travel guide series. My face had aged, but I had literally come clean with myself. I felt free.

When I returned to Harvard, my friends had a hard time recognizing me, expressing disbelief that I'd done away with something that had, up until now, defined me. Before long I was named a member of the campus "cultural elite" by the *Harvard Crimson*, owing to my exotic background and membership in both the Spee and the Signet Club, another elite club of artists and intellectuals I'd found my way into. Yet as junior year gave way to senior year, I realized the reason I wanted to get into the Spee and the Signet clubs and the time I spent socializing with Harvard's elite had been a subconscious effort to fit into a culture I did not belong to. I wanted to be accepted as a member of the intellectual elite, as a prep-school grad who went to Harvard and achieved academic success, to ultimately even be accepted as an American. But I wasn't any of these things, and no matter how hard I tried, or how genuinely people regarded me, in the end I was simply an Afghan.

Everything I'd done in life so far was in a way an act of rebellion. By striving so hard to be what I thought an American was, I'd come dangerously close to losing my individuality. So instead of trying to fit in and to socialize with people who had a soft spot for anything exotic, I tried to make deeper friendships with people I liked and who genuinely liked me. While most of my Harvard friends were white, I counted among them a Filipino, a Lithuanian Jew, and a black of Nigerian ancestry. They were all Americans, and they were all my friends. Even a first-generation immigrant who spoke English with an accent was as American as someone whose ancestors had been on the *Mayflower*. In America everyone had a fair shot at becoming American.

In Afghanistan, I grew up in a tribal society suspicious of everything foreign. My childhood revolved around members of my extended family. My cousins were my best friends. Outsiders were viewed with suspicion, if not outright hostility. The world was clearly divided between right and wrong. Defending one's view in Afghanistan is often regarded as a sign of intelligence, not because you respect your opponent's opinion but because you wholeheartedly trust the righteousness of your beliefs. At Harvard, I learned that in America respecting others' views is as important as defending your own. This was a difficult attitude for a former religious student to embrace, but a necessary one if I were to understand what it meant to be an American.

On the surface, becoming an American looked as easy as converting to Islam. In Islam you pledge there is no god but God and Muhammad is his Messenger. To become an American, you raise your right hand and pledge allegiance to the Constitution of the United States of America. Yet just as Islamic converts submit themselves to God and his teachings, Americans submit themselves to values and principles that define their country and culture. It is about embracing a new attitude—a skeptical yet optimistic way of looking at the world—and a belief in fair play, decency, civility, accountability, ethical conduct, and national unity. This set of values and principles keeps America together during times of crisis. The difference between Afghanistan (or for that matter most Islamic countries) and America is that in America these ideas have been put into practice, whereas in the Islamic world they remain suppressed by authoritarian regimes.

During my senior year at Harvard, while working on my honors thesis, Samuel P. Huntington published his controversial essay "The Clash of Civilizations?" Huntington argued that with the end of the Cold War an authoritarian Islam would be in perpetual conflict with a predominately Christian, democratic West. The essay directly challenged the underlying premise of my thesis. I was writing on the influence of the twelfth-century Moorish philosopher Averroës on St. Thomas Aquinas, and my goal was to highlight the intellectual contribution of Islam to Western civilization. The twelfth century was the golden age of Islamic thought and European philosophers and theologians enthusiastically culled ideas from their more sophisticated Saracen counterparts. In the centuries that followed, the two civilizations took radically different paths, but I did not believe Islam was incompatible with democracy.

Although my thesis sparked in me a life-long interest in early Islamic and European intellectual history, it was not exactly a scholarly achievement. It was long on unfocused rambling and short on original ideas. I turned it in just before the deadline at the end of April while trying to get passing grades in a hodge-podge of classes I'd crammed into my last semester: an independent study on constitutional history; an art history class on the altarpiece; a graduate course in Islamic political philosophy.

Needless to say, I did not have to worry about my thesis or about graduating. While my grades had fluctuated between occasional As and more common Bs and Cs, Harvard was not going to fail me. Harvard rarely failed anyone, having replaced the old F with the passing E grade. This was the age of grade inflation, when the vast majority of students graduated with honors—proof that Harvard students were the best and the brightest.

Shortly before graduation, the senior resident tutor at Winthrop House, where I now lived, called me into his office. He had good news and bad news. The good news was that I was going to graduate. The bad news was that I was not going to get my diploma on graduation day. I owed Harvard upward of seven hundred dollars in library fines, and until I paid they would deny me the pleasure of smelling the ink from the president's pen.

Graduation would be an anticlimax. No grand celebration or exotic vacation before going to work at a white-shoe Wall Street firm. Not only was I not getting my diploma or having my parents at graduation, I was one of the rare graduates not going into finance or consulting or law school or med school. I had decided to take the year off to explore America.

Nevertheless, I was pleased to graduate and decided to make

the most of the circumstances. In the absence of my parents, who could not get a visa to attend graduation, I invited the Murphys to join me in the celebration. Mrs. Murphy, who had driven me to Cambridge during freshman week, could not make it, but Mr. Murphy eagerly showed up.

The night before graduation, I joined one of my roommates and his family for a sumptuous dinner at the Charles Hotel. The rest of the evening involved hopping from party to party and getting back to Winthrop in time for a brief nap. The next day, I woke up around six to shower and put on my cap and gown and join the Winthrop procession to the Yard. After an hour-long chapel service and a rousing speech by the Reverend Peter Gomes, the university chaplain, we joined the rest of our sixteen hundred classmates in front of Memorial Church for the three-hour commencement service. Then we headed back to Winthrop House to receive our diplomas and eat lunch. Finally we shuffled back to the Yard once again—to listen to Vice President Al Gore, the commencement speaker.

Chapter Eight

August 1994—The last days of summer were approaching. The sun was warming the morning air. Porter Square was quiet, almost a world away from the bellowing street musicians and sidewalk cafes of Harvard Square a couple of miles down Mass. Ave. At a small, newly opened restaurant, I was having brunch and looking forward to my budding Sunday morning ritual: completing the *Boston Globe* crossword puzzle. I had gotten good at doing them. As usual, I lifted the front section from the bulky paper for a quick perusal before proceeding to the puzzle. As I scanned the news for the latest on violence in the Sudan, Rwanda, and Bosnia, a brief item caught my eye: "BBC Reporter Killed in Kabul."

The BBC was the most popular news source in Afghanistan, and most Afghans were familiar with the names of its reporters. I began reading the article to find out more: "Mir Weiss, a twenty-five-year-old stringer for the BBC Pashto Service, was shot multiple times . . . his bullet-riddled body was found the next day along a roadside . . ."

Could it be Mirweis, my cousin? I couldn't be sure—I didn't want to be sure—no last name was mentioned. Leaving my plate untouched, I settled the check and dashed home to call the *Globe* for more information. After being transferred several times and getting nowhere, I decided to call the Boston bureau of the Associated Press. Over the phone the editor on duty read out the full story and confirmed that the journalist in question was indeed Mirweis Jalil.

Too distraught to cry, I put down the receiver and just sat on my bed. I wanted to break down but couldn't. I sat there feeling intense pain in my chest. I knew this crippling pain. I had first felt it at the age of ten with the death of my Uncle Kamkay. With the deaths of another uncle and many other relatives and friends over the next decade, the experience became routine: denial followed by conviction that nothing mattered anymore, not my own life nor anyone else's. I decided to call Mirweis's sister, who lived with her Afghan husband in Rockport, north of Boston. She picked up the phone and sounded her cheerful self, no hint of anything amiss. "Oh, Masood Jaan, it was so nice to see you last week. When are you going to visit us again?" I played along. I did not know why no one had called her. Perhaps the family in Pakistan was too busy trying to retrieve the body. Not wanting to be the bearer of bad news, I asked to speak with her husband, Anwar. I quietly told him that Mirweis had been in an accident and that he should get in touch with my uncle as soon as possible.

As I learned a few days later, Mirweis had been killed on the orders of Gulbuddin Hekmatyar, the former mujahideen leader who had become prime minister and was then fighting for control of Kabul. Hekmatyar had been displeased with Mirweis's coverage of his group. They got into a shouting match during an interview on the outskirts of Kabul. Shortly thereafter, Mirweis was dragged out of his car by masked Hekmatyar men, tortured, and shot forty times before his mutilated body was dumped by the side of a country road.

What a way to go down. Not martyred by Soviet bullets, but dead at the hands of fellow Afghans. I'd lost friends and family to infighting but I never imagined it would be my cousin's fate. It was Mirweis who had first encouraged me to join the jihad. He rendered jihad as a great religious obligation, and whenever martyrdom was discussed, he cited it as every Muslim's highest calling, even giggling a bit when he spoke of the rewards that came with it. "Those houris," he once said. "How many of them do you think you can handle? God Almighty is too generous."

Martyrdom is defined broadly in Islam. According to one authentic saying of the Prophet, anyone who dies in pain is a martyr, even someone who "dies of diarrhea." But while we used to apply the term to the war dead, I struggled over what to call Mirweis when I wrote to his father a week later. I couldn't honestly tell him that he and my aunt should be proud that their son had "laid down his life in the way of God," or worse, congratulate them on the martyrdom of their son. So I began my letter with the Koranic verse, "Verily, to God we belong, and to him shall we return," and went on to quote the poet Sa'di's remark that a man with a good name never dies. I went on to tell my uncle how much Mirweis's death pained me personally. I told him that Mirweis had served his country with sword and pen and that we should all be proud. Throughout my letter I avoided the words *martyr* and *martyrdom,* but I couldn't help signing off with a classic verse from the Koran regarding martyrs: "And never think that those who were slain in the cause of God are dead; they are alive and well provided for by their Lord, pleased with His bounties and rejoicing."

As I rummaged through a folder of old letters and photographs looking for my uncle's address, I came across a couple of graying photos: one of Mirweis standing at the top of a ditch, not far from Tora Bora, catching a mortar round thrown to him by someone next to me. His face is bright with a smile. Another picture showed a massive explosion. "To my dear brother Masood," he'd written on the back. "A SCUD blast outside Jalalabad." In the accompanying letter, he'd asked me to look into a way for him to move to the States to study orthopedic surgery. I couldn't help feeling guilty. Would he still be alive had I pursued his request? If I had any interest in going back to Afghanistan in the middle of the factional fighting, Mirweis's death put an end to it. Spared of martyrdom in the jihad, the last thing I wanted to do was go back and be killed by a fellow Afghan. My parents couldn't agree more.

After graduation I wrote a letter to my mother and father, telling them of my plan for a yearlong road trip across America before entering the workforce. In truth, I had been turned down for foreign travel and study fellowships and was at a loss for what to do. While I'd been steeped in life at Harvard, I wanted to be different, not another Harvard student who worked at an investment bank or consulting firm. So when my friend Michael, a classmate and Spee brother, suggested that we take a road trip and make a movie about it, I agreed. I even read Jack Kerouac's *On the Road* to help prepare myself for the journey.

In October, after a summer working at the library to save money, I climbed into a 1987 Oldsmobile station wagon that Michael had bought for our journey, and headed west. It took us almost an hour to get from his parents' house in Queens to the freeway.

"An inauspicious start," Michael deadpanned.

Within hours we were in southern Pennsylvania, the gateway to America's heartland, skipping industrial Pittsburgh in favor of a circuitous but scenic route to Illinois. I'd always taken Pennsylvania to be a northern state but realized it was more western than northern. We made good time and arrived at the border of Illinois by sundown.

Chicago was our destination, and by the time we drove into the city the next evening and met up with two Harvard friends, we were ready to relive our college days. The Windy City, smaller than New York but bigger than Boston, had plenty to offer by way of entertainment for two young adventurers, and Michael and I took full advantage of it. But by the end of the week, I realized that I'd blown nearly five hundred dollars, or one-sixth of my budget. This was no way to spend a year on the road. So Michael and

I decided to avoid the temptations of big cities, zip across the country, and get to Motel DuBeau, a youth hostel in Flagstaff, Arizona, that we'd both visited during our stints with Let's Go.

DuBeau, a turn-of-the-century motel once popular with gangsters, now catered to young European backpackers visiting the Grand Canyon and other attractions in northern Arizona. The proprietor, Mike, was a slight man with a burned face and a crooked nose. He let us stay for free on account of our positive reviews of the hostel in Let's Go.

The new plan was to spend a few weeks in Flagstaff while exploring northern Arizona and then move on. But I was running out of money and Michael decided to return to New York. I moved into a one-bed minitrailer, left behind by an Australian backpacker on the hostel's back lot. To make some pocket money, I took over the kitchen and cooked five-dollar dinners of pasta or tacos for hungry backpackers.

If DuBeau had a theme song, it would be "Hotel California" by the Eagles: you can check out any time you like, but you can never leave. In fact many backpackers who intended to stay only a night or two at most found themselves spending a week or longer. I couldn't blame them. There was the Grand Canyon, a mere ninety miles north, a natural wonder that could not possibly be explored in only a day or two or three, except, of course, by American tourists in their trademark white T-shirt and pants. Then there was Monument Valley, farther northwest, on the border with Utah, a starkly beautiful gem of red and blue rock formations, its every ridge and cliff made famous by John Ford in his classic westerns. Finally there were the Indian reservations, sad and lifeless but a curiosity nonetheless, and the "holistic" red rocks of Sedona halfway between Flagstaff and Phoenix. Many visitors tried to pack all this into one day, but at the end of a long hike, on returning to a festive party at the hostel, they realized they needed more time.

More than anything else I enjoyed going to the Grand Canyon, the mirror image of Afghanistan's Hindu Kush mountain range. It took me several visits to get used to the way it opened up, or rather opened down, in the middle of the desert, as the ground caved in and the red rock walls rose up a mile apart. Looking at it was breathtaking, and I couldn't get enough of it. In the eight months I lived in Flagstaff, I visited the canyon dozens of times, often taking backpackers with me or joining a group of local hikers I'd befriended.

When I wasn't visiting the canyon or Sedona or the Petrified Forest or Monument Valley, I took long walks in the woods of the San Francisco Mountains on the edge of Flagstaff. Sometimes I brought Buddy, the hostel's golden retriever, who had adopted me as his companion, and we would play hide and seek. As he led the way, I'd throw a tennis ball up the trail, and when he ran after it, I'd hide behind an aspen. It was a game I enjoyed playing and might have won except for Buddy's impeccable sense of smell.

As winter turned to spring, and spring to summer, and summer began to wind down, I started to wonder how long I could idle away in Flagstaff. My yearlong "practical training" visa, which was granted to all graduating college students, was running out. Returning to Afghanistan was not an option. In the year since Mirweis's murder, the war had taken a turn for the worse with a new warring group, the Taliban, entering the fray.

The Taliban described their mission as putting an end to anarchy and establishing an Islamic government in the country. The press at the time made the Taliban sound like little more than a fringe movement. The big fight was going on in Kabul where government forces, led by Commander Masood, fought a varied and shifting alliance of militia groups. In a statement that would come to haunt him one day, the Afghan president at the time, Burhanuddin Rabbani, called the nascent Taliban "angels of peace." He made the statement at a time when the Taliban were fighting one of his enemies on their way to capture Kabul. Rabbani didn't foresee what was coming, and the West, preoccupied with Bosnia and other conflicts, couldn't have cared less.

I didn't know what to do next. Moving to New York, where many of my friends from Harvard lived, was the only choice that made sense. They could help me get a job, I thought. But the thought unnerved me. Michael had moved into a family apartment in Queens and begun writing, but most of my friends who had moved there had high-powered jobs at investment banks and consulting firms. I knew I'd have a hard time landing a conventional job. Except for my summer of writing for Let's Go, I had little to show by way of work experience. But I needed a job to avoid deportation, and as fun as Flagstaff was, I decided to fly to New York, with three hundred dollars in my pocket.

I was twenty-six, young but unambitious. Money had never enticed me. In fact, an aversion to wealth and status was the reason I'd decided not to become the doctor or engineer that my parents had wished I would be.

Moving to New York is like going to a fancy party with a cash bar: you get to enjoy it in accordance with the contents of your wallet. I'd visited the city several times while at Harvard, during the infamous Dinkins era, and now I immediately noticed the changes the city had undergone with its new mayor, Rudolph Giuliani. Gone were the hookers and pimps and drug dealers that brazenly operated in Times Square and the drunks that urinated on filthy subway platforms.

Giuliani described his work as urban renaissance. Despite the visible improvements, certain things hadn't changed. New York was still about money, the Wild West of the American East, where you moved to make your fortune, where people made money on Wall Street and bought fancy apartments, dined at chichi restaurants, and sent their kids to prestigious schools.

Of course, for many Afghans and Pakistanis and Indians and Bangladeshis, the process of settling in New York involved little more than flying to JFK, driving to Queens or Brooklyn, and taking a job at a friend or relative's business. But mine wasn't an immigrant's experience. I was in New York, not to make it big, but for the sole purpose of avoiding deportation while gaining experience that I could bring back to Afghanistan one day. The love and dedication I had for Afghanistan and my desire to return home still burned within me.

I spent my first night in the city with a college roommate, the second with another college friend, and the rest of the week with Michael in Queens. By the second week, with my pocket money down to less than a hundred dollars and no job prospects in sight, I began to worry that I'd be deported before I found a job. I called Nancy, an old friend from New Jersey. In the years since first arriving in the States, I'd grown close to her family. Tall and beautiful with a charming smile, Nancy took me under her wing. She gave me small projects at the book packaging company she ran. The earnings gave me enough money to make ends meet, but I needed a full-time job to be able to stay in the country.

Other friends and acquaintances wanted to help me too, and they all had their own ideas about what I should be doing. A new girl-friend suggested I get a job in security or intelligence, or even bet-ter, in the CIA. A young lawyer suggested I tweak my résumé to get a job as a paralegal. A former banker promised to help me land a big job on Wall Street, but he dropped dead before making good on his promise. And then there was the prominent journalist and fellow Harvard grad who encouraged me to "think big" and write an essay about my experiences, which he was certain would be published in a national magazine.

As weeks then months passed, my failure to find permanent work began to concern me. Realizing my lack of employment was dire, I rang the editor of a local Afghan newspaper I'd picked up at a restaurant in Queens. I told Nisar Zoori I'd recently graduated from Harvard and wanted to meet with him to see if we could work together.

"Oh sure," Mr. Zoori said. He sounded pleasantly surprised. "It would be an honor. Yes, let's meet to talk about it."

We met a few blocks from the studio apartment that doubled as his office, at a popular Afghan restaurant on Queens Boulevard. He was a stocky man and looked ten years older than his age of forty-five. A typical Afghan émigré, I thought. Right off the bat, he began talking about the life he'd been forced to leave behind in Kabul.

Born into a prominent Kabul family, Zoori attended the prestigious Hibibia Lycee, Afghanistan's first high school, and had planned to attend university. But the war forced him out of the country, and while he managed to take a couple of college classes in exile in America, he continued to chafe about his circumstances.

"In Afghanistan, my family ran a large publishing house," he said without looking me in the eye. "Here I have nothing. The newspaper is the only thing I've got here. It keeps me alive."

I eyed the recent issues of the newspaper he'd laid on the table.

"You should be proud of the work you do," I said, trying to boost his ego. "It's a great service to the community."

Mr. Zoori put down his spoon. "You see," he said, his voice rising, "Afghanistan is burning." He went on to explain that his day job didn't leave him enough time to report Afghanistan's tragedy.

I asked what he did for a living, besides running the newspaper. He was evasive.

"I work in Long Island City," he said.

Guessing he must be holding a menial job, I didn't want to press the issue. As we left the restaurant and walked to his apartment, I was glad I hadn't asked him for a job. The place was dark and dank, littered with books and graying copies of *Time* and *Newsweek* and the *New York Times*.

He put me to work right away, handing me a copy of a *New York Times* story to translate into Farsi and type up on his late-model IBM desktop with a green screen. When I was ready to leave, Mr. Zoori didn't pay me, but I had gotten a nice meal out of the meeting. For the next few months, when I wasn't doing chores or running errands for Nancy, I'd take the subway to Mr. Zoori's apartment, pulling an occasional all-nighter to get the newspaper out, for which he did pay me a little.

Mr. Zoori seemed to know everyone in the Afghan community and in exile-newspaper circles, but he denounced their increasingly partisan politics. More than Afghans in Afghanistan, activists in the Afghan diaspora had split along political and ethnic lines, most supporting the Tajik president Rabbani but a small and growing minority backing the emerging Taliban. He considered himself above ethnic labels, something we shared, and split his time between rival mosques.

As if to condemn the ethnic tensions spilling over into Afghan communities in the States, he would often say, "Afghanistan is burning. We don't need to add fuel to the fire."

There were plenty of stories to translate out of the *Times* and the *Washington Post* and *Time* and *Newsweek* and reprint (illegally, I realize in retrospect), but Mr. Zoori had a hard time attracting advertisers to buy even half a page for a hundred dollars. The only regular advertiser was a local Afghan hairdresser whose infectious smile was displayed in her monthly ad.

"She likes her picture," Mr. Zoori said as we put together an issue. He almost smiled when he added, "I made her beautiful."

At the end of each visit, whether it involved a few hours or a two-day sleepover, Mr. Zoori would hand me a twenty-dollar bill, always apologetic. "I wish I could give you more," he'd say. I wanted to turn it down but had to accept, realizing I needed it as much as he did. It could get me through a day or two.

My work at the newspaper paid other dividends. When Ramadan ended, I wrote an article about the post-Ramadan festivities known as Eid al-Fitr for a English language community newspaper in Queens. It was my first newspaper credit, and it came in handy when I applied for a job at a bond industry trade publication and later at AP/Dow Jones, the international business wire run jointly by the Associated Press and Dow Jones. At the time, AP/Dow Jones (subsequently renamed Dow Jones Newswires) hired a couple dozen journalists a year and trained them in various business beats before shipping them out to foreign bureaus. It was the fastest track I could find to become a foreign correspondent.

I sent in my résumé and was called for an interview and later for a test, a daylong affair common among major wire services. In a couple of months I was offered a position. It came just in time—I had only days left on my visa.

Within months the Taliban overran Kabul. The embattled government forces, led by President Rabbani and Defense Minister Masood, withdrew without putting up a fight. Although it wasn't clear at the time, a new chapter in the war had opened.

An earlier phase had begun after the Soviet withdrawal in 1989. It was commonly and incorrectly labeled a civil war by Western journalists and experts alike. It was not a civil war in the conventional sense of a conflict between major groups of the population within a country. Prior to 1989 the battle lines were clearly drawn: on one side stood the Soviet occupation army and its Afghan Communist allies. On the other side were the mujahideen, loosely organized into seven major groups (and eight Shiite ones), sometimes fighting one another but more often fighting the Soviets.

After the Soviet withdrawal, and especially after the collapse of the Communist regime in 1992, all that changed. No longer united by a common enemy, the mujahideen turned on one another as they scrambled for control of territory. The laws of the jungle determined which group controlled which pocket of the country. In the southeast around Jalalabad two factions of the Hezb-I Islami, including the one to which I belonged, held sway in an uneasy alliance. In the southwest things were more chaotic, with control of Kandahar changing hands every month or so among three opposing groups. Control of the north was divided among three groups, with Uzbek warlords ruling the cities of Mazar-I Sharif and Sheberghan in the center, and two factions of Jamiat-I Islami (later known as the Northern Alliance) operating in the east and west.

In this struggle for power, Kabul was the biggest prize and became the epicenter of factional fighting. In theory there was a unity government in Kabul, made up of members of the seven Peshawar-based mujahideen groups as well as an alliance of Shiite resistance parties. (Hamid Karzai, the current president of Afghanistan, rose to power through his association with one of the Peshawar groups.) No sooner had the government assumed power than its internal factions burst into open conflict. Unsurprisingly, the ensuing fight for control of Kabul pitted three of the most ideologically extreme mujahideen groups against one another: the Jamiat, led by Rabbani and Masood; the Hezb, led by Prime Minister Hekmatyar; and the Ittihad, headed by Sayyaf. Occasionally in alliance with the Shiites or Uzbeks, these groups fought street battles and exchanged artillery fire for the next two years. By the time the Taliban rolled in, these rival factions had killed upward of fifty thousand civilians, bombed the city to rubble, and exhausted themselves.

The country had essentially broken into several power centers. While the epicenter of the war was Kabul, most mujahideen stayed out of the fighting in the capital, content with controlling their own domains in various cities. My group controlled eastern Afghanistan, including Jalalabad, with Commander Hajji Qadir serving as governor and Commander Engineer Mahmoud running Jalalabad University. But when the Taliban advanced on the city, Hajji Qadir and Engineer Mahmoud virtually handed over the keys to the militia before running for their lives.

Weeks later I learned that Engineer Mahmoud, my Tora Bora commander, had been killed during the Taliban assault on Jalalabad. I was devastated. His death had received only a cryptic line in a wire story. It was sad to see a key mujahideen commander, a man who once led more than ten thousand fighters, die with hardly any recognition. When I called my parents, they seemed relieved that the mujahideen had been forced out of Kabul, but they were under no illusion that the war had ended.

Father said philosophically. "This is a lull masquerading as peace."

Then I asked him about Engineer Mahmoud. Father said he didn't know how he had been killed. Rumors about the circumstances of his death abounded. Some said the Taliban had killed him; others that drug lords operating in Jalalabad had ordered the hit. But what I confirmed, much later, was hardly surprising: he'd been killed by a personal enemy, ambushed while driving toward the Pakistan border with a couple of comrades. I was heartbroken that another of my heroes had failed to become a martyr. I didn't want to think about how many enemies he'd made over the years or how much blood he had on his hands. To me he was still the tough and honorable commander, hopping from post to post in the heat of battle, carrying himself with poise and dignity. I'd written to him a couple of times since I left the country, and when he'd become provost of Jalalabad University, I had thoughts of joining him there.

With the Taliban in power, the country was effectively divided. But that did not appear to have much effect on people's ability to travel. When fighting erupted in the north, some of my relatives who had fled Kabul during the height of the fighting moved back. Others joined a new stream of refugees pouring into Pakistan. Many came from Sheberghan where they'd enjoyed relative peace during the decades of Soviet occupation and the post-Soviet fighting that swept much of the rest of the country.

"Everyone is here," Mother would say over the phone whenever I called her. "Your aunts and uncles and cousins. No one left in Sheberghan. When are you going to visit us? How long are you going to make us wait?"

"Soon," I'd reply. Soon.

Then, in August 1998, al-Qaeda operatives struck two American embassies in East Africa, an event followed within a week by retaliatory missile strikes against Sudan and Afghanistan. I was afraid that it was the start of a new American assault on Afghanistan, but it was the height of the Monica Lewinsky scandal, and many dismissed the strikes as "wag the dog."

A week later Nancy called.

"I don't know if you heard, but Carlos's body was found in Peshawar," she said.

"What?" Carlos Mavroleon. My friend Karimullah.

"No one knows what happened," she added.

"Oh shit" is what I said and sank into despair. Once again I was overcome with the loss of someone dear to me. Karimullah had been dead forty-eight hours, probably longer. He'd flown to Pakistan a couple of days after the missile strikes, on assignment for *60 Minutes,* and had gotten as far as the border town of Miranshah in Waziristan. Posing as a doctor, he'd sneaked into a hospital and interviewed several Pakistani militants wounded during the attack on a training camp across the border in Afghanistan. But his bold scheme to film the aftermath of the missile strikes unraveled as agents of ISI (Pakistani Military Intelligence, which operated the training camps) discovered him, threw him in a jail, and after a twenty-four-hour interrogation put him in a minivan bound for Peshawar. The next day, according to a local press account, his body was discovered slumped over a bed in a dingy Peshawar hotel next to bags of heroin and used syringes. A death by drug overdose did not make sense to me because I thought that Karimullah had kicked his heroin addiction ten years earlier. Could it have been a hit ordered by ISI to silence him? After all, the ISI had a history of ruthlessly crushing its critics.

I hadn't seen Karimullah in several years nor spoken to him since Mirweis's murder in 1994. In the meantime he'd become a roving war correspondent covering the Sudan, Somalia, and Bosnia, among other conflicts. And while our paths had crossed only a handful of times in recent years, I had kept our jihad days close to my heart: Karimullah entering the smoke-filled tent in the White Mountains at our first meeting, looking like Lawrence of Arabia; Karimullah cracking jokes about becoming a martyr by the side of a little creek outside Jalalabad; Karimullah warbling the call to prayer at a village mosque in Kunar Valley and then leading a small group of us in predawn prayers.

His death, at the age of forty, left me numb. To grieve you need to be able to feel, but I could not even bring myself to cry. Then the inevitable self-recriminations: Why he and not I? Why Karimullah with his sunny disposition and zest for life? Why were so many of my friends falling, all years after the jihad? First it was Mirweis. Then it was Engineer Mahmoud. Now Karimullah.

"May God lessen our grief" had become a common refrain in Afghanistan, and so I prayed as I organized a memorial service in New York and tracked down his many friends. Whatever the circumstance of his death, Karimullah, like Mirweis, Engineer Mahmoud, and countless others, had been willing to sacrifice his life for a good cause, and he needed to receive due recognition. When I met Karimullah's grieving mother, sister, and brothers, I didn't know what to say. His younger brother Nicholas was convinced Karimullah had been murdered, although the rest of the family seemed less sure. In an attempt to assuage their grief, I told them that Karimullah had not died in vain. I for one owed my life and everything I had accomplished to him.

The following summer, I decided it was time to go home. It was an overdue journey. Afghanistan seemed a lost cause, and reading the daily accounts of the war and the world's indifference to it made it difficult to hope for a peaceful future. But while I'd come to terms with my inability to serve my country, I realized that my prolonged stay in America had taken a different toll on my life: it had driven a wedge between me and my family. The longer I lived in America, and the more at home I felt there, the more removed

I felt from my family. It didn't hurt that a semblance of peace had returned under the Taliban, a quiet I wanted to experience first-hand as a way of deciding once and for all if I should settle down in America or stay in Afghanistan.

To prepare for my visit, I spent the summer growing a beard. It was more than a whimsical effort. Under the Taliban, Afghanistan had become a nation of bearded men, and a religiously correct beard served as a passport into the country. I'd read and heard all sorts of crazy things about the Taliban's enforcement of the facial hair requirement, how they measured the length of a beard with a Coke can, how the vice and virtue police issued certificates of authenticity. Some of these were undoubtedly legends. Nevertheless, a beard shorter than a Coke can, I was told, was punishable with flogging and a week at a religious enlightenment center.

Over the phone from Peshawar, Father, still a clean-shaven man, told me not to worry. The Taliban were lenient with Afghans visiting from abroad, he said. Twenty-five days of growth would be more than enough. As hirsute as the next Afghan, I could easily grow a good beard in that time. I didn't want a short, clipped beard that would be the laughing stock of Peshawar. I wanted a real beard, the kind I had when I first moved to America. As I let my beard grow during the unusually hot summer, I drew more than a few amused looks from friends and strangers. One day in the elevator at work, a colleague, unaware of my plans, wryly remarked, "Hell of a time to grow a beard!" I only smiled. How odd, I thought, the comment would sound to someone in Afghanistan, where facial hair was not determined by season but was a legal requirement enforced under penalty of imprisonment.

When I disembarked at Peshawar International Airport and stepped into the heat wave, I remembered what my colleague had said. But I liked my beard. It would easily get me into Afghanistan —I looked like a shabby Afghan refugee. Though I was wearing jeans and a white, open-collar shirt, I looked somewhat scruffier than my fellow passengers, most of whom were actually clean-shaven.

In the crowded arrival lobby, I spotted Mother, Father, my little sister Lachi, and several other relatives. Mother and Lachi had tears in their eyes. Father broke into a smile when he saw me. As I made my way around the rope, Mother, wearing a long white chador over a pink dress, ran up to me and held me in her arms, tears running down her face. Her skin was darker than I remembered, and she had circles under her charcoal eyes. As we embraced I realized how much I had missed her, and I couldn't help shedding tears of my own. Mother had dyed her hair in an effort to make her look like the mother I had left ten years back. She had also painted her hands with henna—a little over the top, I thought, but I was moved by the celebratory gesture. I learned later that she had been telling everyone she'd probably faint on sight of me.

I walked up to Father and gently kissed his hands, and he responded with a warm kiss on my head. He looked happy. He was not a man given to emotion or sentimentality, and his affection toward my sisters and me had always been formal and detached. But now, at the age of sixty-five, with his hair gray and his pink cheeks sunken, Father had taken on a grandfatherly air. When I last saw him, he had started losing his teeth—thanks to a lifetime of smoking cigarettes and chewing *naswar* snuff—but now he wore a full set of dentures. Standing next to Father, Lachi was fidgeting and wiping tears with her embroidered white chador elegantly wrapped around her head. I held her in my arms and kissed her several times. She was a grown-up woman, no longer the little sister I used to lavish with candy bars and ice cream. But I couldn't help thinking of her as my little sister, especially when she affectionately called me "Laalaa"—Big Brother.

We rented a large van and drove up to my parents' bungalow in Hayatabad, a suburb of Peshawar populated mostly by well-off

Afghan refugees. When we arrived, Uncle Shah Lala's wife walked up and tossed a fistful of candies over me, a custom traditionally reserved for newlywed couples. Mother followed by tossing a handful of Pakistani rupee bills. The pomp and circumstance was a little too much.

Inside the house, more relatives awaited me: Uncle Shah Lala, Mother's diminutive older brother; his two daughters and young son visiting from Siberia; and several others I didn't immediately recognize. As we sat down for a sumptuous late breakfast of eggs and homemade pastries, I told them about the corrupt immigration officer who'd held me up at the airport. I should have known better, Uncle Shah Lala proclaimed. I should have just slipped a five-dollar bill into my passport and walked out.

He was incredulous that I got through immigration without paying a bribe. But there was more to the look on his face. Like my other relatives, he seemed in awe of me. I could feel it in their gazes and body language and the manner in which they addressed me. Everyone called me Masood Jaan, a somewhat formal term of endearment, and addressed me in the formal second person plural. I had become a beloved stranger. It was a formality created in part by the passage of time. I tried to put myself in their shoes and imagine what could be so dazzling about me. Was it all the bundles of money they thought I must have brought from America? But I hadn't even taken out my skinny wallet with its handful of hundred-dollar bills. It couldn't be my looks, that was for sure. Having changed into traditional clothes, and fingering my beard, I did not look like an Afghan-American. Perhaps it was my paunch—a sign of good living and, if it was large enough, even of wealth. But my potbelly was hardly big enough for me to pass off as a khan or *khojayeen* or any other wealthy man. Perhaps it was because they knew (and my beard confirmed) that I had once taken part in the jihad. Was it that I had an American degree? Was it Harvard? Had they even heard of Harvard? Whatever the case, I was seduced by their mesmerized looks and formal mannerisms. I even tried to flaunt my knowledge and education by giving them a rather incoherent explanation of digital technology. They seemed lost.

The next day, still jet-lagged and sleepy, I decided to take a break from the nonstop stream of relatives and family friends and other well-wishers who came over to wish my parents "bright eyes" and to offer them loaves of naan bread, an age-old Afghan custom for greeting new arrivals. I was lying on Lachi's bed when Father knocked on the door and walked in. His face bore the biggest smile I'd ever seen on it. I moved to get up.

"Don't get up," he said standing in the doorway.

"No, no, I'm fine. I'm just a little tired," I said. "By the grace of God, we have a lot of guests."

"In our house, it's like this every day," he said.

He walked over and quietly sat down on the bed, and before I knew it we were both leaning back against the wall, our legs swinging from the bed, chatting about life, man to man, father to son.

"You know, my son," he said softly, gazing at the undecorated wall, "there is a purpose to life."

I was jolted. He'd rarely called me "my son," and I realized he wanted to make amends. I wanted to listen.

"When we're young," he continued, "we disobey our elders and parents, and our only purpose in life is to have fun."

I said nothing. Father was clearly talking about himself. He knew nothing about how much fun I'd had during my college and postcollege days.

"You're a grown-up man. Your mother and I are very proud of you and everything you've achieved. I'm sure you've given some thought to your future. Your mother is worried about you living alone, and I'm concerned too."

"I know," I said.

As a boy I had resented my father for his stern discipline and his proclivity to lecture me, but now I listened with the eagerness

of a loyal friend. Without saying so, Father wanted to put the past
behind us and treat me like an adult. For the first time in my life,
I realized how much I admired him. He was a man of intelligence
and integrity. A straight talker, he did not mince words and never
bowed before authority. And as rebellious as he had been in his
teens, he'd inherited his own father's uncompromising moral
scruples.

"I have one piece of advice for you," he said. "In marriage, the
key to success is compatibility—social compatibility, economic
compatibility, and intellectual compatibility. You want someone
who is your equal, not someone who is more intelligent or less
intelligent than you, not someone poorer or richer than you, and
not someone a class below or above you."

"I agree," I said.

I got up and kissed his hands.

"Now let's go out and see if the butcher has arrived," he said as
we left the room.

The butcher looked serious as he sharpened his knife in the front
yard. "*Allahu Akbar,*" he muttered as he pressed the blade against
the throat of the terror-stricken lamb. It took him only seconds
to slit the throat, sever the windpipe, and decapitate the animal.
As I looked at the dying lamb through the viewfinder of my camcorder, I thought it would make for good footage to show my
American friends. A film about Afghanistan wouldn't be complete
without a lamb slaughter. I hadn't seen one of these slaughters in
ten years. In America, I told my relatives, you couldn't kill an animal in your backyard or in front of your house. "Animal cruelty,"
I said sarcastically. Afghans knew all about kindness to animals,
but when I said "Animal cruelty," even my father looked puzzled.

Having severed the head, the butcher skinned the animal and
cut up the meat, making three piles: one for the poor, one for
relatives, and one for us. This was the *khayraat* in my honor that
Mother had promised over the phone. A *khayraat* is a sacrificial

meal given on various occasions such as a recovery from sickness or a close call with death. But this *khayraat* would serve a more practical purpose: it was a welcoming party designed to attract as many eligible girls in the extended family as possible.

The party began early that evening. The guests arrived two by two—the girls were escorted by their mothers. They wore their most expensive dresses, the kind they wore at weddings. I greeted them politely as they walked in, all the while trying to look disinterested. The first girl that caught my eye wore a white dress. She had sad green eyes. As she and her aunt made their way into the living room, I asked a cousin who she was. He told me and said, "She's seventeen but she's no good," adding that he'd fill me in on the whole thing later.

Mirweis, my younger first cousin from Sheberghan, and Ahmadullah, a second cousin, seemed to know the dirt about every girl in the family. I didn't trust their judgment, but I knew that reputation mattered a great deal in Afghan culture, and what these two men told me about these girls, whether true or false, mattered as much as what I thought about them. And if I was to marry an Afghan girl, I'd better listen to them as much as to my heart.

Dinner was served as the last guests trickled in. Women and children gathered on the floor around large tablecloths with floral patterns. The dozen or so men ate on the verandah. Nowrooz, Mother's cousin, had prepared two large pots of my favorite dish, *qabili palow* (rice with lamb, carrots, and raisins). He had also cooked spinach, beef stew, and eggplant *boorani*—dishes commonly served at parties. There were crates of Fanta and Pepsi, which were less common. But this was my party, and I wanted to make sure the guests were satisfied. When we ran out of drinks, I handed Mirweis some money to get more.

When the meal was finished, two musicians whom Ahmadullah had hired for the occasion showed up with their instruments. The harmonium player was wearing a crumpled green sports jacket over a gray vest and white shirt. He had a little moustache that did not quite serve the intended purpose of giving him a manly look. The tabla player was clean-shaven and quiet.

They started with a slow song but worked their way to folk dance tunes. When the girls got up to dance, I stood in a corner and started filming, zooming in on several who called for a closer, postparty examination: the girl in the white dress; the tall, dark-complexioned twenty-two-year-old second cousin with beautiful black eyes in a dark blue dress; the plump, fair-skinned eighteen-year-old in a blue dress who was my father's favorite; the neighbor's daughter who seemed to have danced since her birth; and finally, two slightly chubby sisters, the older of whom was Father's second choice for me.

Sitting next to the musicians, Ahmadullah's two younger brothers, Fawad and Jawad, kept one eye on the entertainers and one on the girls. The rest of the male guests stayed outside on the verandah, but I felt I should take an occasional peek inside. All the girls knew I was single, and while they surely realized I was checking them out, they feigned ignorance. Some of them were too shy to dance for more than thirty seconds or so. But my old cousin Laylaa Jaan forced everyone else to dance for at least one full song. "No exceptions," she announced.

The party went on past four in the morning. By then, only twenty of us were left. A couple of relatives passed out on the porch. Nowrooz was snoring on a straw cot. I was about to stand up from the floor when I heard a knock on the door. Nowrooz answered it. Then we heard voices. The police. Mother pushed me into a back room, and I saw two cops with AK-47s storm in. As I slipped into the back room, I could see one of them hitting the harmonium player with the butt of his rifle. Some of the girls came into the room. Embarrassed to cower in the room, I made a move to get out but they said they didn't want me to get arrested. I could hear shouting and hooting outside the door. The police officers asked who owned the house. An uncle told him the owner was not around. The cops told him they were getting complaints from neighbors. It was prayer time. Hadn't he heard the call to prayer chanted over the mosque loudspeaker? But that was not all. They said they heard alcohol was being served. Where were the bottles? Where was the owner?

In the chaos that ensued, the teenage tabla player took off, leaving behind one of his shoes. The cops managed to get the harmonium player and Ahmadullah, however, and put them in the paddy wagon parked outside. As they left the house, I emerged from my hiding place and walked to the front door. Laylaa Jaan was scolding the cops, trying to grab one of the officers' rifles.

"You have violated our sanctuary," she screamed. "How could you break into a house full of women without permission? Is this how Pashtun men treat their women? Have you no shame? Where is your sense of honor?"

Meanwhile, Ahmadullah and the harmonium player jumped out of the van and sprinted away while the other police officer relieved himself across the street. As the cops searched for them, Uncle Khoja Agha went out to try to retrieve their instruments. He came back half an hour later empty-handed.

"The police said they wanted money," he explained. "They wanted a couple thousand rupees"—the equivalent of twenty dollars—"but I bargained down to a thousand. But they wouldn't give me the instruments. Someone has to go to the police station tomorrow to pick them up. That will probably cost another thousand."

This was the price of living in Pakistan. In exchange for enjoying the relative freedom of their adopted country, my relatives had to accept police harassment and corruption. They were not happy about it. Some lived off money sent by relatives in the West, and many were desperately trying to move to the West. And all of them were waiting out the war in exile.

I asked them what they thought about the Taliban. They all had strong opinions of course and, knowing I was a journalist, jostled to air their views. To some, the Taliban were puppets of

Pakistan. To others, they were doing the bidding of American oil companies. Still others saw them as just another power hungry, corrupt militia looking to enrich themselves.

These were the voices of the educated urban elite who'd fled Taliban rule because they didn't want their women to be covered or their girls to be banned from school. But their views, I thought, were probably not representative of the majority of Afghans, who were enjoying peace under the Taliban. What I found most surprising about the Taliban refugees, however, was that the men had kept their long beards. These men had been clean-shaven when we lived in Sheberghan, and I didn't understand why they hadn't shaved the beards they were forced to grow under the Taliban. They explained that they kept their beards for "emergency purposes"—in case, for example, one of their relatives living in Afghanistan died and they had to attend the funeral at a moment's notice.

The stories I kept hearing about the Taliban only added to my urge to visit Afghanistan and check it out for myself.

But Mother was not keen on the idea. "You're visiting for only three weeks and you want to spend one of them in Afghanistan?"

"I miss Afghanistan," I said. "It's not as if a war is going on there."

I'd learned that some of my relatives had recently moved to Jalalabad and to our ancestral village of Islamabad, and I wanted to visit them, thinking that they—ordinary people living in the sticks—would be better judges of Taliban rule. I told Mother if she didn't want to leave my side, she could tag along. She smiled and said she was game. Worried I'd be stopped by the Taliban and beaten for muddling my prayers, she handed me a prayer book to brush up. I told her not to insult me. Plus I had a letter of introduction from the representative of the Taliban in New York. I'd also met several Taliban ministers while they were touring the United States a couple of years earlier at the behest of Unocal, the American oil company that wanted to build a pipeline in Afghanistan.

* * *

By sundown the next day, our party—Mother, Mirweis, Nowrooz, and I—arrived at Islamabad by hired car, having endured none of the harsh treatment that relatives had warned me about. A river separates the village from the road, but the bridge had been reduced to hunks of concrete with steel rods sticking out. The river was larger and the water muddier than I'd remembered from my childhood visit with Grandpa Agha.

Nearly a dozen boys and girls screamed at us from across the river. I couldn't make out what they were saying.

"They're saying the river is about to flood," Nowrooz explained. "We should hurry across."

Nowrooz told one of the boys to send word of our arrival up to the village. We rolled up our pants and started across the river. It was more than fifty feet wide at this point and knee-deep. Holding Mother's hand, Nowrooz led the way. Mirweis had never been to Islamabad, and as he struggled through the water, he started griping and deadpanned, "Here is our beautiful smelly ancestral land."

I had to agree with him. Most of the trees had been cut down. The fields lying between the village and the river were barren, ravaged by three years of drought. Several gray hills lay to the north, but the snow-capped mountains were too far away to lend the village a scenic backdrop. Islamabad, in short, was not quite the idyllic village I'd remembered. Nevertheless, I was happy to be here for the first time in nearly twenty-five years, and more so at the prospect of visiting relatives—the families of my mother's two uncles.

With Nowrooz leading the way, we walked up the narrow, dung-filled dirt road, past tired cows being led by boys. Within ten minutes we arrived at my two great-uncles' compound. Built at the turn of the century, it was one of the larger compounds in the village and one of the few with a water well, a large verandah, a two-story guesthouse, and a half-acre fruit garden.

The two brothers lived in separate parts of the house. Uncle Qazi, the younger brother, had recently moved in from Sheberghan along with his two wives. He no longer looked the middle-aged former judge that I remembered. Slight and skinny, he had grown deaf and walked with a cane. His beard was completely white. He still wore his trademark silk turban. He kissed me on the head and addressed me formally but seemed genuinely happy to see me. His two wives showered me with kisses and words of kindness and affection. They lived in separate parts of the house with their young children and seemed still to hate each other every bit as much as I remembered.

Uncle Akhundzadeh, the other brother, had moved to Islamabad several years ago. The last time I saw him he served as a preacher and prayer leader at a large mosque in Kabul. An octogenarian, he now looked hunched but still elegant in his white turban wrapped around an embroidered skull cap. His neatly trimmed beard, glowing eyes, and serene face gave him a spiritual look. In fact he was the only member of my extended family who had carried on the clerical tradition. When his brothers left the village to attend the College of Islamic Law in Kabul, Uncle Akhundzadeh had continued to tend to the spiritual needs of the community.

The next day I accompanied Uncle Akhundzadeh to the mosque to offer prayers to the villagers. Islamabad had two mosques, both long run by my extended family: a large congregational mosque about five hundred yards away, which attracted worshippers from outlying villages on Fridays, and a little mud hut mosque not far from Uncle Akhundzadeh's house for regular prayers. It was sunset when I accompanied Uncle Akhundzadeh to the little mosque. The sun was sinking behind the mountains. The sky, bright as the sea all day, abruptly turned gray and released a heavy rain. Uncle Akhundzadeh unfolded his old black umbrella. I took it from him to hold it over his head as we walked down narrow alleyways toward the mosque.

When we arrived, someone was standing under the front awning chanting the call to prayer, holding the thumbs of his outreached hands to his ears, his high-pitched voice muffled by the downpour. We took off our shoes and dashed inside, where about two dozen men were waiting for the start of the prayers. I didn't recognize them. I greeted them with "*Assalamu alaikum,*" and they returned the greeting.

It was dim inside. I helped carry the straw mat inside the mosque where the service was going to be held. Someone had already lit a lantern and placed it on a wooden box to the right of the oval-shaped niche carved into the front wall of the mosque.

Uncle Akhundzadeh stepped to the front of the niche. He straightened his turban and looked to his right and left. We formed three rows behind him and began praying. The service lasted about ten minutes. When it was over, Uncle Akhundzadeh turned around and started murmuring the quiet prayers that typically follow the service. Then he lifted his hands and rubbed his beard. I was about to get up to perform the closing prayer when Uncle Akhundzadeh lifted his hands again.

"Brothers," he said, raising his voice a notch, his eyes looking tired in the flickering orange glow of the lantern. "We have an honored guest here."

A sudden quiet settled on the mosque. No one moved. One or two men who had stood up sat back down, scouring the room for the guest.

I was sitting in the front row, slightly to the left of the niche. To my right sat Nawaid, one of Uncle Akhundzadeh's dozen sons, to my left Mirweis. I shifted in place, holding up my hands, trying not to look conspicuous.

"Masood Jaan is here with us," Uncle Akhundzadeh continued, looking at me. "He's the son of Maulana Sahib, the grandson of Sufi Sahib."

That was all the villagers needed to hear by way of introduction. The son of the Supermullah, the grandson of Sufi Sahib.

I glanced shyly to my left and right, looking at the row of worshippers, and bowing in respect. The men bowed in return.

"Masood Jaan is a very intelligent and well-mannered and pious boy," Uncle Akhundzadeh continued. "Many of you probably don't know this, but he was also a mujahid. He's visiting us from America."

Uncle Akhundzadeh paused to catch his breath.

"Look at him," he said. "By the grace of God, he's kept his beard despite the fact that he's lived in America for ten years. He's visiting us for a few days. On his behalf, let us say a prayer for all the dead and martyrs among us."

Intelligent, a man of proper manners and piety—I was flattered by those words. But a man who'd kept his beard all these years despite the satanic temptations of American society? I said nothing and sat still, resting my hands on my knees. Looking blankly at Uncle Akhundzadeh's wrinkled face, I felt guilty for allowing my beard to become a testament to my piety, or a snare of hypocrisy of which Hafez had spoken.

But embellishment was part of the vernacular: every good man was depicted as a man of God, every bad one as a follower of Satan. While he didn't show it, there was an air of pride in Uncle Akhundzadeh's voice as he introduced me to the villagers. Another member of his educated clan had made it to the West.

Uncle Akhundzadeh finished his prayers and stood, and the congregants gathered around me. Some of them were poor peasants, their faces sunbaked, their hands calloused. They seemed to have come straight from the fields to the mosque. Most of these men were related to me in one way or another. They wanted to know how everyone in my family was, how my father was doing, they wanted to have me over for dinner. They insisted that I accept their invitations. They'd be offended if I turned them down, they said. I told them I was sorry I didn't have enough time, but I promised to stop by the next time I visited Islamabad.

As I left the mosque I felt proud to be an Afghan, proud to be connected to these men. After ten years in America, I'd begun to forget how seriously Afghans took values such as hospitality and generosity. It warmed my heart to see how fiercely these people clung to their culture and sense of honor in the face of abject poverty.

Later that evening, I visited several close relatives to offer prayers and personal condolences on the loss of their loved ones. Before entering each house, Nawaid would tell me who they were and who had died. In many cases I found the relations too distant and complicated to understand. Yet I gladly walked into their houses, drank a cup of tea, said a prayer, made small talk, and walked out, feeling that I had fulfilled my social obligation.

The next day, I went to the village cemetery, stopping by various tombs to offer prayers. There was the surprisingly small tomb of Darwish Khan the Victor, the Central Asian general and founder of Islamabad. Pieces of cloth hung from the tomb's decaying wooden flagpole. The other graves were mostly mounds of earth; only one or two carried tombstones, and a cousin had to point out which relatives were buried under which heaps. There were the graves of my great-grandfather, great-uncles and aunts, and of course more recently built graves of those who had been killed during the war.

My grandfathers' graves were conspicuously absent; my maternal grandfather was buried in Kabul and my paternal grandfather in Sheberghan. As I walked around the cemetery, I realized that while my grandfathers had been men of tradition, they'd left behind Islamabad in search of better lives for themselves and their children, all the while accepting the challenges of modernity that were sweeping the country. I also realized that in many ways my own life was an attempt to emulate theirs.

In Kabul, I went to meet with a top Taliban official for an informal interview and to sound him out on my idea of starting an independent educational radio station. A former Taliban information minister and education minister, Amir Khan Mutaqqi had recently been promoted to cabinet secretary. He was one of Mullah Omar's loyal lieutenants, and one of the Taliban ministers I'd interviewed in New York in 1997. He now lived in the former residence of Sultan Ali Keshtmand, who had been a prime minister in the Communist regime.

The residence occupied an entire block and was located across from the UN compound. There was no street address on the large metal gate. But I could see a wooden guardhouse behind the gate. I knocked and an armed guard opened the door. I told him I was there to see Mutaqqi. Speaking with a northern accent, he said the minister was not around. I handed him my letter of introduction from the Taliban rep in New York and jotted a quick note to the minister. Before Mirweis and I left for a stroll around the neighborhood, the guard asked me what America was like.

"I like it, but it's not our country," I said. "You can't find anyplace like Afghanistan in the world."

The guard smiled and proceeded to tell me that he'd recently learned about some "photocopied forms" going around for sale that could get you to America.

"Is it true that you can go to America with one of those forms?" he asked me excitedly.

I knew what he was talking about: the annual visa lottery that the U.S. Immigration and Naturalization Service held for some ten thousand foreigners from around the world.

"Yes, it is true," I said. "I know several people who have won American residency through the lottery, but of course not everyone wins."

He smiled broadly. He told me his name was Noor Agha. He asked me for my name and address and said that he'd look me up when he came to America. I smiled back and gave him my address. To me, his desire to go to America only confirmed what everyone had been telling me throughout my journey: there was nothing for me to do here. Everyone was trying to get out. But I wondered what Minister Mutaqqi would think if one of his bodyguards left him for America. I wondered if Minister Mutaqqi himself wanted to get to America.

When we came back an hour later, Noor Agha led us into the compound and had another guard take us to the main building. Outside was a volleyball court. Several men sat on the lawn under the shade of some trees. We went up to the residence's second floor and sat in a spartan reception room. Mr. Mutaqqi showed up a few minutes later. He greeted me but didn't seem to recognize me. I told him we'd met in America. He looked puzzled.

"Your beard doesn't look American," he said.

I reminded him about the time we met at the dingy office of the Taliban rep in Flushing, Queens.

"You didn't used to have a beard," he said.

"Yes," I lied, "I did."

He looked even more confused. He was a powerful man who could throw me in jail for past offenses. I didn't want him to think of me as a clean-shaven, earnest young journalist badgering him with questions. I remembered the interview during which he deftly answered my questions. He had been introduced to me by a friend as one of the more moderate and better-educated Taliban officials. When I asked him how they were going to convince the Americans to invest in the pipeline project while a war was still raging in Afghanistan and the political situation was unsettled, he said, "They are businessmen. They don't care about politics."

Now Mutaqqi looked hurried. Several other men were standing in the room. He announced it was time to say the late afternoon prayer and asked me and Mirweis to join him in the "nice mosque" he had built in the residence. I had said my afternoon prayer a couple of hours ago, but no matter.

The mosque was across the hallway in a large room. The floor was covered with straw mats. There was a handsome prayer rug in the center of the room where Mutaqqi stood. The rest of us lined up behind him. When the service was over, Mirweis and I followed Mutaqqi into his office.

It was a small room with a couple of couches, a faux mahogany coffee table, and a large bookshelf filled with religious texts, atop of which sat a copy of the Koran. I took out my tape recorder and placed it on the table. I asked him if it was okay to record our conversation and he nodded. I started off with questions that I knew would please him: Did he think all the talk about the Taliban's abuse of women was enemy propaganda? (Of course.) Would they really open schools for girls some day? (Ditto.) His answers were polite, but he fiddled with his fingers in such a way that it was clear he was uninterested.

Then I asked him a question that was nagging at me: Was it true that Pakistanis and other foreigners were fighting alongside Taliban forces?

With a blank expression on his face, he said it was not true. He granted that some Pakistani classmates of Taliban fighters may have come to Afghanistan, but their number was small and they were not involved in combat.

But what about the Northern Alliance's claims that they had captured many Arab and Pakistani fighters?

Mutaqqi's face darkened and his eyes enlarged with anger.

"It's absolutely not true," he said.

I expected the former information minister to tackle the issue a little more diplomatically.

When I persisted, he shifted in his seat and raised his voice. "Forget about it. Why do you want to know this?"

I was treading in dangerous waters. I realized I wouldn't be able to get more out of him without provoking him further. Meanwhile, Mutaqqi kept glancing at his watch, signaling that my time was up. It was clear that Mutaqqi's answers were disingenuous. I was now convinced that there was some truth to the reports that Arabs and Pakistanis were going into battle to kill Afghans. But in my naiveté I also hoped that reports of foreign terrorists fighting in Afghanistan were exaggerated and that the Taliban would wake up and kick out the terrorists and hand over Osama bin Laden.

I decided to turn off the tape recorder. Muttaqi looked relieved. I then told him that I wanted to discuss something else with him: my idea for a radio station designed to disseminate knowledge to people who couldn't read or write. For example, it would offer simple information to farmers on advances in agriculture technology and give housewives tips on health care and raising children.

"Nothing political," I insisted. "I don't care about politics. I want a radio station that is completely apolitical. I have some ideas about raising funding for it."

Mutaqqi listened carefully and fidgeted. I didn't know how he would respond, but I felt good about the case I was making.

"You have a good idea," he said when I finished. "We have a radio station, and I can arrange for you to do whatever you want. Why don't you work for us?"

This is not what I expected. I knew all about Taliban radio—"the voice of Sharia," it was heavy on religion and Taliban propaganda. I thanked him for the offer but told him that wasn't what I had in mind. I wanted to start an independent radio station that would provide a public service for ordinary Afghans.

"What do you need an independent radio station for?" he asked. He got up from his seat. "We have a radio station, and I'll do everything I can to help you."

The interview was over. So was my little presentation. I realized I had failed to persuade Mutaqqi—he was not persuadable—and felt disappointed. The only idea I had about serving Afghanistan was not going to go anywhere. Mutaqqi confirmed what everyone had been telling me all along: there was nothing for me to do here.

On the way out of the compound, Mutaqqi told me he was about to play volleyball. He said he'd mastered the jump serve. I should come by sometime to watch him play. On the volleyball court, several bearded men were warming up, their turbans and vests lying in a pile on the sidelines. Among the players was Noor Agha, the guard who wanted to desert his patron for America.

Mutaqqi was eager to join them. I thanked him for his time and said good-bye.

The next morning we drove back to Pakistan. I felt disillusioned. The Taliban were in Afghanistan to stay, and I had no choice but to settle down in America. I liked the peace the Taliban had restored, but I wished they were not religious extremists. I also wished they would renounce their alliance with foreign terrorists. But such thoughts were absurd. Without their extremist views and foreign support, the Taliban would not have been the Taliban. I felt there was little hope for my country.

Chapter Nine

September 2001—"Just wait," Uncle Shirinagha muttered ominously. "Now America is going to turn the whole country upside down. You're not going to recognize it."

It was the day after the Twin Towers fell, and Uncle Shirinagha, my mother's witty older brother, was on the phone from Toronto, one of several relatives to check up on me. I still lived and worked in Jersey City, directly across the Hudson River from the World Trade Center. In our expansive eighth-floor newsroom overlooking the river, the usual morning bustle had given way to eerie quiet. Even the most loquacious of the staff had withdrawn into their own thoughts. I checked e-mail and listened to voice messages, trying to account for all my friends in New York. There were some I couldn't.

Uncle Shirinagha was not his usual self, and when he spoke I could sense his fear.

"Just wait and see," he repeated quietly. "America is going to show the Taliban the gates of hell."

What little sympathy I ever had for the Taliban evaporated earlier in 2001, when the militia blasted to rubble Afghanistan's two famed standing Buddhas as part of their effort to rid the country of idols. Of the many atrocities they had committed it was this that revolted me most and left the deepest impression. On the eve of the war, while still living in Herat, Father had enchanted us with the promise of a holiday visit to the massive ancient carvings in the cliffside of the Bamyan Valley, once a vibrant center of Buddhist religion, philosophy, and art. Throughout the war, as we moved from Herat to Sheberghan to Pakistan, and even after I moved to the States, I often dreamed that I'd one day stand at the feet of the Buddhas and marvel at their grandeur and majesty. With the statues gone, so too was my dream. Another part of my home taken away from me.

"These people are barbaric," I told Uncle Shirinagha angrily. "Look what they did to the Buddha statues."

"They are also agents of Pakistan," he said. "They have sold Afghanistan to terrorists."

Indeed, September 11 exposed a dark, sinister face of the Taliban that I had not seen: their close alliance with al-Qaeda. For years I'd viewed the Taliban as a necessary evil, a group of well-intentioned if misguided men trying to bring peace to their country. But they had rented out their country to Osama bin Laden. Although I feared the loss of thousands of my countrymen, I could not help sympathizing with demands for the Taliban's overthrow.

America had come under attack, and there were urgent calls for retribution. On television, pundits in both political parties urged bombing Afghanistan back to the Stone Age as casually as suggesting a fishing expedition. America was not just wounded and mourning; it was extremely angry. The anger was palpable in the voices of TV reporters and commentators, in screaming newspaper headlines and bumper stickers, in the eyes of people on the streets.

The day after the attack, in the lobby of my office building, the express elevator was packed to double capacity. Fifteen people stood shoulder to shoulder. It was as though they wanted to touch each other a day after being evacuated down seven flights of stairs and watching the South Tower crumble to the ground.

In the packed elevator, I spotted a colleague. Knowing I was from Afghanistan, she often cracked jokes about "your mujahideen friends," and on this occasion she had one at the tip of her tongue.

"I knew you did it," she whispered in her accented English, smiling.

On any other day I would have dismissed it as French humor. But on this day, flushed with anger, I wanted to tell her that not I nor anyone I knew had anything to do with it, but I was afraid it would draw more unwanted attention. Her comment had already aroused curious looks, and I couldn't wait to get out of the elevator.

When I got to my desk, I reported the incident to my editor, and the colleague was reprimanded and made to apologize. "I was kidding," she said sheepishly when she stopped by my desk. "Don't take it personally."

"I don't," I said, "and I accept your apology."

Nothing of the sort was going to be tolerated in the newsroom. Not in a civilized corporate environment committed to multiculturalism. We were supposed to keep our feelings to ourselves. If any of my colleagues felt anger toward me, I didn't sense it. On the contrary, they were genuinely sympathetic. A fellow reporter stopped by my cubicle, put his hand on my shoulder, and said quietly, "Everything okay?" Another took me out for a drink and, apparently wanting to put me at ease, mentioned the conspiracy theory then making the rounds that the Israeli Mossad might have orchestrated the attacks.

Later that Wednesday I finally contacted my parents in Peshawar. They were relieved to hear from me.

"I didn't get a wink of sleep last night," Mother cried. "Do you know how many times we tried to call? A hundred times, every hour."

Unable to reach me the day before, my parents had called relatives on the West Coast and in Canada and asked them to try to check on me. Only one got through to me, a cousin in California, and he called them back to tell them I was alive and well.

"Why do you always worry about me so much, Mother? I'm fine. Don't worry about me. Worry about the thousands of innocent people who died."

"I prayed for them, for all of them, and for all the poor widows and orphans."

Her voice trailed. Reluctantly she handed the phone to Father. In the two years since my visit to Pakistan, I'd grown closer to my father and enjoyed talking to him on the phone once or twice a month. He was overjoyed to hear my voice but wanted to know the facts. He peppered me with questions: What is this World Trade Center? Where is it located? How far were you from there when the planes struck?

I reminded him of pictures of the World Trade Center and downtown Manhattan I'd brought along to Peshawar with me.

"The place is still burning," I said. "I can see the smoke."

"Really? That's amazing," is all Father would say in response. He was more interested in analyzing what it meant, not for the world but for Afghanistan, which, in his view, wasn't much. Twenty-three years of endless fighting had made an incorrigible cynic out of him. Rather than an opening for peace, he saw in the coming American campaign against the Taliban the start of a new phase in the ongoing Afghan war.

"Let's see what America does," I said. "It's obviously not going to sit idle and do nothing."

"All I know is this," he said philosophically. "The Taliban's days are numbered, but I fear this will lead to nothing better for our country. The Taliban will be gone, another group will take their place."

Even when I disagreed with Father, I took his analyses seriously, recalling how on the evening of the Soviet invasion he accurately predicted that the war would last twenty or thirty years. The war was now in its twenty-second year. By his most pessimistic prediction, we had three years to go.

*   *   *

A few hours later I spoke with my elder sister. She lived in England with her husband and two young daughters, recent refugees from the Taliban.

"Let's hope this evil leads to something good," she said. "Let's hope America understands our pain. If America goes back and rebuilds Afghanistan, why would people not support it? People are tired of fighting."

America finally understanding our pain—it was a line heard from many corners of the world over the coming days, usually from people who felt aggrieved by America. Palestinians, for example, said they'd lost many more thousands at the hands of Israelis. In Afghanistan we had lost 1.5 million people in the war, one out of ten of us, five hundred September 11s. Everyone had lost loved ones—"Not a crow without a scar," as Mother liked to say. And no one seemed to care, not even Afghans. There was no national day of mourning for the victims of the war, no monuments or shrines. Just scrawny green flags fluttering in overflowing cemeteries.

"We don't value life in Afghanistan," I said to my sister. "In America people value life. Thousands of our people are going to die. Innocent people. As you said, let's hope this evil leads to something good. But I have my fears."

I hung up and thought about something a colleague had said as we stood in the crowd outside our office building the day before and watched the second tower fall. "Our lives will never be the same again." Within hours the line became cliché. Everyone in America was thinking the same thing, although I wonder how many really understood what they meant by it. Clearly they meant more than increased security at airports. A people unaccustomed to large-scale violence on their home soil were girding for war. Some saw this as the first shot in a war of civilizations. Osama bin Laden had declared war on America on behalf of the world's one billion Muslims, and America was going to fight back.

*   *   *

That evening I took the PATH train to the city. I had been moved by the grief and surge of patriotism displayed on our side of the river, but I was not prepared for what I saw as I came out of the Fourteenth Street station and walked down Sixth Avenue.

Smoke lingered in the air. Most stores were closed. People milled around in the empty avenue. The whole area had been transformed into a long stretch of makeshift shrines at bus stops, phone booths covered with MISSING flyers, couples holding hands, and clusters of mourners in candlelight vigils. But what most moved me were the flags. They were everywhere. Giant flags on storefront windows, bandana flags on the foreheads of sidewalk vendors, little flags sticking out of backpacks, piles and piles of stars and stripes on sales tables.

As an Afghan, I had never carried the black, red, and green banner of my native country. Suddenly, though, I wanted to feel what it was like to proudly hold a flag and wave it at passing ambulances, police cars, and fire trucks. I wanted to show my solidarity with Americans. So I bought a passport-size flag for two dollars and sheepishly held it up as I walked to an East Village bar to meet a friend, self-conscious of the spectacle of a nonresident alien carrying an American flag. What was I doing holding an American flag? I didn't even have a green card.

But as I passed several angry-looking vendors who seemed to be studying the faces of every passerby, I realized that the flag could serve a larger purpose. It would give me a sense of security at a time when Muslims were drawing the violent ire of bigots. I have always been proud to be an Afghan, but on this evening, walking down Sixth Avenue in my Gap khakis and Brooks Brothers button-down, I feared that someone might mistake me for an Arab.

"It's good protection," my friend said when she saw my flag.

"I guess," I said, "but I didn't buy it for that reason."

The next evening I had to go to the city again. When I got to the Jersey City PATH station, still carrying my flag, the rush hour crowd was thinner than usual. It was unusually bright inside. The two benches had been removed from the middle of the platform, and the World Trade Center sign had been switched off. As I walked to the far end of the platform, the train pulled in. I stepped into the car, sat down, and surveyed the handful of passengers.

Everyone looked tired. A scraggly couple sat at the other end of the car in silence. Across the aisle an elderly man slouched under an antidrug poster aimed at schoolchildren. Next to them were two Asian women and a white man and, closest to the door, a young man immersed in a book.

On any other day I would not have given the man a second look, but something about him piqued my curiosity. He wore an oversize black coat and dark slacks, and sported a long, neatly trimmed beard. He was hunched over a little leather-bound book. I couldn't make out the book's title, but as he looked up I noted the dark eyes behind his thick glasses and his light complexion. He could have passed for an Orthodox Jew but there was something un-Orthodox about him. The missing yarmulke. I couldn't be sure if he was European or Arab. He could be Egyptian, I thought, or a Ukrainian Jew.

Seeing a bearded Muslim, or even a clean-shaven one, reading the Koran on the PATH train was not unusual. I never made much of them. But it was two days after America had come under attack, and Muslims around the country, afraid of violent reprisals, were keeping a low profile. The Syrian falafel shop in my neighborhood had yet to reopen, the cab stand was devoid of its Egyptian drivers, and the Egyptian shoe repairman near my apartment had plastered an enormous American flag on his window. It struck me as reckless, foolish, even rude for a Muslim to flaunt his faith on this day.

My curiosity increased as the train neared Manhattan, and the man continued his quiet reading. I got up from my seat to steal a glance. When I walked past him I saw the distinct Arabic letters and the zippered black leather case of the Koran. I was stunned. What did he think he was doing? Wasn't he afraid? Was he suicidal?

The train continued to my stop at Fourteenth Street. As I got off, the man shifted in his seat as if aware of my scrutiny, but he remained engrossed in his reading. I wanted to talk to him, ask if he was afraid. But I knew his answer. Why should I be afraid? I'm not a terrorist. Why should I hide my faith? I am a Muslim and not afraid to practice my religion. I read the Koran because I love it, and it is every Muslim's duty to read it. The Prophet said reading the Koran cleanses the heart. God will protect you when you are in danger, and when your time to die comes, it comes. No one can stop it.

He was retaining, on a PATH train to Manhattan, the faith I had learned as a Muslim but had since lost.

In the days that followed, I was inundated with e-mail from far-flung friends and acquaintances hungry for authentic analysis. As America prepared for war with the Taliban, my mostly liberal friends wanted to pick an Afghan's brain. "So what do you think about the state of the world?" a girlfriend wrote. "Do you think Osama bin Laden was behind the attacks?" asked a college acquaintance. Another wanted to know if "we can do what the English and the Russians failed to do." A friend's father inquired about winter conditions in the Khyber Pass and the White Mountains. Flattered by the attention, I tried to give my best assessment —variations on the same theme: "I fear the worst, but I hope for the best."

In reality I knew no more than they did about how long the fight against the Taliban would last. Although I was convinced the regime would eventually fall, I suspected it would take months, maybe much longer. In the Afghan mountains winter was approaching and with it the end of the fighting season. Time was not on America's side.

That sort of analysis was all over the tube. Armchair generals pointed at potential targets on satellite maps and struggled with Afghan names—Burhanuddin Rabbani, Jalalabad, Mazar-I Sharif, General Abdul Rashid Dostum. They offered plenty of commentary and analysis. The best came from "Afghan hands" heretofore unknown to American audiences. The worst offered a revisionist history of the Afghan jihad. According to this line of analysis, the mujahideen were reactionaries fighting the progressive secular government of Afghanistan. There was no mention of the atrocities committed by the Communist regime and its Soviet masters. What seemed important was that the Communist regime was "secular" and the mujahideen were "fundamentalists." And in this simplistic good guy versus bad guy view of the situation, America once again took the wrong side, with deadly consequences. If only America had not supported the Afghan mujahideen, many commentators pontificated, 9/11 could have been prevented.

This kind of commentary was hard to take seriously, or to be disheartened by, except that it presented the accepted wisdom. The world had indeed changed. Once hailed as freedom fighters and Cold War heroes, Afghans were now demonized as fundamentalists and terrorists. I was appalled. It was true that radical mujahideen often hated America as much as they hated the Soviet Union, but the jihad was fundamentally good, a cause that America should be proud to have supported, I told my friends. I was not naive. I knew that many supported the jihad for reasons having nothing to do with Afghanistan's freedom, but I wanted my friends to know that ours had been a genuine war of liberation against powerful oppression.

A week after the attack, I went to the city to meet with my immigration lawyer, who had agreed to work pro bono on my asylum case. The idea of filing two separate applications—one for a green card and another for asylum—was hers. "To increase our chances," she had said earlier that year. Now, having gathered the supporting documents, we were only days away from filing my application.

"So what do you think?" she asked. My lawyer was a blonde, middle-aged Englishwoman. Her paralegal, a Turkish-American who wore a conservative Islamic head scarf, earnestly took notes.

"I don't know what to think," I said. "Everything has changed. I'm worried about how this will affect my status."

"You shouldn't worry," she said. "If anything, this may help your application, but I think we should hold off filing it. Things are unfolding fast, and my advice is to stay put."

The meeting lasted fifteen minutes, and when I left her office I felt anything but reassured. In the week following September 11, I'd started thinking about going back to Afghanistan to report on the imminent U.S. military response. I had been inundated with e-mail and phone calls from journalists, filmmakers, and TV producers bound for Afghanistan. Given my pending green card application, going back was not an option. I had no idea how long the process would take—anywhere from months to years.

I was frustrated, even angry with myself for not taking care of my immigration status sooner. After all these years of wanting to go back, how could I have left myself unable to act? At moments, rash in retrospect, I wanted to ditch everything and just take off, and I had opportunities to facilitate such a move.

A friend with CIA connections offered me a green card in exchange for helping the U.S. military at Tora Bora. But while I wanted every al-Qaeda terrorist dead, I didn't want to show up alongside an occupation force in Afghanistan.

The most attractive offer came in the spring of 2002, in the form of an opportunity to serve as Hamid Karzai's spokesman. The package came with a green card. I was too suspicious of proximity to political power, and the sycophancy that comes with it, to seriously consider it. Nor did I wish to compromise my independence as a journalist by working for the occupation government.

"There are other ways you can serve your country," a friend said, affirming my belief that it was not the right job for me. "You can serve here, by educating people about Afghanistan." Another, pointing out that losing the opportunity to get a green card was not worth the risk, said, "You'll have plenty of time to serve your country."

And so for the next two and a half years, I stayed in America and safely watched the bombing of Afghanistan, the fall of the Taliban, the liberation of Afghan women, and the return to power of Afghan warlords.

Chapter Ten

February and March 2004—The afternoon sky over Kabul is bright and clear. The gray mountains north of the city sparkle with dots of snow from a mild winter. Walking down the tarmac of Kabul International Airport, Uncle Jaan Agha and I board a rickety bus for the ride to the airport's only functioning terminal. A throng of tired Western aid workers, peacekeepers, and Afghan exiles are kicking up dust in the dimly lit building. Uncle Jaan Agha is here to lead a workshop for high school teachers, his third visit to the city since the fall of the Taliban.

We clear customs and immigration in less than an hour, and when we step outside into the warm winter afternoon, we're swarmed by half a dozen pestering cab drivers. I immediately recognize their accents. They're mostly from the Panjsher Valley, the bastion of the Northern Alliance and home of their martyred commander, Ahmad Shah Masood. Reluctantly we go with a young Panjsheri even though he refuses to tell us the fare.

"Just pay whatever you think is right," the driver insists. "Anything."

An old Afghan trick. You're made to believe you're getting a cheap fare only to be ripped off when you reach your destination. Which is exactly what happens to us. The fifteen-minute ride to Aunt Makay's apartment building in Makroyan ends up costing us ten times the going rate.

Makroyan has come to epitomize Afghanistan's travails. Once a quiet middle-class neighborhood, its Soviet-style four- to five-story blocks were shelled and burned at the height of the factional fighting in the 1990s. Today it lies in squalor: trash strewn on sidewalks and lawns; a pair of dusty, grassless soccer fields; clothes hanging from balconies; dark, unlit hallways. Still, this is one of the few Kabul neighborhoods with at least intermittent electricity and running water, and Aunt Makay has paid fifty thousand dollars for her three-bedroom apartment.

When we reach her by telephone at her office, a British NGO that distributes prosthetic limbs to war victims, she apologizes for not being there and asks her husband's driver to fetch us some kebabs. Her husband, an orthopedic surgeon who was until recently the head of the military hospital in Kabul, is on one of his frequent hunting trips south of Kabul.

The next morning, I take a cab to Shar-I Now in the bustling city center. I'm curious to see the much ballyhooed changes. As we drive down potholed streets, the cabbie informs me that the forty-four thousand taxis in the city are driven mostly by underpaid teachers and government employees. Judging by the dense traffic and earsplitting honking of horns, I am inclined to believe they are all on the streets right now.

Kabul is in a construction boom, fueled by foreign aid and heroin money. New businesses have opened, and new exotic restaurants—Thai, Indian, Italian, Chinese—are sprinkled amid music and video stores with unusual signs. Most everything is labeled "super." There is a "super" camera shop, a "super" ice cream parlor, a "super" *gosht* (meat) market. Every other weight-lifting parlor is called Gold Gym, complete with large posters of Arnold Schwarzenegger. Photographs and music, unthinkable under the Taliban, are now ubiquitous. But as I look around, I notice something odd: most women are still hidden under the all-enveloping *chaadaree* veil, and the few who do show their faces wear large, colored headdresses, and look wary. The Taliban may be gone, but the women of Kabul are still afraid to go back to liberal ways.

Nor has poverty eased. Approaching Shar-I Now, our taxi grazes several crippled beggars and women in *chaadarees* sitting on the dividing line, their dirty arms stretched toward us. More of them are on the streets than the last time I visited the city. Off Chicken Street, once popular with foreign tourists shopping for Afghan rugs and antiques, we come face-to-face with more beggars. Trying to dodge them, I dash into a charming bookstore and spend an hour talking to the lonely owner and browsing old books, posters, and paintings banned under the Taliban.

Around noon I have lunch at a crowded kebab joint across the street from the famed Great Afghan Department Store, once the premier shopping stop in Kabul. Reopened after incurring serious damage during fighting in the 1990s, it looks shabby—three dimly lit, dusty floors of gaudy shops manned by bored-looking men. Outside I buy sunglasses and have my picture taken by men running box cameras. There are seven box cameras but no customers—the fall of the Taliban apparently has not been a boon for these guys.

The Taliban are gone. The war is over. Kabul does not have the feel of a city under occupation, as it did in the 1980s. Mindful of the Soviet experience, the Americans are keeping a low profile. The "low-intensity warfare" they are waging against the "remnants of the Taliban" in the south seems a sideshow. No one here talks about it, and few seem to know much about it.

Yet I also sense that without the American military presence, the Karzai government—indeed, Afghanistan itself—can't survive. The Taliban may have disappeared, at least as an organized military presence, but the Northern Alliance, still maintaining a large force outside the city, can be expected to step in. And if not the Northern Alliance, then another group. Everyone knows it: if the Americans pull out, they risk losing the country; but if they overextend their reach and resort to heavy-handed tactics, they risk alienating the population and sparking a new jihad. It is a trade-off, a delicate balancing act the Americans haven't mastered yet.

When I return to the apartment, Ahamadullah is there, the second cousin whom I saw in Peshawar. He's back in action, chubbier and balder than the last time I saw him but very much his old blustering self. Sinking into the leather couch, he rests his arms on its arms and excitedly tells me that he just got back from Khost, a region to the south of Kabul, where he went to track down two of the three teenage Taliban members recently released from Guantanamo.

"By God, it is a wild place," he says excitedly.

I'm a little surprised by this. While not off-limits to outsiders, the south is still considered dangerous.

"How the hell did you get there and back?" I ask.

Ahmadullah only shakes his head.

We leave the apartment for a ride around town. Inside his four-wheel drive Toyota Prado, he proudly shows me his U.S. Army Corp of Engineers ID and tells me about the vehicle's military license plates, which allow him to get into restricted neighborhoods of Kabul. He then explains how he got his ID: shortly after the fall of the Taliban, he helped distribute tens of thousands of school bags filled with stationery donated by American schoolchildren, and he later worked with the U.S. military to distribute food in the north. Ahmadullah is clearly happy with the collapse of the Taliban regime.

As we weave through traffic, Ahmadullah tells me how he ended up going to Khost to look for the boys. He is bidding for a big United Nations contract to oversee militia disarmament in the south, and he made the trip to prove his bona fides to skeptical UN officials.

"There are some really incredible passes there," Ahmadullah says. "Impossible to cross in the winter, especially this winter when it snowed a lot."

Ahmadullah drove to Khost by himself, dropped his car at a bus station, and paid a driver a hundred dollars to take him to the remote village of Angorkhel, where one of the boys lived. In the Khost region, Ahmadullah looked up a mujahideen commander he'd heard about and presented his own jihad credentials (he had been a mujahid in the 1980s).

"That helped me tremendously," he says. "They trusted me, and said, oh yes, you are one of us."

Having tracked down the boys, he tried to talk their families into releasing them into his care for a year of rehabilitation. Much to his surprise, one of the boys agreed to move to Kabul to live with his own brother. Ahmadullah was supposed to go pick up both boys in Khost in a couple of days, but the second boy changed his mind and moved back to his village farther south.

Ahmadullah has moved into a dead uncle's house in Shar-I Now, and I decide to stay with him. He says he'll leave for Pakistan in a couple of days, and then he plans to travel north for the Nowrooz New Year festival. I don't have enough time to stay for Nowrooz, but I like the idea of traveling with Ahmadullah for the next couple of weeks.

Later that night we are joined by a tall, lanky family friend of Ahmadullah's who recently visited America. The three of us get into a heated debate about the need for Afghan exiles to help with the reconstruction effort. I tell Ahmadullah and his friend that I don't want to work for the government. When I call Hamid Karzai a foreign puppet, Ahmadullah loses it.

"It's by calling Karzai a Shah Shujah"—the Afghan king installed by the British during the first Anglo-Afghan War—"that you undermine the government," he says, his voice rising. "Haven't you read Afghan history? We've always had foreign backers. Better to have America than anyone else. America has no economic interests in Afghanistan. The iron and copper mines that we are so proud of are of no interest to America. Yet it is helping us."

I am surprised at the passion with which Ahmadullah defends the system. But I shouldn't be. He is one of its beneficiaries. Locals have divided the population into three parts: al-Qaeda, which includes the terrorists and their Taliban allies; al-Faeda, the politicians and others who have benefited from the new government; and al-Gaeda (literally, "the fucked"), the rest of the population. Ahmadullah is a member of al-Faeda.

His friend is nodding. "America is going to stay in Afghanistan for a hundred years," he says matter of factly.

"I agree," I say. "But are people really going to accept one hundred years of occupation? Or fifty years or twenty years? I think America has five to ten years at the most. They know what happened to the English and the Russians. That's why you don't see their soldiers roaming around Kabul."

"Americans are smart people," he says. "They have analyzed these things, they have strategists."

He then asks me why I don't want to return to Afghanistan.

"I hope to," I say. "I had a lot of opportunities, but I couldn't come back because I didn't have a green card. As soon as I get my green card, I'll start making plans."

"You have a strong emotional attachment to Afghanistan, and I have no doubt you'll return soon," he says. "Just wait. I'll see you here next year or the year after."

I feel inspired. For the first time since arriving in Kabul, I begin to seriously think about moving back.

"Why do you have to wait?" Ahmadullah interjects.

"I don't want to work for the government," I say. "There are other ways I can serve Afghanistan."

Ahmadullah certainly thinks he serves his people.

"I know people think I'm in it for the money, but I know what I do is a service to the people," he says.

I believe him. Still, when he tells me that his goal is to make two hundred thousand dollars over the next year, I can't help but wonder about the source of his inspiration. Perhaps it has something to do with all the Afghan-Americans who are said to be making millions.

After a week of visiting relatives and seeing Ahmadullah make one plan after another, we finally leave for Peshawar. Even then, I have to force him out the door. I agree to pay for a rental car with a driver.

At the Jalalabad bus station in Kabul, we pick up some juice and crackers. While I've been cautious to avoid street food and uncooked vegetables, Ahmadullah seems even more fastidious, complaining that his stomach can't handle it. Sitting in the front passenger seat, Ahmadullah repeats something he told me a couple of days ago: only when Afghan refugees in Pakistan return to Afghanistan can there be stability in Afghanistan.

"The most perceptive observation I've heard you make in years," I tell him.

He smiles. "I'm telling the truth," he says.

As we drive out of the city, the ramshackle storefronts and mud huts give way to lush fields of corn and wheat on the right side of the road. Rugged mountains soar in the distance ahead. After a few miles the paved part of the Kabul-Jalalabad road ends; from there on it is unpaved and potholed. A Chinese company, contracted by the Afghan government, recently began work on the road, a project that is expected to take more than a year.

I have driven this road several times before and am now reminded why the British and later the Russians had a hard time controlling this part of Afghanistan: the gorges are narrow and easy to get trapped in; the mountaintops and ridges make perfect sniping positions. It was along a road running parallel to this one that the first invading British army was cut down in the 1840s, and where the Soviets suffered heavy casualties. Most of the destroyed tanks and trucks have been removed, often by scrap metal merchants, but signs of war are everywhere: spent artillery shells, abandoned military posts, signs indicating minefields.

Shortly before sundown, we reach the Torkham border crossing. I look at my watch: it is minutes until six p.m., the closing time for the gate.

"Let's hurry," I urge Ahmadullah.

We pay the driver and sprint toward the open gate about two hundred yards down the road. A heavy rain is falling. Along the side of the road, shopkeepers and vendors are shutting down their stalls. I can hear the sound of the *azan* over loudspeakers on both sides of the border.

At Ahmadullah's suggestion, I had put most of my money in an inside pocket of my vest, keeping two hundred-rupee bills in my hand in case I need to give a souvenir to the border guards. But as we reach the gate, no guards are in sight. Men and a few women hurry in both directions, the way they always have. We simply cross the border and walk to the Landi Kotal bus and van station, where we hire a car to take us to Peshawar, a two-hour drive.

In the five years since my last visit, little seems to have changed in Peshawar. A few new shopping centers and American-style gas stations have sprung up, as has an underground passageway lined with music and clothing stores. But everything else looks frozen in time: the buggies and rickshaws, the nostril-blackening smog and earsplitting car horns, the noisy bazaars teeming with men in turbans and *pakool* hats. And the sight of Afghan refugees.

All this is familiar. Yet since my family left the city for England, I no longer think of Peshawar as my adopted hometown. But I still have many relatives here, and wherever I go I hear the same message: no one is about to move back to Afghanistan. Things are still too unstable. The Taliban may be gone but the warlords are back in power, and memories of living under the warlords are fresh.

At my cousin Laylaa Jaan's house, where I spend the week, her mild-mannered husband has nothing good to say about Pakistanis —Pashtun and non-Pashtun alike—but he is convinced that there is no better place for Afghans to live than Peshawar.

"You feel like you're living in Afghanistan," he says. "Why leave Peshawar where you have water, electricity, schools, hospitals, and roads?"

Peshawar is a thriving refugee oasis, a quick getaway for many Afghans. Almost another Afghan city. Even with the poor road conditions, if you leave Kabul early enough in the morning, you can get to Peshawar by late afternoon. There is no work in Peshawar, but that's not a problem; many live off money sent by relatives in the West. And those who don't have relatives in the West hope their pretty young daughters catch the eye of eligible bachelors in the West.

No one bothers Afghans here, I keep hearing, especially since the post-9/11 electoral victory of the local Islamist parties in 2002. The police have stopped harassing refugees. But even in my scruffy three-week-old beard and unwashed *shalwar kameez,* I have a hard time avoiding attention. A couple of days after I arrive, while riding in a cab with a cousin, we're stopped by police and let go only after I hand over five hundred rupees. My relatives dismiss the incident as an aberration.

Still, there is another aspect to Afghan life in Peshawar.

"People have grown spoiled here," says Noor Agha, my mother's swaggering cousin with a Taliban-era beard. "They can't go back to their old lifestyles. They can't live in a mud hut and shit in an outhouse. Even in Sheberghan, you know, people have stopped using clay to wipe themselves clean."

His blunt statement gives me pause. While I know many people have discovered the joy and luxury of toilet paper, the prospect of squatting in a stinky Afghan outhouse leaves me unsettled.

"Let me tell you something," Noor Agha continues. "Don't even think about coming back to live in Afghanistan. It will take you fifteen years to readjust to the lifestyle."

"I don't know about that," I shoot back. I explain to him that I'm not worried about reacclimatizing, but I agree with him that I can't imagine spending the rest of my life in Pakistan or even

Afghanistan, not least because the world in which I was supposed to live has vanished. My parents gone, and with the exception of two aunts and one uncle, all my aunts and uncles and their children have moved overseas and live as far apart from each other as Sydney, Australia, and Washington, D.C.

Later that week, in another refugee neighborhood, I track down Saboor, my cousin and our mujahideen group's logistics and political officer. He hasn't changed since I last saw him. A few strands of gray hair but still pencil-thin, melancholy, and as serious as a funeral director. He has closed his old convenience store and opened a secondhand furniture and junk shop.

By the standards of Afghan refugees in Peshawar, Saboor seems to be doing well. Even so, he tells me that he's thinking about moving back to Kabul to reclaim a small piece of property he inherited. In the meantime, he says, refugees are staying put.

"For two reasons," he says, looking me straight in the eye. "The economy and education."

I am surprised by this comment. If there are two things that have improved in the past two years in Afghanistan, they are education and the economy. But like other Afghans, he insists that Afghanistan is far behind Pakistan.

Over a meal of lamb, rice, and spinach, Saboor tells me that he also wants to start an NGO that will offer refresher classes for high school teachers.

"Sounds like a good idea," I say. "But you should probably go through the ministry of education in Kabul."

"I was wondering if you could bring it up with the professor," he says. The professor in question is Uncle Jaan Agha. "He must have some ideas and know people."

"I certainly will," I respond. "But I still think you should go through the ministry of education. I'm sure they'll like your idea."

He looks disappointed. He informs me that his daughter, a fourth-grader, just published a collection of folk poems and nursery rhymes. He proudly hands it to me. I ask for two autographed copies—one for me and one for my father—and I hand him the equivalent of twenty dollars to buy books and stationery for her.

Saboor is a man of few words, and as we sip tea and seem to run out of conversation, he gets up and pulls out a stack of old military maps and bags of pictures from the jihad days. I haven't seen many of these faces in fifteen years and don't know if they're alive or dead. I ask Saboor what everyone is up to: Qari Nazeef, my old Stinger gunner buddy; Doctor Hamid, the medic and mortar operator; Awalgul, the mortar operator from the battle of Jalalabad.

"Qari Nazeef was here in Pakistan for several years, but I heard he moved to Europe, I don't know where," Saboor says. "Awalgul is in Guantanamo."

My jaw drops. Saboor tells me the little he knows about how Awalgul ended up at Gitmo. After the fall of Jalalabad to the Taliban in 1996, Awalgul, like several small-time commanders from our group, stayed behind and joined the Taliban. He served as a commander for the local army corps. When the Taliban fell and Hazrat Ali, the military commander of Jalalabad, returned to the city, he handed Awalgul over to the Americans, labeling him a Taliban and al-Qaeda sympathizer.

I've long felt that many of the al-Qaeda-affiliated Arab fighters captured in Afghanistan belong behind bars. But now I wonder how many other Awalguls languish in Gitmo. Who would have thought that a man who once fought for his country, and was an ally of America, could end up in an American detention facility?

Another former American ally who has found himself on the wrong side of America is Mawlawi Muhammad Yunus Khalis, the leader of our old resistance group who was welcomed to the White House by President Reagan as a great warrior and who made a splash for urging the Gipper to convert to Islam. After the Soviet withdrawal, Khalis distinguished himself from the rest of the mujahideen leaders by avoiding factional fighting and living a quiet retirement in Jalalabad. I tell Saboor that I read about the kidnapping of Khalis by the Taliban, but he informs me that Khalis is alive and well. Apparently Khalis's son, a fire-breathing pro-Taliban mullah, had a falling out with the political authorities in Jalalabad and persuaded his ailing father to leave Jalalabad and declare a jihad against the Americans.

These days no one knows where Khalis is, and his call for jihad has fallen on deaf ears. I pity him when I picture the mighty, red-bearded warrior on his deathbed surrounded by his son and a couple of loyal disciples. But I also know that Khalis is a man of conviction; perhaps he really believes that America's occupation of Afghanistan is bad for Afghanistan and that if his call is heeded, the American venture in Afghanistan will collapse.

As we talk about Khalis, I remind Saboor of the little tract Khalis once wrote and which I translated into English. He remembers it and says that a Peshawar-based publisher of Islamic books might have it. We decide to walk over to the office of the publisher, about half a mile down Jamrood Road. The publisher's office is on the fourth floor of a shopping and office complex. Inside, we find only the original version of the tract I'd translated.

I buy several recently published collections of Khalis's essays and poems, and the publisher looks surprised, not knowing my affiliation with the party. He tells us that just a few days ago a couple of Americans stopped by the office and bought several copies of Khalis's books. "We want to know what this man thinks," they told him. I wonder who these guys were. Americans usually see Khalis as a caricature: a fiery fundamentalist who was good at killing Russians; a lecherous octogenarian married to a fourteen-year-old. They probably had no idea that he was a writer and a poet as well as a mullah and a warrior. I wonder if they were really after what Khalis wrote; they were probably after him.

"Do you remember anything?" Fayeq asks as we get out of the cab.

It's late afternoon in my third week and Fayeq, my thirty-year-old cousin who resembles the hard-line Iranian president Mahmoud Ahmadinejad, and I are standing in Bandar Akhchah, one of Sheberghan's four ancient gates. Each of the four gates is named after a nearby town and this one serves as a gateway to Akhchah. It also serves as a market. I look around in disbelief, and not only because I am finally back in my hometown after more than twenty years. In Peshawar, I was told that the Sheberghan I left behind was not the Sheberghan of today, but more than any place I've visited, Sheberghan looks frozen in time. A few things have changed, but everything else looks pleasantly familiar: my old school, with its low whitewashed walls and rusting cast-iron gates; the one-story bank building opposite the school; the pharmacy at the corner; the poplar trees, looking a bit withered and sleepy, but still standing. The only big change: beat-up Toyota yellow cabs have replaced Sheberghan's brightly decorated buggies of yore.

"It's the same old Sheberghan," I murmur as I snap out of my daze. "Nothing has changed."

The cabbies, standing a few feet away, look at us anxiously. I study the faces of everyone in sight, trying to see if I recognize any. I don't. Fayeq, holding our duffel bags, looks amused. He's on his first visit to Sheberghan since the fall of the Taliban, but he looks more intent on capturing my reaction.

"There are hardly any buggies left," he says. "It's all taxis now. Sheberghan has progressed a lot."

"Yes, it certainly has."

Fayeq insists that we get moving. Sheberghan is small, he reminds me, and I'll have plenty of time to see everything.

We hop into another taxi and drive down the wide, unpaved road to Fayeq's house. I take in all the houses around us but don't recognize many. Fayeq's parents' house is in better shape than I remember, with some new rooms and a large concrete verandah. The courtyard is planted with flowers and flanked by a chicken coop.

We are greeted by Fayeq's father, Uncle Khan Agha. Gone is the big, bushy Taliban-style beard he sported when I last saw him in 1999. Instead he sports a goatee. He is wearing vintage sunglasses and a karakul lambskin hat, the kind made famous by President Karzai. To honor our arrival, his wife runs up and throws candy and money over us.

We walk into Uncle Khan Agha's house and sit down, but before finishing the first cup of tea it's time to leave for the nearby town of Saripul to pick up my cousin Sa'dat, Fayeq's brother. Mayar, a second cousin and my closest childhood friend, will be driving us. When he shows up, Mayar is as stylish as I remember. He wears an expensive leather jacket and tan slacks. His thick black mustache makes him resemble his father. We have not seen each other since our early teens, and we greet each other with awkward formality and try to break the ice.

The road to Saripul is good, I'm assured, but after a few short miles of pavement, it gives way to the most difficult road I've driven on in Afghanistan. Craters and potholes and ditches continually greet us, a vivid reminder that even small stretches of backcountry road are not immune to the brutality of war.

"Where are the Americans to repair the road," Mayar murmurs as he calmly steers the car. "This is a story you should write about."

The sun begins to set and Uncle Khan Agha, sitting in the front passenger seat, fills me in. The warlords have plundered the country's resources. Three of the northern warlord General Dostum's commanders have taken over the Angoot oil field, one of the few working oil fields in northern Afghanistan, and they sell the crude oil for two thousand dollars a tanker to a makeshift refinery built by a local businessman with close ties to Dostum.

Saripul is pitch dark and quiet. It is no longer the pretty little town of mulberry and apricot orchards that I remember from my childhood. When we finally track down Sa'dat at his office down a dark, narrow street, he bears no resemblance to the seven-year-old boy I remember. Sporting shoulder-length hair and a full beard to mask a skin condition, he resembles a rock star. But he's anything but flamboyant, and, much to my surprise, he greets me with the deference of a younger person. I'm touched by this and reminded that social mores remain deeply rooted in this part of the country.

"Afghanistan is far from stable," Uncle Khan Agha says as we head back. "But just being able to drive down this road is a remarkable accomplishment."

A couple of years ago it would have been inconceivable to make a trip like this, not to mention at the height of the war in the late 1980s and early 1990s.

Back in Sheberghan, we're served tea again, then instant coffee, pulled out of a dusty cupboard.

"It will relax you," my uncle's wife says as she proudly pours me another cup.

When I tell Uncle Khan Agha that I am planning on spending only two days in Sheberghan, he smirks and says, "That's impossible." Then he asks: "Where were you all this time?"

"With Ahmadullah," I say. "You know Ahmadullah."

"No wonder," he says. "You may want to leave in two days but no one is going to let you go. Two days after twenty years? That's impossible."

We decide to play it by ear.

The next day, in keeping with age-old Afghan tradition, Uncle Khan Agha suggests that I visit and offer condolences to older relatives who have lost loved ones since my family's flight to Pakistan. It is a small number. The Sheberghan branch of our extended family—the network of aunts and uncles and cousins that formed the world I grew up in—has shrunk to fewer than ten families, most of the rest having escaped to Peshawar in the 1990s.

I don't have much time, so I limit myself to what Uncle Khan Agha calls "must visits": Uncle Khan Agha's father-in-law, whose wife died about ten years ago; a middle-aged relative whose mother died a couple of years ago; another relative whose son died in a car accident. The visits are cold and somber, limited to formal prayers and pleasantries over tea, and end with insistent dinner invitations that I politely decline.

After half a dozen such visits, I call upon Qadir Jaan, a relative whose younger brother Malik was a childhood friend. An avid soccer and volleyball player, Malik and several teammates were killed in a firefight while traveling from Sheberghan to Mazar-I Sharif in the mid-1980s.

Tall and sturdily built with a salt-and-pepper mustache and a friendly manner, Qadir Jaan is married to one of my mother's youngest cousins. He works as the principal of a girls' school. They live with their two teenage daughters in a large house left behind by an aunt now living in Australia. I sit on a leather couch across from him and his wife and raise my hands in prayer and stare into them. When I'm done, I rub my face with the palms of my hands and wish them life and tell them how devastated I was by Malik's death.

"He was like a brother to me," I say sincerely. "I loved him. I remember hearing about his death in Pakistan. It greatly saddened me."

At the time of Malik's death, I viewed those who stayed behind in Sheberghan, our own relatives included, as virtual Communist sympathizers. I did not understand how difficult it could be for people to abandon the comfort of their homes for the strange world of exile. Nevertheless, when I heard about Malik's death, a couple of years after the fact, I was heartsick and began to realize that those who stayed behind in Afghanistan were also victims of the war.

Qadir Jaan is clearly touched by my expressions of sympathy but, like everyone else, he seems to have taken tragedy with stony equanimity and gotten on with his life.

Not remembering the names of his other brothers, I ask him how his parents are doing.

"They are fine," he says formally.

I learn later, much to my embarrassment, that his father had long been dead and that I neglected to offer separate prayers for him.

Later an old relative comes to see me. I don't know exactly how I'm related to Shah Koko, but I feel close enough that I walk up to her and kiss her hands as she kisses me on the back of the head. She is elegantly dressed and frail, and her hair, which she used to dye with henna, has turned gray. When I was little, her sons Salih and Atta used to tease me about my fair hair and call me German.

We sit down and engage in formal pleasantries. She asks how my parents and sisters are doing. I ask how her husband, whom I used to call Uncle, is doing. Then I inquire about Salih and Atta.

"They're fine," she says in her quiet, toneless voice.

When she leaves, I learn that one of her sons was killed in a battle a long time ago. I feel embarrassed and guilty and want to visit her house and apologize but decide against it. She probably understands. Everyone here seems to have lost loved ones. Some were unlucky passengers caught in crossfire on the road to Mazar-I Sharif. Others were local men forced into the Communist army to fight the mujahideen. Still others were killed fighting the Soviets.

People talk about these incidents with the matter-of-factness of describing a bicycle accident. They lost their relatives, they mourned their deaths, and they moved on. In their loss they too are victims of the war.

The extent of my family's suffering is all the more apparent when I visit our clan cemetery to pray at the tombs of my grandparents. The cemetery sits on the edge of town and has grown over-crowded, the mounds of rain-washed dirt that pass for graves packed tightly like sardines in a can. Many hold the remains of martyrs and are topped by green banners. I'm struck by their number and ask Mayar who they all are. Mayar, who has lived in Sheberghan all his life save for two years during the Taliban rule, has an encyclopedic knowledge of our family history. As he points at each grave and rattles off names, I try to remember them, but my mind wanders back to the lost time when this cemetery was small and pretty and we came to this part of town in the spring to run in the surrounding fields, red with tulips, and the air was filled with the scent of wild roses and fruits.

"I used to love the tulips," I say when Mayar finally stops his narration. "You know something? America is a beautiful country, and I've traveled all over it, but I haven't seen anything like our tulips in America. When do they start sprouting?"

"They already have," Mayar says. "I saw a couple the other day. We had a drought for several years and we hardly got any, but maybe this year will be different. There are tulips in those fields. You can't see them; it's getting dark."

The neighborhood echoes with the sound of the *azan* from a nearby mosque. Standing on the edge of the cemetery we hold up our hands a second time and say a final prayer. On our way out, we bump into the lonely middle-aged caretaker. A native Uzbek with a thin beard, he has worked at the cemetery for twenty-five years except for two years during which he was drafted into the army. He knows where everyone is buried, not just the prominent citizens of the community. He says that the cemetery has grown beyond capacity and will soon run out of spots to squeeze in more graves. Our clan, the Laghmanis, have been trying to buy the outlying fields, but the owners have not agreed to sell. The caretaker is not sure where our family will bury our dead when the graveyard runs out of space. Perhaps in a different part of town. In any case, he reminds me, tradition dictates that every forty years or so graveyards are flooded, planted with wheat for two seasons, and then readied for fresh burial. The time to flood this graveyard will come soon.

I'm saddened to hear this. I tell my cousins that in America many cemeteries are hundreds of years old, and then I realize a paradox of Afghan culture: Afghans revere their ancestors and bury them nearby where they can visit them often, but Afghanistan is a poor country and habitable land is scarce. After a generation, we have to let go of them. Physically but not spiritually. As much as we revere shrines, what matters most is their spiritual presence.

The morning of my third day in Sheberghan, I visit with our old Uzbek house servant Hasan Lala. (*Lala* is a term of endearment for an older brother.) He holds me in his burly arms and insists that I accept his dinner invitation.

"I really would like to," I say. "I have great respect for you, but I have already made commitments."

"Can you visit us at least for breakfast?" he pleads.

I agree.

The next morning we take a cab to his house on the eastern edge of town, across the road from a housing complex. Hasan Lala is doing well for an illiterate former house servant. He owns a grocery store and two small houses, one of which he rents out. We sit down around a big spread of food, and he asks his daughter to fetch "the glass." The glass is a shot glass. Hasan Lala has something special in mind. He pours a bit of lager into the shot glass and mixes it with Pepsi. Hasan doesn't drink, and the cocktail tastes nasty, but I am touched by his gesture and make myself drink several glasses of it.

Sitting across from me are his shy wife and two pretty daughters. He married his wife, the daughter of a local truck driver, shortly before we left Sheberghan. He tells me that he views me as a young brother or even a son, and reminds me that he used to push me and my sister Farkhundah in a stroller around our old neighborhood. He smiles when I mention the tambourine he used to keep in his room when we were growing up. "Oh, I didn't know how to play it," he says. "I'd just bang on it." I think of him as an older brother, not a servant. I hope his polite children do not know our relationship. I ask Hasan Lala about life after the Taliban, about the warlords and their militiamen. He says they are fine people; they don't bother anyone. We talk for several hours, and it is one of my most enjoyable visits in Sheberghan.

Sheberghan is a microcosm of what the overthrow of the Taliban has meant for most of Afghanistan. In political terms, it has meant the restoration to power of violent warlords, such as the notorious Abdul Rashid Dostum. When we were living in Sheberghan, in the first two years of the occupation, Dostum led one of several ethnic Uzbek militias established by the Soviets to protect key outposts against mujahideen attacks. The effort was not always successful, but having proved themselves as tough combat fighters, Dostum's men began taking part in military operations alongside Soviet and Afghan Communist forces. By the time the Soviets left the country in 1989, the Kabul regime depended on the militia for its own defenses and dispatched it to Jalalabad to ward off the mujahideen attack in which I took part.

Indeed, Dostum became so crucial to the survival of the Communist regime that when he switched sides in 1992 and allied with Masood, the mujahideen were able to enter Kabul and overthrow the government.

After a year of supporting one mujahideen group or another in the rising factional fighting in Kabul, Dostum pulled out his militia in order to consolidate his power around his home base at Sheberghan. During this time, from the early to mid-1990s, Sheberghan was a peaceful oasis in the country, as long as you didn't mind Uzbek rule. The Uzbeks, nationally a minority but regionally a majority, dislodged just about every non-Uzbek from virtually every position of power, much to the resentment of other ethnic groups. It was blatant ethnocentrism to a degree that the multiethnic populace had not seen before. At its height "Uzbekism," as non-Uzbeks labeled Dostum's rule, turned into a reign of terror, Dostum's commanders ruling with impunity.

During this time several frightened relatives, including an uncle, either fled to Pakistan or sent their marriageable daughters there to evade Dostum-allied suitors.

In Afghanistan most regional movements crumble within a few years, and that is what happened when one of Dostum's key commanders defected to the Taliban in 1997. Almost overnight the militia fled across the border to Uzbekistan. After a short-lived attempt to regroup and retake Sheberghan, Dostum was forced out of Afghanistan again the following year. This time he sought asylum in Turkey.

The American-led military campaign that brought men like Dostum back to power was not flawed from the outset. It was smart to avoid putting a large number of American boots on the ground and instead to rely on heavy bombing of Taliban positions and a ground push by what was left of the Northern Alliance. Unfortunately the remnants of the Northern Alliance included Dostum's militia and other long-disbanded groups. In the short term, the strategy paid off and avoided an immediate security vacuum. But instead of quickly moving to disarm the militias and replace them with an international security force, as many Afghans urged, the United States buttressed the warlords. The idea was to avoid a military confrontation with the militias. This fear was misplaced. The truth is that the militias had been decimated by the Taliban and enjoyed little popular support. In any case, the window of opportunity shut on the Americans in the first year, allowing Dostum and other warlords to consolidate their power, which made the task of stabilizing Afghanistan all the more difficult.

Sheberghan is in the midst of weeklong festivities. Commander Laal, one of Dostum's top lieutenants, is having a lavish circumcision party for his two preteen sons. Ten thousand invitations have been sent out to guests across Afghanistan; every citizen of the country is invited. Uzbek men take the circumcision of their sons seriously, and Commander Laal, a former day laborer who rose through the ranks of Dostum's militia, sees himself above most khans. Traditionally, hosts of such large gatherings ask their family and friends to house their out-of-town guests. And so Commander Laal has ordered every prominent family of every neighborhood in Sheberghan and the surrounding villages to provide lodging to his hundreds of guests. They're supposed to feed the guests and their horses and to lavish them with gifts of expensive silk turbans and karakul hats and wool robes.

The centerpiece of the party is *buzkashee,* a central Asian game that is played on horseback with a headless calf or goat. Several thousand villagers and townsfolk have assembled at Pul-i Khurasan for the spectacle. The stands are reserved for VIP guests, including a group of Westerners in civilian clothes and one or two in military fatigues. There is live music by Bahauddin, a renowned tambourine player, and Bismil, a dark-complexioned folk-singer who croons in praise of Dostum.

The game goes on for several hours. Brawny horsemen in thick corduroy robes and pants and protective boots jostle for control of the dead animal. The crowd of excited spectators standing on three sides of the grounds sways back and forth as the horsemen lunge toward the goal circle and attempt to drop off the carcass. The intensity of the game picks up as the prize money increases from three hundred dollars per goat to a thousand.

Around five in the afternoon, Dostum rides in atop a white horse, trailed by a posse of fawning acolytes and subcommanders. Wearing a black cap and long brown corduroy robe, he gives a pep talk in Uzbek to a group of horsemen. I walk down the field to capture the scene on my camcorder. As I zoom in from twenty feet, the thuggish features of the once obscure oil field worker come into focus: the large piercing eyes, the bushy eyebrows, the thick black mustache, the coarse, round Uzbek face. For a leader with a vast following, he shows surprisingly little swagger. Perhaps he fears his days are numbered as the powerful warlord of northern Afghanistan. But behind the blank expression, I can't help seeing the war criminal and brutal murderer. I despise him for the atrocities he committed, first in support of the Soviet occupation and later as he tried to consolidate his hold over northern Afghanistan.

Dostum raises the prize money again, and the announcer urges the spectators to applaud. They release a thunderous roar. Dostum rides off the grounds and the game resumes. It is a game that our country's greatest modern poet, Khalilullah Khalili, humorously described as "one animal riding another animal chasing the carcass of a dead animal." But this is more than a game. It is a display of power and status, not that folks here need a reminder of who is in charge.

At Mayar's house that evening we talk about the game and the warlords. Mayar's father, a former senior police official now working for the state oil company, thinks the warlords can easily be driven from power. He thinks the solution is to expand the NATO-led International Security Assistance Force beyond Kabul and the best place to start doing that is Sheberghan.

"First of all, Sheberghan is a town where only one group holds power, and confronting one is much easier than confronting several," he says. "Second, Sheberghan is a relatively small town. And third, it is close to a border port that generates revenue that now enriches only the warlords."

He is an optimist. He says the warlords will be removed from the scene one way or another in the next year or two. I want to agree with him. Of late, Karzai seems to be asserting authority. He's fired several local police chiefs and governors and replaced them with professionals from Kabul. But Karzai is "too nice for Afghanistan," as a close friend and admirer of his once told me. "He's fifty years ahead of his time." What Afghanistan needs, I hear from more savvy Afghan observers, is another Abdur Rahman

Khan, the Iron Amir who did not hesitate to use brute force to tame rebellious tribes and bring the country under state control.

Several days later Fayeq and I travel to Jalalabad to track down a couple of my Tora Bora friends, but we are unsuccessful. "I need a lot more time if I'm going to find them," I tell Fayeq. We spend a night with relatives in Jalalabad.

In the morning I propose that we continue our search by visiting Mehtarlam, the capital of our ancestral Laghman province. Fayeq is not keen on this trip. He's never been to Laghman and tries to dissuade me. I can't tell if he is worried for me or for his own safety. The night before, we had been told that rockets were fired on Mehtarlam.

When we finally get into our rented car in Jalalabad, I tell Fayeq that we need to see some action. "A trip in Afghanistan can't be complete without some boom-boom," I tell him.

He smiles. "Don't forget that you want to get home safe."

Outside Mehtarlam, armed men stop us and demand a ride. The driver pleads with them to let us go, telling them that his passengers are journalists. I am surprised by the comment—I have not told the driver what I do for a living or that I am visiting from America. Later he tells us, "Those guys are afraid of journalists." He's used the same cover story many times to get past these checkpoints.

We stop in Mehtarlam to look up a cousin of my father's, a prominent doctor. We find his clinic but he's out to lunch. We track down his brother-in-law, who runs a pharmacy a few blocks from the clinic. Armed militiamen mill about. In the pharmacy two of them, blue-eyed and young, are sitting on the floor drinking tea. The pharmacist later tells me that they hang out in his store and drink tea when they have nothing else to do.

As we talk, a large bearded man comes in. He's a doctor and runs a clinic above the pharmacy. The pharmacist introduces us. His name is Mangal. I tell him that I am visiting from America, which brings a pleased smile to his face. I ask him about life in

Laghman. He's not happy and tells me that it takes extreme courage to live here. He shows me a gun under his coat and says that he does not dare to walk unarmed. Since the local Pashtun police chief of Laghman was arrested by the Americans, the ethnic Nooristanis have descended from the mountains like foreign occupiers. I ask him what can be done about the militiamen.

"Send in ten American Humvees," he responds. "And if that doesn't work, fly in B-52s. That should take care of the problem."

I am struck by his comment. More than two years after the fall of the Taliban, people remain in awe of American power and prefer benign foreign occupation to anarchy and lawlessness. But while they long for foreign protection, I wonder how much more they can take before things blow up. Again.

The next twenty-four hours are a whirlwind across the region, first to Islamabad, then back to Mehtarlam and Jalalabad and on to Kabul to catch a flight home the next day. I don't like packing all this into my last day but I want to see everything and everyone and complete the journey.

I take the makeshift tram across the river to Islamabad and find the village peaceful and deserted. Uncle Qazi and Uncle Akhundzadeh are not in their house, and I am disappointed to learn that Uncle Qazi died recently and Uncle Akhundzadeh left for Peshawar mere days ago. Many of their children have moved to Kabul and Pakistan. I stay a while in their largely empty house, drinking tea and offering condolences to one of Qazi's wives. On the way back, I stop at Mehtarlam to make a last attempt to track down my father's cousin, but then I must board a van to Jalalabad and after that a taxi to Kabul.

When I reach Kabul, I marvel at the distance I've traveled in hardly two days, a journey that would not have been possible before the fall of the Taliban. I feel optimistic but fear the window of opportunity is closing on Afghanistan. All the talk after 9/11 of building a democratic and prosperous Afghanistan is contradicted by what I've seen on the ground. Afghanistan is a long way from reaching that goal, and I'm not sure it will get the help it needs. As for me, I am renewed in commitment to my country, remembering Sabir's words when I first arrived in Kabul: "Your heart is tied to Afghanistan. I have no doubt you will return."

Chapter Eleven

June 2007—The story ends here, but life goes on. Three years after my last visit to Afghanistan, three years while I have bided my time, and two and a half decades after our flight from the Soviets, I am going back, not for a quick visit but to live. I have taken a six-month assignment, which can be extended to a year and possibly longer, to mentor Afghan journalists in Kabul. This finally is a way to give something back, to serve my people, and perhaps to chronicle a critical time in the history of my country. I longed to serve, remember, even as a boy: "When I grow up, I want to serve my country." When I shyly uttered those words as a seven-year-old outside our house in Sheberghan, I didn't know what they meant. Years later I learned their intent and was ready to put it into practice, but my timing was off. Harvard was followed by the outbreak of civil war and later Taliban rule—seven long, brutal years for Afghanistan. Then came 9/11 and a time that I did not have a green card. The last three years were subsumed by one excuse or another, what Afghans call "turning today into tomorrow."

Every excuse exhausted, all obstacles surmounted, I am flying home, free as the parrot in the well-known Rumi poem. But unlike Rumi's parrot, I return to a changed and unwelcoming home. For Afghanistan this is the most unstable and uncertain time since the fall of the Taliban. A few days before I write these words in June 2007, a suicide bomber blew himself up near a police bus in

Kabul, killing twenty-four people, mostly police instructors. A few days before that another suicide attack killed five people.

Suicide attacks, once as alien to Afghans as the Arabic *niqab* is to our women, have become common. Afghans have even coined a literal translation of "suicide bombing": *hamlah-I intihaaree*. So far this year, there have been more than fifty in the country, up from less than thirty in the same period last year and a mere ten in 2005. When I visited Afghanistan in 2004, there had been only one or two and those were thought to be the work of Arab and Pakistani militants. On my way back to New York, I had met two friendly Afghan laborers during a layover in Dubai. They hailed from Khost, a hotbed of Taliban activity, and I was curious to find out what life was like there. Over tea at a busy airport cafe, they took turns describing, in tones hushed and horrified, a recent suicide bombing in Khost, apparently the first to strike that part of the country. A gangly man on a bicycle rode up to a military truck parked in the town's market and detonated his explosives. The bomb killed only a handful, but it left a scene of horror.

"By God, I've seen nothing like it in my life," said the more garrulous of the two. "Body parts were everywhere. People couldn't believe it."

"It was an Arab," the other interjected.

I don't know if the attacker's nationality was ever ascertained, but I was inclined to agree that the bomber could not have been Afghan. It was one thing to sacrifice your life on the battlefield, but strapping on explosives and blowing yourself up in the middle of a crowd—in defiance of the Koran's injunction against suicide—was unfathomable to the people of Khost. Yet it has since been established that while most suicide attacks have been carried out by radicalized Pashtun tribesmen from Pakistan, Afghans are increasingly the perpetrators. The Taliban, scriptural literalists in matters of outward piety, have found an expedient way to justify suicide bombings. They call them "self-sacrifice operations" and, if you believe their spokesmen, boast thousands of *fedayeen* (literally, "those who sacrifice themselves") ready to blow themselves up at a moment's notice.

I often wonder who these people are. They can't all be junkies who picked up dope in Pakastani refugee camps, as the Afghan government propagandizes. Many must be ordinary Afghans brainwashed by a pernicious ideology that has afflicted the world of Islam: the belief that taking one's own life and the lives of others is justified in the fight against the enemies of Allah. It chills me to think that fellow Afghans, men of faith and honor, would become so perverted in their worldview.

The rapid increase in suicide bombings in 2007, we keep hearing, reflects the Taliban's desperation. They failed to pull off their much anticipated "spring offensive" and had to resort to desperate measures. The suggestion is that this year has not been as bloody as last year. But if violence has declined, it's not showing in the stream of daily news reports coming from Afghanistan. Not a day goes by that NATO does not report heavy fighting and the killing of dozens, sometimes hundreds, of "extremists" and "enemy fighters." But the victims more often than not are civilians. According to one count, more than four hundred civilians have been killed this year, a paltry number by Iraqi standards but enough to provoke outrage in Afghanistan. Following a week in June during which more than a hundred civilians were killed in NATO and U.S. air strikes, Karzai condemned the "careless operations" and warned that "Afghan life is not cheap."

The violence has not been limited to the Taliban stronghold in the south. It has spread east and north, engulfing Nangarhar, Kunar, and my native Laghman. In early April a suicide attack on an Afghan military convoy in Mehtarlam killed nine people, including five children. In mid-April another suicide bomber blew himself up at a police academy in the northern town of Kunduz, killing eight police officers and injuring dozens. Even Sheberghan, largely peaceful in the five years since the fall of the Taliban, has not been spared. In late May seven people were killed and nearly thirty injured after police fired on a group of Dostum supporters demanding the resignation of the provincial governor, Juma Khan Hamdard, an erstwhile Dostum ally who had a falling out with him. Order was restored only after four days of sporadic fighting kept the panic-stricken residents indoors and quadrupled the price of produce in the local market.

How did we get here? In a word, Iraq. In two words, Iraq and Pakistan. In three, Iraq, Pakistan, and warlords. In four . . . The list of blunders goes on ad infinitum. But whether it is Iraq or Pakistan or the warlords or any other thing that upended early hopes of a peaceful Afghanistan, it all stems from the same source: an obsession on the part of U.S. policy makers with short-term tactical victories at the expense of long-term strategic vision. Little thought goes into what actions today will mean in the future. That Afghanistan fell victim to an ill-conceived, ill-timed, and ill-executed Iraq plan has become accepted wisdom. It is true that the Iraq war diverted needed attention and resources from Afghanistan, but it is less clear how, without an Iraq invasion, Afghanistan would have received what it needed to get the job done. In April 2002, a year before the Iraq invasion, President George W. Bush grandly announced a Marshall Plan for Afghanistan to "give the Afghan people the means to achieve their aspirations." But the promise was never fulfilled. The Taliban were gone; the mission was accomplished or almost accomplished; and if a war was going to be fought, it would be fought on the cheap. As the veteran Associated Press correspondent Kathy Gannon observes in her book *I Is for Infidel:* "The tragedy of Afghanistan is that to the world's powers, it has really never mattered—or mattered for long."

Other countries seem to matter more, at Afghanistan's expense. Take for example America's post-9/11 alliance with Pakistan. The task following the terror attacks was to get Pakistan to drop its support of the Taliban, and when Pakistani President Pervez Musharraf made an about-face, America rewarded him with economic and military aid. The matter was never pressed again even as the Taliban regrouped. As long as Pakistan handed over an occasional al-Qaeda operative we cared little if Pakistan harbored the Taliban rank and file. What drives the American policy toward Pakistan? One thing: a deep-seated American fear of the mullahs getting their hands on nukes. According to this line of thinking, it's far better to keep Musharraf in power than risk nuclear ambitious, anti-American elements replacing him. Pakistan has legitimate concerns about security on its border with Afghanistan, not the least of which is the Afghan government's long-standing refusal to recognize the Durand Line that marks the Afghan-Pakistani border.

Another problem is America's continued support of Afghan warlords. Following my trip in 2004, I wrote an op-ed piece for the *Wall Street Journal*. Recalling the circumcision celebration I witnessed in Sheberghan and the atmosphere of fear surrounding it, I urged expanding the UN–mandated International Security Assistance Force and stepping up the effort to improve the nation's security instead of pushing for presidential elections scheduled for the fall. Noting that the routed Northern Alliance had returned to power only with American support, I also wrote that the warlords "are not as powerful as they're made out to be" and could just as easily be dismantled. Mine was one voice in a chorus of calls for increasing the security force. The Pentagon, long opposed to such nation-building measures, finally acquiesced. But instead of disarming the warlords and providing security, the expanded security force, now under the command of NATO, propped them up and devoted its men and resources to fighting the Taliban in the south and east. No wonder even in the more secure northern areas people view ISAF not as a peace keeping force but an American-led army that is occupying their country.

* * *

Today Afghanistan sits on a knife edge. In the next year or two, it could go either way. There are various nightmare scenarios. Foremost is that the Americans, losing the will to fight, pull out of the country, leaving the Karzai government to fend for itself. The result, by almost universal consensus, would be the immediate collapse of the government and its takeover by any number of groups, including the Taliban and their Pakistani allies. Another scenario could involve the spread of the Taliban insurgency throughout the country. This scenario is not as far-fetched as it sounds. As reports of civilian casualties rise, signs indicate that support for the Taliban and other antigovernment groups is growing, and not just in their southern and southwestern stronghold. Even among my relatives, no fans of the Taliban, I occasionally hear whispers of sympathy. The Americans have kept a low profile through most of the war and are virtually invisible in much of the country. But if the fighting spreads and casualties rise, will the calls for a jihad grow? It is likely. Drops make a river, as we say in Afghanistan, and graves a graveyard—and Afghans know their country has long been the graveyard of invaders.

A more likely scenario, however, is that the country will chug along with only a "moderate level of instability," as UN officials like to put it. The American military will keep a low profile, the Pakistanis will check the flow of the Taliban across the border, Afghan forces will grow in numbers, and fighting will decrease. It won't be the prosperous democracy America promised after the fall of the Taliban, but it will be a half-functional nation-state.

Even the latter scenario is nothing to write home about, to use an Americans saying. As I began planning my return journey, I contacted an old American friend and mentor in Kabul. He knows

Afghanistan as well as any American and was an early booster of the American enterprise there. In 2002 he even encouraged me to take the press secretary job with Karzai. In an e-mail, he described Kabul as "dirty, smelly, noisy, ugly, even risky" and griped that "whatever progressive idealism existed in, say, 2002 has given way to opportunism." Not exactly surprising coming from someone who has lived there for the past five years, but not the most encouraging words for a homeward-bound Afghan.

Years ago when I started to cover the energy market, I proudly sent him one of my early *Wall Street Journal* clips, a story about oil prices and pork belly futures. "How can a nice Muslim boy like me be writing about pork bellies?" I quipped. A couple of weeks ago when I wrote to him that I was moving to Kabul, he reminded me of my playful remark and wrote, "No longer will you be asking that question."

I can't say I am as optimistic about the future as I was three years ago, but I'm an idealist and I still feel I can make a difference, even if it's small, even at this stage. I have spent the last three years trying to write this story of my life, a selfish endeavor, not to mention a painstaking one, while holding down a job that offered little by way of moral gratification. Along the way I have tried to keep my hope alive even as the situation in Afghanistan has deteriorated. For all I know, everyone's worst nightmare could unfold. Alternatively, the country could regain its footing. Whatever happens, if I don't go back now, I know I never will, and I would regret it.

To that end, I must close this chapter in my life. A difficult part has been convincing my girlfriend that I have to move on. When I first told her my plans, she felt her life was being turned upside down. After initially refusing to accept that I was serious, she tried to change my mind.

"Why go now?" she kept asking. "Why not wait until things calm down?"

To remind me of the dangers facing Afghan journalists, she e-mails me news reports she comes across on the Internet. I know all about them. Last month the Taliban abducted and beheaded an Afghan journalist, Ajmal Naqshbandi, after the government refused to release several Taliban commanders. That was followed by the killing of two women journalists, including one affiliated with the organization I will be working for. And according to the latest news reports, an Afghan journalist with whom I will work just received a death threat on her cell phone: "Daughter of America, we will kill you, just like we killed her."

"They're targeting everyone who is working for progress," my girlfriend says. "In their eye, you're an American son, a traitor, and your death will be a huge win for them."

I'm undeterred. I have no time for melodrama and no interest in debating, and like a true believer, I ask her to stop her propaganda.

She obliges, reluctantly, painfully.

Others who care about my safety are less resistant to the idea. Uncle Jaan Agha, who recently returned to England from his latest visit to Afghanistan, warned about the threats facing journalists.

"They accuse people you'll be working with of spreading pro-American propaganda," he said the other day over the phone.

"I know," I replied. "I know all about it."

"One of their journalists had to quit his job after repeatedly being threatened," he said. "He went underground and started an Internet site and posted the warnings online. You should check out his site." Aware of what the return of the Taliban would mean for the country, however, he added, "It's better to be spreading pro-American propaganda than pro-Taliban propaganda."

As for my parents, I have had little trouble convincing them to visit me once I am settled. Like other Afghan parents, although they live in England they have long dreamed about spending the twilight of their lives with their only son. But they're torn. On the one hand, they like the comfort of living in the West and being close to my sisters; on the other, they miss Afghanistan and want to live with me. Mother takes pains to mask her anxiety but says she'll come along. Father is anything but hesitant.

"It's not an ideal time to go," he says, "but then, we'll probably never see an ideal time. We will go wherever you go. We will follow you."

Acknowledgments

This book unintentionally grew out of an article I wrote in the winter of 2001. As American bombers began pounding the mountains of Tora Bora and TV experts made wild speculations about the "terrorist hideout," I felt an urge to set the record straight and to write about my own experiences there. A friend and former colleague, Erik Baard, put me in touch with *The Village Voice,* which published my account of life at Tora Bora under the title "Fire on the Mountain." Another friend and sharp-eyed writer, Tom Reiss, saw a book in the story and generously introduced me to his literary agent, the inestimable Tina Bennett, who pitched it to Grove's Morgan Entrekin among other major New York publishers. The rest is history. It was an honor to be represented by Tina. Through the years, she never lost faith in the book or me, even when I had doubts of my own about its publication. All four deserve my thanks for bringing the book to fruition, as do the dedicated editors at Grove, including Jofie Ferrari-Adler and Brando Skyhorse. I'd like to thank several other friends who read the original book proposal and/or excerpts of the manuscript and through their love and support and social distractions made sure the book only occasionally was not on my mind and that it took me a mere seven years to complete: Philip Munger, Michael Stockman, Christopher "Belly" Bell, James "Jimmy" Covert, Salman Farmanfarmaian, Dick Levine, Courtney Pyle, Sarah Cohen, Emily Tucker, Leah Long, Diane

Munro, and Sheryl Amada. Elsewhere, my heartfelt thanks go to my old friend Ekram Shinwari of Voice of America; my former boss at the Afghan Media Resource Center, Haji Sayyid Daud; my uncle and mentor Professor Ishaq Negargar and his family; my numerous other uncles and aunts and cousins; and last but not least my beloved parents and my three lovely sisters.

Masood Farivar
Kabul, Afghanistan
August 2008